NEW
PROFICIENCY
ENGLISH

BOOK ONE

Language and Composition

NEW PROFICIENCY ENGLISH

BOOK ONE

Language and Composition
W. S. Fowler and J. Pidcock

Nelson

Thomas Nelson and Sons Ltd
Nelson House   Mayfield Road
Walton-on-Thames   Surrey   KT12 5PL

51 York Place
Edinburgh   EH1 3JD

Thomas Nelson (Hong Kong) Ltd
Toppan Building 10/F
22A Westlands Road
Quarry Bay   Hong Kong

© W.S. Fowler and J. Pidcock 1985
First published by Thomas Nelson and Sons Ltd 1985
ISBN 0-17-555605-9

NPN 9 8

Printed in Hong Kong

Contents

CONTENTS

CONTENTS

CONTENTS

Introduction

New Proficiency English

New Proficiency English is planned as a replacement of *Proficiency English*, published in 1976–8, and as a logical continuation of *New First Certificate English*, published in 1984. In effect, it is the result of several years' experience of using the previous course and gradually adapting materials to the needs of students taught at earlier stages in the learning process by different methods from those current in the early 1970s. As in the case of *New First Certificate English*, my co-authors, John Pidcock and Robin Rycroft, and I have preferred to write a new course, taking this experience into account, rather than to revise the original. While some elements that have proved particularly successful have been retained – above all in *Book 3, Use of English*, where the revised Cambridge syllabus of 1984 for the paper shows no innovations – over 80% of the material in the course is new.

By this time, it will be evident that the examination as such has not changed to a noticeable extent either in level of difficulty or in form, except in the design of the aural/oral tests (covered in this course by *Book 4*). The main change in approach, especially in *Book 1*, has therefore been to shift the emphasis away from the formal presentation of grammar towards the acquisition of skills. At the same time, the overall coverage remains the same.

The main problem for teachers at advanced level and for students attempting the Proficiency examination is that the former are inclined to relax the pressure once students have passed First Certificate because the Proficiency examination is still a long way away, while the latter underestimate the difference in standard. This course has been written for students likely to attempt the examination two years after First Certificate if they attend classes five hours a week (300 hours) or three years afterwards if they attend three hours a week (270 hours). The material has been pretested and graded through use with students at each stage to allow for the time-span envisaged, but it is above all important to point out that the language-learning process should be continuous. Our experience leads us to believe that it is necessary to develop skills methodically throughout the period and that it is unwise to imagine that students can be left largely to their own devices for a year or so before making a systematic approach to the examination.

The design of the course

The four books comprising the new course can be used independently, in order to concentrate on a specific paper in the examination, but they have been written in such a way that they relate to each other. *Book 1, Language and Composition*, consists of 28 units, the last four forming a separate section intended for those students who wish to attempt the Prescribed Books option in composition. The units of the other three books have been written in parallel to those of *Book 1* in such a way that every unit of *Book 1* is supported by two out of the three possible units devoted to the skills required for Reading Comprehension, Use of English and Listening Comprehension/Interview. The chart accompanying the *Teacher's Guide* shows the relationship. In this way, the themes of units in *Book 1* are frequently reflected in the choice of reading passages in *Book 2* so that there is an opportunity for revising and expanding vocabulary; the structures necessary for the composition tasks in *Book 1* are revised and practised in *Book 3*, and the topics for summary in *Book 3* also have a thematic relationship in the majority of cases with parallel units in *Book 1*; the opportunities for free discussion and the listening material provided in *Book 4* are also related to themes and group-work tasks originally presented in *Book 1*. The design of the course, comprising 24 basic units for study in *Book 1*, permits teachers to make a convenient break either after Unit 8, if students are studying three hours a week, or after Unit 12, if they are studying for five hours a week.

The organisation of units in *Book 1*

The book contains 28 units, the last four, as previously stated, relating entirely to Prescribed Books. The first 24 units are divided into six stages, reflecting the different kinds of composition students may be asked to write, description, narrative, discussion, and guided composition of various kinds (a task formerly set as the last section of the *Use of English* paper). The stages have been designed so that students can make progress towards more sophisticated techniques in self-expression and in the later stages there is an emphasis on the need to blend techniques (for example, of description and narrative) in order to handle certain topics.

Although the persistence of elementary mistakes may at times suggest that the problems of students at advanced level resemble those of the intermediate student preparing for First Certificate, they are essentially different. The main difference lies in the fact that students now have sufficient knowledge of structure to write accurately, and the structures they have learnt already are quite sufficient for them to achieve fluency if they know how to use them; the few structures that have not previously been taught are, for the most part, seldom used in good modern English and are best dealt with as items for structural conversion (*Book 3*), a matter of recognition rather than use. On the other hand, primarily because the majority of students do not read widely enough in English and do not analyse the techniques of discourse employed in what they read, they are often incapable of developing their writing skills towards fluency. The difference between the accurate writing required to pass First Certificate and the level demanded by Proficiency is not one of more complex forms of expression, as many students imagine, but of having a much greater variety of technical resources at one's disposal, and a wider and therefore more precise vocabulary. Consequently, we have provided a large number of tasks aimed at helping students to identify techniques used in writing of different kinds and to use them for themselves, while at the same time we have stressed the importance of expanding vocabulary thematically through the interrelation of *Book 1* and *Book 2*.

These tasks, developing naturally from the content of the book, have six main objectives:

1 to introduce the theme of the unit and source of potential composition topics in an interesting way and to help students to clarify their ideas;

2 to help students to analyse the construction, development and organisation of paragraphs within different kinds of composition;

3 to help them to analyse the style and content of passages written for a specific purpose, either in isolation or by means of comparison, in order to understand the techniques involved;

4 to help them to analyse the techniques themselves in such passages so that they can employ them in their own writing;

5 to use information retrieval techniques and contrasted models as a basis for exercises aimed at helping students to reorder and rewrite information in a different form;

6 where necessary, to revise grammatical points essential for specific composition tasks.

The relationship between skills and grammatical accuracy

As in *New First Certificate English Book 1*, the principal emphasis of this book is on acquiring the skills necessary to write English in a wide variety of circumstances. At First Certificate level, because of the different levels of English of students entering the class and the inevitability of remedial work, we provided a checklist of grammatical items at the beginning of each unit which had to be thoroughly understood before the unit could be started. It seemed to us discouraging to students to repeat such a list at a more advanced level, however, even though many of the misconceptions and consequent grammatical errors may still persist in some cases. What we have done instead is to provide a thorough reference section at the end of the book for students to refer to; we expect students to make use of this, whenever they are in doubt. This decision was based on practical experience; in common with the vast majority of the teachers of advanced classes we have consulted on the subject, we are convinced that long-standing structural problems (as distinct from students' ability to develop writing skills and to clear up points of vocabulary and usage by asking the teacher) can only be cured by students making the effort to check such things for themselves. This is not to say that remedial practice is discounted. There is an ample section devoted to the problems commonly found among advanced students at the beginning of *Book 3*, but this is primarily intended for revision of points that affect the majority of a class, not as an essential part of the initial presentation.

The units therefore form not so much a grammatical progression, although this feature is incorporated within them, as a gradual approach to handling more and more complex topics in a more sophisticated manner. Whereas in *New First Certificate English Book 1*, we ourselves wrote almost all of the models on which students were expected to base their own compositions, in this book we have chosen the majority from modern English journalism, creative and technical writing, as examples of what constitutes an appropriate style for a given task. We have also paid great attention to the organisation of paragraphs and the ways in which paragraphs are related to each other to form a coherent whole. While we believe that the techniques we have taught here are flexible enough not to restrict the freedom of expression of students who already have the capacity to organise their ideas effectively in English, they should provide a reliable framework for those who have not learnt them in their own language.

The First Certificate examination is limited for lexical purposes to fewer than 4000 words selected from the *Cambridge English Lexicon*, while in theory there is no limit whatever for Proficiency. In the same way, the scope of this course, and the challenge confronting students, must necessarily be wider than at First Certificate level. We hope that the material and the guidance we have provided will stimulate students to meet this challenge.

Will Fowler
Barcelona, August 1984

Acknowledgements

The publishers wish to thank the following for permission to reproduce photographs:
BBC Hulton Library pp 1, 72, 73, 151; Rex Features Ltd pp 1, 24, 117, 126; Zefa pp 8, 53, 83, 117; Barnaby's Picture Library pp 8, 70, 117, 118; Kobal Collection pp 134, 142, 146, 156, 158, 159, 160, 162; National Tourist Authority p 117; VRU (Thomas Nelson) p 117
Photography Goran Mihajlovic pp 1 (bottom), 5, 10, 11
Research and photographic art direction Terry Gross

Thanks are also due to the following for permission to reproduce copyright material:

The estate of Virginia Woolf and The Hogarth Press for an extract from 'The Death of a Moth' in *The Collected Essays of Virginia Woolf, Vol I*
Mrs Laura Huxley and Chatto & Windus for the extract from *Brave New World*
Readers Digest Association Ltd for the extract from *Folklore Myths and Legends of Britain*
The executor and trustee of Gordon Rattray Taylor for an extract from *The Doomsday Book*
The *Guardian* for an editorial, and articles by Hella Pick and David Irvine
Times Newspapers Ltd for articles by John Coyle and Glenn Gale which appeared in the *Sunday Times* and two articles by Jane Last and Jonathan Croale which appeared in *The Times Education Supplement* May 1983 and 3 June 1983

A.D. Peters & Co Ltd for the extracts from *The Liners* by Terry Coleman and *In Character* by John Mortimer, copyright © Advanpress Ltd
Faber and Faber Ltd for the extract from *Spirit of Place* by Lawrence Durrell
Penguin Books Ltd for *Woman's Consciousness, Man's World* (Pelican Books, 1973), copyright Sheila Rowbotham and *Uses and Abuses of Psychology*, copyright © H.J. Eysenck, 1953
The Bodley Head for *Zen and the Art of Motorcycle Maintenance* by Robert Pirsig
Andre Deutsch for *Plain Tales from the Raj* edited by Charles Allen
The *Sun* for an editorial, and articles by Hugh Jamieson and Trevor Kavanagh
Hodder and Stoughton Ltd for *Gifts of Unknown things*, copyright © L. Watson, 1976
The estate of the late Sonia Brownell Orwell and Martin Secker & Warburg Ltd for the passages from the works of George Orwell
The estate of Rachel Carson and Hamish Hamilton Ltd for the extract from *Silent Spring*
Granada Publishing Ltd for the extract from *The Female Eunuch*

Every effort has been made to trace owners of the copyright, but if any omissions can be rectified the publishers will be pleased to make the necessary arrangements.

People

Who's who?

1

2

1 Look at the list of adjectives below. Work in pairs to check which of them could be used to describe the face in the computer portrait.

curly-haired	dark-eyed	broad-shouldered
swarthy	bushy-browed	bull-necked
thickset	hawk-nosed	sallow
bearded	plump	thin-lipped
bald	smooth-skinned	fattish

2 Now compare the computer portrait with the four photographs on the right, and try to identify which face it corresponds to. Work analytically, and give reasons for your final choice.

3   **4**

3 You are going to hear five brief extracts of people talking.
  a) After each one, note down your mental picture of the person you have heard: age, appearance, character, etc.
  b) When you have heard all five, compare notes with a partner and then work out together which of the five faces below might belong to which speaker and why.

A

B

C

D

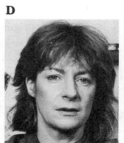

E

Appearance and personality

Activity 1 – pair work

Popular newspapers in Britain often use a number of adjectives in succession to describe people.

1 In the first article here, note a) which adjectives come nearest to the noun and which furthest away; b) where else adjectives can be placed, if not before the noun, and when they are linked together by **and**. Study the Reference Section, page 168, before continuing with the Activity.

2 Many adjectives in such articles are irrelevant. In the second article, decide how many of the adjectives can be cut out without changing the essential facts of the story.

To her workmates at Krashen Electronics Factory in Batley, Yorks., good-looking, auburn-haired, computer assembly worker, Stella Percival, was just 'that nice, clever lass with the friendly smile'. Imagine their surprise last Saturday when they saw her coast home, calm and relaxed, an easy first in the European Women's Marathon. Interviewed in the front room of her parents' cosy semi-detached house in Ilkley Road, Stella was still quiet and unassuming. 'I kept my training a secret at work' she said. 'I was afraid the other girls would be disappointed and upset if I raised their hopes too high.'

For balding, 48-year-old furniture factory worker, Arthur Hawkins, yesterday began like any other day. But when he bought his copy of the *Daily Moon* on his way to work, bearded, bespectacled bachelor, Arthur, found that the day's Bingo number was the one he was waiting for, the last one on his card. So he ran to the phone to claim his prize from the *Moon* . . . and dialled the wrong number! 'I got so excited,' said Arthur 'that I misread the number!' Arthur, keen on angling and an expert darts player, shares his semi in Ashford, Kent, with his 80-year-old, white-haired mum, Eileen, and uncle, Norman Burgess, 73.

Activity 2 – pair work

Choose the most appropriate adjective, from those given below, for each space in the article on the right. Put those in groups in the correct order. Then decide how many of them are relevant to the story.

55-year-old/plump/office/jolly;
keen-eyed;prompt; suspicious;
grateful; public-spirited;
conscientious/punctual;
ex-rugby/craggy;
quick-thinking/dark-eyed;
yellow/slim;
open-plan/newly-built

_____(1) _____(2) _____(3) _____(4) worker, Mrs Molly Davies from Newport, leaves home at 8.00 every morning to catch the 8.25 train to Cardiff. Mrs Davies is _____(5) and _____(6), but yesterday was different. On the way to the station, _____(7) Mrs Davies noticed a _____(8) _____(9) spiral of smoke coming from the _____(10) _____(11) primary school. 'There wasn't much.' Mrs Davies told me, 'but enough for me to be _____(12).' So _____(13) _____(14) Mrs Davies phoned the fire brigade, and her _____(15) action saved the school. Newport's fire chief, _____(16) _____(17) star, Mr Barry Thomas, commented, 'Firemen are _____(18) to _____(19) people like Mrs Davies.'

Professional writers often build up a picture of people by using significant details about their appearance, their past and present experience and their conversation to create an impression of their personalities as a whole. Read the passage below and then work in pairs on the activity.

Portrait of the Artist

'As I grow older the glasses get smaller. Of course, I'm still blond. I've been blond for twenty-three years. My mother thinks it's natural.'

In fact David Hockney, at forty-three, has changed little. His is still the dry, comical voice of everyone's favourite North Country auntie. He wears small gold glasses instead of the big horn-rimmed, **pop-period gig lamps**, his features are sharper, he is thinner and stoops slightly; but moving round his studio hung with some new paintings ('I did them to cover the wall. For my own amusement. If you do things for your own amusement other people often like them too') he became younger by the minute, until the time when he switched on the lights and rang up the curtain in his model theatre, and changed the enchanting scenery for his New York Metropolitan production of a triple bill of the ballet *Parade* and two short operas. And then he waltzed, wearing his dark-blue baseball cap and yellow T-shirt and voluminous grey-flannel trousers, to the music of **Maurice Ravel**.

'My father was an eccentric,' said Mr Hockney. 'He worked for twenty-five years as an audit clerk in Bradford; but he was always making things. He made prams. Not very good prams. And he did posters – for **CND** and the Bradford Diabetics.'

David Hockney has a portrait drawing by his father grandly entitled 'Bertrand Russell. Peace Campaigner' which he managed to get into a corner of one of his own exhibitions in the Hayward Gallery. Once Hockney *père* set out by train for the **Aldermaston** March and in charge of all the Nuclear Disarmament banners, some of his own making: unhappily he fell asleep before Reading and was carried on to South Wales with his banners, where he became involved in a violent argument about the fare.

'My father took some art lessons and when the **Leonardo cartoon** was in the news, Dad said, 'I know what that's called. It's called *Light and Shade*.' They taught him light and shade from that picture at his class; they don't teach it any more, although, as a matter of fact, light and shade are still there.'

Keen on light and shade himself, David Hockney has a respect for conventional art teaching; by the age of sixteen he had committed himself to Bradford Art School and spent four days a week learning to draw, lessons which can rarely have been put to better use, the line in a Hockney drawing, as in a Picasso, being never less than superbly confident and always truthful.

'Drawing's important. It's about looking. That's what drawing does,' he says. 'It teaches you how to look.'

'Can you teach drawing?'

'You can teach some things about it. The poetry you can't teach.'

'You enjoyed **the Royal College?**'

'It was a good time. I sold a drawing to another student for £10 and went to Paris: on the way home I had enough money for a bed for the night or the duty-free cigarettes. I bought the cigarettes and slept in a doorway.'

From *In Character* by John Mortimer (abridged)

pop-period gig lamps: large glasses popular during the 1960s
Maurice Ravel: French composer of the operas for which Hockney had designed the sets for the New York production
CND: Campaign for Nuclear Disarmament, which organised an annual march to **Aldermaston** in the 1960s to protest against nuclear weapons in Britain
Leonardo cartoon: of the Virgin and Saint Anne, the subject of an appeal for money by the Royal Academy in the 1960s in order to keep it in Britain
the Royal College: of Art, in London

Activity 3 – pair work

1 Find references in the passage to David Hockney's age, physical appearance, dress, art training and present work.

2 In what ways does the reference to his father as 'an eccentric' a) indicate parallels in the son; b) show that the son is conscious of these similarities?

3 How is the father's eccentricity indicated to us?

4 How does the author persuade us that Hockney is more youthful than his age suggests?

5 How does he suggest that Hockney is unconventional in some of his behaviour but has respect for convention in artistic terms?

6 Do you think the title is an appropriate description of the impression of Hockney given here? If so, why?

Linking description

Compare the two versions of a composition printed below. Note that neither version uses complex sentences or difficult constructions, but the second is much more complete than the first.

My younger brother

Alex is my younger brother. I have known him for as long as I can remember. I do not remember what he was like as a baby because I am only a year older, but later we became close friends.

5 Alex is like my mother, with dark hair and brown eyes, but he has inherited my father's height and broad shoulders. He looks older than he is. When we go to parties together, girls think he is my elder brother.

10 Alex is very strong. He swims well, and likes climbing and skiing, but he is not very fond of ball games. He spends his time reading and talking to his friends about books and films. He also takes part in plays and says he would like to

15 be an actor. My father tells him that he will soon be too big to take most parts.

He has a gentle personality , but underneath he is tough. He is determined to succeed but hates studying subjects he is not interested in.

20 He often has arguments with my father about it. My father has a violent temper. When Alex is angry he grows cold and hard and does not forgive people easily. My father knows him well and keeps his own temper under control.

25 I do not know whether Alex will achieve his aims in life. He has the ability and persistence to do so. He is attractive and has a good sense of humour. These are great advantages. I hope he will be successful. I am very fond of him.

My younger brother

Alex is my younger brother so I have known him for as long as I can remember. I do not remember what he was like as a baby, except from photographs, because I am

5 only a year older, but later we became close friends, apart from being brother and sister.

Alex is like my mother in complexion, with dark hair and brown eyes, but he has inherited my father's height and broad

10 shoulders. As a result, he looks older than he is, and when we go to parties together, most of the girls think he is my elder brother and has come along to look after me!

Alex is very strong. He swims well and

15 likes climbing and skiing, but he is not very fond of ball games. He spends most of his spare time reading and talking to his friends about books and films. He also takes part in plays at school, and sometimes says he

20 would like to be an actor, but my father tells him that unless he stops growing soon he will be too big to take any parts but monsters.

At first sight, he has a gentle personality,

25 but underneath there is an element of toughness in his character. He is determined to succeed in everything he does but hates studying subjects he is not interested in and often has arguments with

30 my father about it. My father has a violent temper, but when Alex is angry he grows cold and hard and does not forgive people easily if he thinks they have been unfair to him. Fortunately, my father knows him well

35 and keeps his own temper under control.

I do not know whether Alex will achieve his aims in life, but he certainly has the ability and persistence to do so. Apart from that, he is attractive and has a good sense of

40 humour, and these are both great advantages. Naturally, I hope he will be successful because I am very fond of him.

Activity 4 – pair work

1 Each paragraph in the compositions here has a purpose. The first, for example, introduces the subject. Give each of the other paragraphs a short title defining its purpose.

2 Study the position and use of the following in the second composition: **as a result** (line 10), **at first sight** (line 24), **apart from that** (line 38). How do they add to an understanding of the passage?

3 What difference is made to the sense of the passage by the use of: **except** (line 4), **most of** (line 16), **fortunately** (line 34), **certainly** (line 37), **naturally** (line 41)?

Pen pictures

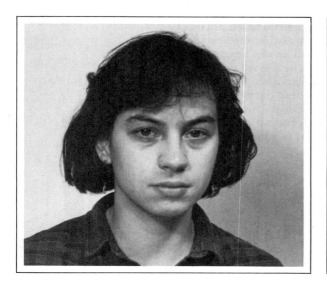

Activity 5 – pair work

You work for a university newspaper. Every week it is your job to write two brief feature articles entitled 'Personalities of the Week', in which, in about 200 words, you describe two students who have distinguished themselves in one way or another.

Use the facts from the table below, together with your impression of the photograph to write a draft article about one of these people. Your partner should write about the other one. Follow this plan for the article:
1 INTRODUCTION, 2 PHYSICAL DESCRIPTION, 3 INTERESTS, 4 PERSONALITY, 5 CONCLUSION. Compare your versions with those of another pair.

Kirstin Macleod	**Name**	Jess Adams
20	**Age**	22
1 metre 73	**Height**	1 metre 85
53 kilos	**Weight**	74 kilos
British	**Nationality**	Australian
dark	**Hair colour**	fair
brown	**Colour of eyes**	green
Mathematics	**Studies**	Anthropology
Aquarius (refined, lovers of freedom, strong on both theory and practice, idealistic, retiring, sincere)	**Horoscope sign**	Capricorn (practical, persistent, hard-working, long-suffering, not easily discouraged, expressive and dynamic, tactful, self-controlled)
Chess, computing, cinema, photography, astronomy	**Interests**	Tennis, swimming, sailing, surfing, folklore, rock guitar, exploration
Co-director of short documentary film *The Reality in Science Fiction*	**Why in the news**	Named leader of Anglo-Australian universities climbing expedition to the Andes

Annoying characters

A description of a person can be based not on physical and mental characteristics, interests and personality, but on the effect he/she has on other people. In that case, it is necessary to give examples of his/her actions and, probably, conversation. Details expanding the description to make it more lively, and to give necessary additional information, are generally contained in subordinate clauses or phrases in apposition.

Activity 6 – pair work

A number of phrases have been omitted from each of the paragraphs in the description on these pages. Choose the most appropriate phrase from the list given on the page opposite to complete the description below. Then answer the questions on the completed passage.

There are very few people I really dislike but Mr Mackenzie, _____(1), is certainly one of them. I have been working for Mardex since I left school five years ago as secretary to Mr Norton, _____(2), and our branch has always been – _____(3) – a happy place. Mr Norton, _____(4), always encouraged us and stood up for us _____(5). Then, one morning last April, _____(6), Mr Mackenzie arrived.

I always arrive first, a minute or two after 9.30, _____(7), and everyone else turns up in the next quarter of an hour. That morning I was surprised to see a thin man waiting outside, _____(8), _____(9), _____(10). 'Ah,' he observed sarcastically, 'a sign of life! What do you do here – _____(11)?' I told him who I was and showed him into Mr Norton's office. Mr Norton arrived ten minutes later, _____(12), _____(13).

Since then Mr Mackenzie has visited us quite often. He calls us together and makes a little speech, _____(14). He tells us how idle and useless we all are. The first time, he said we were 'a lot of dilettantes', _____(15). He explains that when he arrived in Dundee, _____(16), everything was a shambles. Now it is the most efficient branch in Britain, _____(17).

The whole atmosphere in the office is different now. Mr Norton, _____(18), shouts at me irritably and smokes three packets a day. The worst of it is that we never know when Mackenzie is coming, _____(19). Our only hope is that he is so ambitious that he is bound to be promoted to Head Office in London, _____(20).

Paragraph 1: the Branch Manager in Farley; the Area Manager for my firm; who is a kindly, good-humoured man of about 50; that is to say, it was until recently; when no one expected it; when there were problems with Head Office .

Paragraph 2: which disappeared from his face as soon as he saw Mr Mackenzie; which is the official opening time; who was impatiently tapping his foot on the ground; with his usual cheerful smile; with a wispy beard and fierce, penetrating grey eyes; if, in fact, you do anything; dressed in a dark blue suit

Paragraph 3: which is all due to him, no doubt; which sounded bad but did not upset us much because we did not know what he meant; which is always the same; where he was Branch Manager before his present appointment

Paragraph 4: which makes it difficult to put on a show of efficiency; who used to be so pleasant and gave up smoking because of his bronchitis; where he can make other people's lives miserable and leave us alone

Activity 7 – pair work

1 Among the phrases listed above, find those that, to make the description clearer:
   a) explain who someone is
   b) explain what he is like
   c) give a more precise time reference
   d) explain the circumstances in which an action took place
   e) define something more precisely
   f) imply someone's personality
   g) imply someone's reactions
   h) describe someone more precisely
   i) give a more precise place reference
   j) contain a personal comment on the situation.
In some cases, these categories will overlap and more than one answer will be applicable to the same phrase.

2 Five of the phrases listed begin with **which**. Decide which of them refer to the word immediately before the phrase, and which refer to the whole of the previous clause – i.e. Does **which is the official opening time**, in the second paragraph, refer to **9.30** or **the fact that the narrator always arrives at that time**?

Activity 8

The paragraph below is written in simple sentences. Join each pair together with **who**, **which**, **where** or **with**. When you have done this, decide which sentences with **which** refer only to the previous word or phrase, and which refer to the whole of the previous clause.

When we first got married we lived next door to an elderly couple, the Christies. They were about 60 and had three grown-up daughters. Mr Christie owned a cement factory. His sons-in-law worked there. He used to smoke big cigars. He imported them from Cuba. He never took them out of his mouth when he was talking. This made it difficult to understand him. Mrs Christie must have been very pretty when she was young. She always dressed well. She kept the house spotlessly clean and whenever she came into ours looked around for signs of dust. This irritated my wife. She also liked to describe her daughters' beautiful houses. They had all been built with Mr Christie's money. My wife eventually got so bored with this that she said it was not surprising the houses were so beautiful. There was so much cement in the family.

Composition

Write about a) someone you know very well; b) someone you dislike; c) your neighbours.

Work

What's his/her line?

1 Look at the following pictures. Work through each, making notes about what the person may be doing in each case, and guessing each one's job. Then compare conclusions with a partner.

A

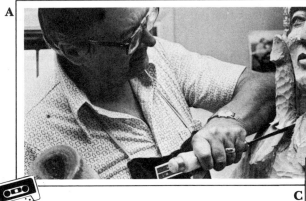

B

C

2 Listen to these four people talking about typical days in their lives. They do not mention exactly what they do as a job but it is possible to make an informed guess. Make your first guess individually and then compare notes with a partner. Explain your reasons for the guess.

3 **Game:** WHAT'S MY LINE?
In this game, each person should prepare a mime to illustrate a job. The rest of the class has twenty guesses to identify the job, but the person miming can only answer YES/NO.

Activity I – pair work

Compare the two passages opposite.
1 How much do we learn about the work these two people do?
2 Do they work regular hours?
3 What is their attitude to their work, and why?

4 In what ways would the first writer probably envy the second?
5 Which one gives a clearer impression of his/her life?
6 What evidence is there that neither is really suited to the job he/she is doing and would really rather do something else? What else?

8

A life in the day of . . .

IT IS 1.45 on a Monday afternoon and I am getting changed into coveralls at the factory where I work. As I don my coveralls I can smell the factory on them. The buzzer sounds. We reluctantly make our way to the shop floor. I step on to the shop floor and I am surrounded by rubber, in racks piled five high, one on another. There must be thousands of them.

I work at the powder post, which is the area where they make up the chemicals that go into the rubber mix for tyres. Through a cloud of dust, as I move nearer, I can make out three men working with these chemicals. They are wearing masks because the air is toxic. They wear large gloves and aprons which cover the entire length of the body, giving them the appearance of aliens from a distant planet. I put on my own apron and mask, and look up towards the windows of the roof to catch a glimpse of the sun. But to no avail – there is too much dirt on the windows.

The job I do is a menial one: it requires very little intellect for its proper performance, so I can afford to let my mind wander. I think about the play I was going to write about Edith Piaf, the 'Little Sparrow', and how I was pipped at the post by a play on the same theme produced in London and starring the lovely Jane Lapotaire.

The last buzzer of the day, as far as I am concerned, sounds at 10.00: the end of the shift. I have a shower – the only way to rid myself of the powder and debris which has clung to my body throughout the shift. But even then it is still evident. Finally I clock off. There are those who run to get out of the gates as though to escape a great catastrophe. I do not run: for are we not to return here on the morrow?

When I get home my little girl is in bed. My wife makes something for me to eat. I do not talk about the work: how can you explain about hell? There is some decorating to be done and the child needs another pair of shoes, my wife tells me, and the cat has hurt its paw but will be all right.

I wake to a long, low whistle. I get up and go downstairs. I light a cigarette. I know now what has awakened me: as I draw back the curtain it looms before me. Like a monument to a bygone age the factory lies in front of my window. Even in sleep I am not to escape it. I want to be in the country, to be by the sea. I want to see the sun shine. In the echoes of my mind I can hear someone say: 'Ha! He wants the reward but not the labour.' Is the sunshine then an award for labour?

A Day in the Life of J. . . C. . . in the Sunday Times

WE LIVE IN a two-bedroom house, so as soon as James aged two starts calling 'Mummy, Mummy' around 7.00 in the morning, he wakes everyone up. I take him downstairs and start getting breakfast ready. Before long the other three kids are also down. If Paul's recording or we are touring, I try to make sure he's not disturbed. But if he isn't working, he gets up at the same time and joins the kids at breakfast.

It seems mad to have moved from a large house in London to a small place on the south coast, but it's much cosier. Paul and I are in the kind of business where we can be totally detached from our kids and hardly see them grow up. But the kids travel everywhere with us. When touring abroad we usually rent a house and make it our base so we can return to the kids each night.

We're all vegetarian, so breakfast is eggs laid by our own hens, home-grown tomatoes fried, vegetarian sausages, cereals and whole-wheat bread.

Because we have a big breakfast and a big dinner we don't have lunch. So about this time I'm doing jobs around the house. Paul never helps me. He likes tidiness, but is not too tidy himself. If I'm working or going out, I have a woman in to do the cleaning. But I always do the cooking because I enjoy it.

I love being close to the earth. In fact we spent a year on our farm in Scotland when Paul started getting itchy and asked me if I wanted to start a group. The idea of me being in it was totally his. After all, they could have the greatest keyboard player if they wished. I think he felt he would be more secure if I was in it too. He suggested I played keyboards because he thought I could learn it quicker than the guitar.

Because we live in the country we don't socialise that much. But I think that's also partly because I'm too lazy. There's so much I'd like to do, especially in the photography field, but I'm loath to leave the life I lead in the country unless I absolutely have to.

From A Life in the Day of L . . . M . . ., interview by Glenn Gale in the Sunday Times

A typical day

Erica Fern is a Member of Parliament. Yesterday was a typical day in her life. She describes it as part of an interview for a magazine.

I got up at 6.30, as usual. I always make the breakfast for my husband, who is a teacher. He looks after the house most of
5 the time, so I think it is the least I can do! We read the papers, and he went off to school about 8.30. We live quite near the House of Commons, so my
10 secretary, Jill Barnett, comes to the flat every morning, and I dictate letters until about 10.00, when we drive to the House together. At the House, I col-
15 lected some telephone messages and made a few calls myself before going to a party meeting at 11.00.

The meeting lasted till 1
20 o'clock, and Jill **had collected** some more letters and phone calls for me to deal with before I had time for a quick lunch around 1.45. I always like to
25 attend the Prime Minister's question time from 2.30 to 3.30, and yesterday I **had put down** a question myself, so I had to be there. I did not get a very satis-
30 factory answer, as I expected, but this gave me the chance to make some points that I thought were important.

After that, I went to the lib-
35 rary to draft a lecture for the youth group of my local party next week, and gave my notes to Jill to type while I went to listen to the debate on shipbuilding
40 policy at 5.00. I had to leave this about 6.00 to sign the letters I **had dictated** earlier before Jill went home. Then I had a drink in the bar with some journalists
45 before driving to the TV studios about 7.00 to do a current affairs programme. This was televised live, and we had a good debate, but I could not stay for
50 very long afterwards because I wanted to be back at the House for the vote on the shipbuilding bill. Once that was taken, about 10.00, I drove home and had a
55 late supper with my husband. Rod always has a snack earlier but prepares dinner for us both unless I ring him to say I will be at the House all night. It is the
60 one time of the day when we get the chance to talk, but yesterday there were still half a dozen phone calls to answer before we finally got to bed about mid-
65 night.

Activity 2

1 Make a timetable of Erica Fern's day to account for everything she did.
2 Decide which of these activities are the same every day when the House is in session, which of them happen quite often, and which only happen occasionally.
3 Notice that the account is given mainly in chronological order and the verbs are mostly in the Past Simple tense, but a) many are in the Present Simple (Why?);
b) some, printed in **bold** type, are in the Past Perfect. Suggest a time when the actions referred to in the Past Perfect took place, or could have taken place.

An eventful day

Some days are more eventful than others, and then certain things stand out in the memory. Gary Marshall, 18, a professional footballer, explains here in a magazine interview why last Saturday was not a typical day for him.

I always sleep late on Saturday mornings when the Reserves are playing at home, but last Saturday a phone call
5 woke me at 8 o'clock. It was the Manager. 'Get your kit and come straight down to the club,' he said. 'Johnny Lane's fallen downstairs and twisted
10 his ankle, so I need you as substitute for the first-team game in Manchester.'

I shaved and had breakfast and almost ran to the club. It's
15 not far from my lodgings. I felt shy in the coach with all the first-team players. On the journey they were all playing cards and making jokes, but
20 I was too excited to play or talk. We got to Manchester about 12.00, had lunch, and went to the ground to get changed about 2.15.
25 When we ran on to the pitch, the noise was frightening. There were 50,000 people there. I sat on the substitutes' bench and
30 watched the game. The boss was smoking cigars, one after the other. We were playing quite well, but United were on top. Somehow we managed to
35 survive till half-time.

Then, halfway through the second half, the Manager suddenly turned to me and said, 'Bob's limping badly.
40 Take your tracksuit off, son, and let's see what you can do.' In the first few minutes, I hardly touched the ball, and when I did, I made a mess of
45 it. I wasn't used to the speed of the game. And then, just before the end, Brian Cooper got away from the fullback and put over a lovely centre. I was
50 on the edge of the box and the defence weren't marking me. Maybe they didn't think I was worth the bother. It all happened in a second. A
55 couple of defenders were turning towards me, the keeper was coming out, so I just hit it and hoped, and it went straight into the back of
60 the net. What a great feeling! I couldn't really believe I had scored the winner when the ref. blew the final whistle a minute or two later.

Activity 3

1 Unlike Erica, Gary does not describe the whole day, but only what were the most important moments for him. Make a timetable for his day, picking out the important moments.

2 The three events in the day that made it memorable for Gary are distinguished from the rest, either by the use of dialogue or by the amount of space devoted to them. Check that these are the moments you have picked out. Why do you think he quotes the manager's words, and describes one incident in great detail?

Jess Winter runs a small farm with her husband, Tom. They have a son, Neil, aged 11. Yesterday morning began typically for her, but then some unexpected events took place.

Study the timetable below, comparing what usually happens (on the left) and what was unusual yesterday (right).

7.00	Gets up. Makes breakfast.	
7.30	Has breakfast.	
8.00	Tom and Neil feed pig, hens, calves and sheep.	
8.20	Begins to milk cow.	Noticed cow was 'in season'. Rang Cattle Breeding Centre for artificial insemination service.
8.45	Neil leaves for school.	
9.00	Tom separates milk from cream.	
9.30	Cleans house. Tom goes to plough field.	
10.30	Begins working in vegetable garden.	
11.00		Two youths rode up on motorbikes. Demanded food. Jessie suspicious. Shouted for help, but Tom too far away to see or hear her. One youth pushed her to ground and went into house. Jessie ran to barn and got hay fork. Other youth came towards her.
11.05		Man from Cattle Breeding Centre arrived. Blew horn – motorbikes blocking entrance. Saw Jessie. Blew horn repeatedly. Tom heard.
11.10	Tom usually has morning cup of tea.	Youth outside caught between Tom and man. Jessie held hay fork to throat. Youth inside came out. Tom knocked him down. Man rang police.
11.20		Police arrived.
1.00	Neil comes home for lunch.	'Have you had a good morning, Mum?'

Activity 4

Tell the story of Jessie's morning, in chronological order, but concentrate on the main events. Not all details listed here need to be included. Use dialogue where necessary to heighten interest.

Begin: *Yesterday morning began as usual. I . . .*

Composition

1 Write about a typical day in the life of: a) an actor/actress; b) a pilot/air hostess; c) a doctor/teacher.
2 Write about an unusual day in the lives of one of these people.
3 Write about a day in your own life that began normally but was memorable because of an unexpected event.

3

The British

(The answers are at the back of the book.)

How much do you know about Britain?

1 The population of the United Kingdom is 55,676,000 (1981) but what proportion lives in England?
   a) 60–70%. b)70–80%. c) Over 80%.
2 The largest city is London (population 6,696,000). Put the next five in descending order:
   Liverpool, Glasgow, Leeds, Birmingham, Sheffield.
3 Britain is notoriously wet. But which is the wettest month of the year, and where does it rain most? Which are the driest months?
4 'An Englishman's home is his castle', but what proportion of people in Britain own their own home?
   a) 40–50%. b) 50–60%. c) Over 60%.

5 The British read a lot of newspapers, but which are most popular? Put the following in order of circulation figures, beginning with the highest: *The Times*, the *Guardian*, the *Daily Telegraph*, the *Daily Express*, the *Daily Mirror*, the *Sun*.
6 Britain imports food from other countries. Which of the following do we need to import most, and which do we not need to import? Meat, fish, eggs, milk, potatoes, sugar, wheat.

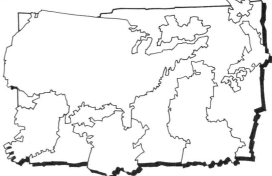

7 With which countries do we trade most? Put the following in descending order of importance: France, Holland, West Germany, Eire, Japan, the USA.
8 Where do most people in Britain work? Put the following in descending order of importance: in factories, in shops, in transport, on farms, in the civil service.
9 What do they spend their money on? Put the following in descending order of importance: food, drink, tobacco, housing, fuel and light, running the car.
10 The English love animals. Which of the following are most common? Put them in order, beginning with the most common: dogs, cats, cows, sheep, pigs.

(The answers are at the back of the book.)

Writing a paragraph

Activity 1 – pair work

> Well-organised paragraphs generally begin with a topic sentence, which introduces the subject. This topic is then developed in a variety of ways: by extending the exposition, by using examples, making examples, indicating a contrast, etc. Subsequently, the writer frequently needs a transitional sentence or two to prepare for the conclusion. The organisation of paragraphs in this way enables the writer to express his thoughts in an ordered manner.

1 What is the topic of the paragraph above? Is it expressed in the first sentence?
2 What examples does the writer use to develop the paragraph in the second sentence?
3 Is the third sentence transitional? If so, in what way?
4 Express in your own words the meaning of the whole paragraph, as contained in the last sentence.
5 Does the paragraph exemplify the explanation given within it?

Activity 2

A new paragraph may relate directly to the previous one, linking with the concluding sentence, or may begin a new approach to the main topic as part of the whole article.

The following paragraphs are alternative second paragraphs to the one in Activity 1 above. Decide which technique is being used: relating the paragraph to the previous one or beginning a new approach to the main topic. Give reasons for your answer.

> a) Just as well-organised paragraphs depend on a logical sequence of sentences, so the paragraphs themselves should follow an ordered plan. It is a good idea for students to make a plan of the paragraphs in their compositions, giving each one a title. This has the advantage of reminding them of what they plan to include in each paragraph as they write. It also serves the more important purpose of providing the framework for a convincing argument.

> b) This is essential in writing effective articles, especially those dealing with general topics. A good argument depends on logical presentation and the provision of examples that help the reader to follow it. Students often put forward their ideas as a series of generalisations without any evidence to support them. Instead of convincing the reader, this frequently provokes him into finding reasons for disagreement.

National and regional characteristics

Activity 3

Read the following four paragraphs about life in Britain.

1 Find the topic sentence in each and decide what the purpose of the other sentences is – development, transition or conclusion.

2 In the first three paragraphs, decide how the topic is developed, e.g. by example, by showing a contrast, etc.

3 The fourth paragraph is printed with the sentences out of order. Find the topic sentence, decide what the purpose of each sentence is and reorder the sentences correctly.

When foreign students talk about people in Britain, they often do so in terms of stereotypes. The Englishman
5 is thought to be a man in a bowler hat sipping tea, for example. The Scot, on the other hand, wears a kilt and carries a bottle of whisky
10 everywhere. Such simplifications occur whenever people refer to the inhabitants of other countries. They are unlikely to be true of
15 individuals, though there *are* such things as national and regional characteristics that can be identified.

Within England itself, for
20 instance, the differences between North and South are a perennial source of argument. To a Southerner, Northerners are uncultured
25 barbarians with harsh accents. Northerners, on the other hand, regard Londoners, in particular, as lazy, selfish and insincere. Such definitions
30 break down even further when we consider the traditional rivalry between two groups of Northerners, those from Yorkshire and
35 Lancashire. At least in their own opinion, the people from each county have separate characteristics.

To a Southerner like myself,
40 these characteristics are not immediately obvious. Apart from that, it is dangerous for anyone not directly involved to express an opinion or
45 appear to take sides. There is a joke about a Southerner who applauded a good shot during the annual Yorkshire–Lancashire cricket match, and
50 was asked belligerently by the man next to him which county he came from. When he said 'Neither', he was told to mind his own business! While
55 rivalries exist between different regions of a country and the inhabitants themselves even enjoy them, outsiders are warned not to
60 take part.

In the same way, individuals you meet in Britain may or may not live up to your idea of a stereotype
65 but this does not necessarily mean your idea was mistaken. While everyone agrees about those of other countries or regions, the same people
70 resent foreigners or strangers mentioning their own. All the same, it suggests that the wisest course is to judge them as individuals, wherever they
75 come from. The fact is that national and regional characteristics are a risky topic in conversation.

Developing paragraphs

**Topic sentences can be developed in a variety of
ways to reach different conclusions within
paragraphs. Below, starting from the topic
sentence, three separate paragraphs are developed.
One depends primarily on *example*, one on
comparison and one on *contrast*.**

Activity 4

1   Read the beginning and development of each paragraph
and decide which of these three techniques is used in
each case.

a)   The English public schools in the nineteenth century
were largely responsible for the organised development of
most of the outdoor games popular all over the world
today. This does not necessarily mean, however, that they
invented them. On the contrary, there is evidence that the
Chinese, for example, played a form of football as long ago
as 500 BC, and games similar to tennis and golf were also
played in ancient times . . .

b)   The English public schools in the nineteenth century
were largely responsible for the organised development of
most of the outdoor games popular all over the world
today. Association football, the most popular of all, stems
in its modern form from the establishment of the Football
Association in 1863. In the same way, the Rugby Union
was set up in 1871, and the Lawn Tennis Association a few
years later. These associations at first met to agree on the
rules, but soon established competitions which form the
basis for the appeal of modern professional sport . . .

c)   The English public schools in the nineteenth century
were largely responsible for the organised development of
most of the outdoor games popular all over the world
today. In some cases the form of a game played in different
schools led to different games emerging, so that the game
of football played at Rugby School evolved according to a
separate code from the standard form. Even then, in the
case of rugby, there was a further division between north
and south, leading to similar games played by 13 players in
the north (Rugby League) and 15 in the south (Rugby
Union) . . .

2   Choose the most appropriate sentence from the three
given below to form the second to last sentence of each
paragraph.

i)   Of these the most
significant were the FA Cup,
first played in 1871, and the
Wimbledon Tennis
Championships, which began
in 1877.

ii)   This difference was further
emphasised when northern
rugby clubs adopted
professionalism while the
southern ones remained
amateur.

iii)   Evidently, as Desmond
Morris argues in his book *The
Football Tribe*, games
combining skill and strength
fulfil an inherent human need.

3   Write a concluding sentence to summarise the meaning
of each paragraph as a whole. Begin each sentence with
one of the following suggestions.

i)   In effect, the differences
between the games played in
individual schools led . . .

ii)   Consequently, although
the public schools . . .

iii)   It can therefore be claimed
that . . .

The English

National characteristics are not easy to pin down, and when pinned down they often turn out to be trivialities or seem to have no connection with one another. Spaniards are cruel to animals, Italians can do nothing without making a deafening noise, the Chinese are addicted to gambling. Obviously
5 such things don't matter in themselves. Nevertheless, nothing is causeless, and even the fact that Englishmen have bad teeth can tell one something about the realities of English life.

Here are a couple of generalisations about England that would be accepted by almost all observers. One is that the English are not gifted artistically.
10 They are not as musical as the Germans or Italians; painting and sculpture have never flourished in England as they have in France. Another is that, as Europeans go, the English are not intellectual. They have a horror of abstract thought, they feel no need for any philosophy or systematic 'world-view'. Nor is this because they are 'practical', as they are so fond of claiming for
15 themselves. One has only to look at their methods of town planning and water supply, their obstinate clinging to everything that is out of date and a nuisance, a spelling system that defies analysis and a system of weights and measures that is intelligible only to the compilers of arithmetic books, to see how little they care about mere efficiency.
20 Another English characteristic which is so much a part of us that we barely notice it, is the addiction to hobbies and spare-time occupations, the *privateness* of English life. We are a nation of flower-lovers, but also a nation of stamp-collectors, pigeon-fanciers, amateur carpenters, coupon-snippers, darts-players, crossword-puzzle fans. All the culture that is most truly native
25 centres round things which even when they are communal are not official – the pub, the football match, the back garden, the fireside and the 'nice cup of tea'. The liberty of the individual is still believed in, almost as in the nineteenth century. But this has nothing to do with economic liberty, the right to exploit others for profit. It is the liberty to have a home of your own,
30 to do what you like in your spare time, to choose your own amusements instead of having them chosen for you from above.

From The Lion and the Unicorn by George Orwell.

Activity 5 – group work

1 What is the writer saying about national characteristics? Are they a) non-existent; b) of no importance at all; c) part of a complex picture?

2 What English habits are evident from the fact that the English have bad teeth?

3 Which form of art, for which the English have a great reputation, is excluded from the writer's generalisation?

4 What evidence does the writer give for the English not being 'practical'? Have any of the examples he mentions been changed since 1940, when this was written? What do you imagine were the causes of the English not being 'practical' in the way he mentions?

5 The writer forecast that the effect of mass media would be to change the picture he gives in the last paragraph. How far has this happened, from your experience of Britain?

6 Does the writer develop his ideas in these three paragraphs by means of example, comparison or contrast, or by a combination of these? Give examples from the text in your answer.

Activity 6 – group work

Look at the following table of contrasting adjectives, which could be used about the people of any country. Then work in groups to decide what your picture of the average British person (man or woman) is. Put a ✓ in the appropriate box.

	*** Very	** Fairly	* Average	** Fairly	*** Very	
talkative						shy
sincere						hypocritical
romantic						practical
emotional						phlegmatic
broad-minded						narrow-minded
egalitarian						class-conscious
bohemian						conventional
hard-working						lazy
polite						rude
humorous						humourless

Then compare your picture with the picture you have of your own country and people, or of another, thinking about *how* you came to form these impressions.

Discussion

Discuss with others in the group whether you think British people are 'more talkative' or 'shyer' than you are; 'not as romantic' or 'not as practical' as you are. Find out if you agree with others in the group that British people 'are different from us' or 'similar to us' in various respects. Are there any characteristics where they seem to you to be 'the same as we are'?

Composition

What is your impression of Britain and the British people? You can answer in terms of: a) the impressions you have gained on visits to Britain in personal terms; b) if you have not visited Britain, the idea you have gained of it from reading, meeting people from Britain, etc.

Telegrams and notes

Telegrams

Read through the following telegrams and make informed guesses as to who was sending the message to whom. Then try to fill out each message to make it into a story.

1 SANDRA DARLING COME BACK ALL FORGIVEN MY SIDE STOP NO GOOD WITHOUT YOU STOP SORRY DRAMA LOST TEMPER STOP LAST TIME EVER STOP PROMISE STOP NEVILLE WITH LOVE

2 CANALETTO CERTAINLY GENUINE STOP COLOURS INCREDIBLE STOP PROPRIETOR UNAWARE OR GOOD ACTOR STOP MUST MAKE CREDIBLE OFFER STOP YOUR ADVICE WELCOME SOONEST STOP ALEX

3 FANTASTIC NEWS STOP CONGRATULATIONS YOU AND MORRIS STOP SO HAPPY MORRIS FINALLY TOOK PLUNGE STOP BUT MUCH REGRET CANNOT MAKE WEDDING BECAUSE STILL FILMING CALIFORNIA STOP BEST WISHES FUTURE HAPPINESS TIMMY SENDS LOVE NANCY

4 SCHINDLER NOW UNSEEN FOUR DAYS STOP CAR NOW GONE TOO STOP HOUSE APPARENTLY EMPTY BUT HOUSE DOBERMANNS FED DAILY STOP TOWN DEAD QUIET STOP REQUEST AID FROM INTERPOL ALLOWING ENTRY STOP MACK

Read the following series of four telegrams from a newspaper editor to a foreign correspondent and work out what you think happened.

21.11 1715	PRESIDENT OMALI REPORTED ILL STOP YOUR COMMENTS SOONEST STOP LANGHAM
21.11 2325	REQUEST CLARIFICATION STOP OMALIS ILLNESS NOT REPEAT NOT UNIMPORTANT STOP FRONT PAGE IN RIVALS STOP YOUR COMMENTS RUMOURED COUP D'ETAT POSSIBILITY SOONEST STOP SUPPLY 800 WORDS IMMEDIATELY STOP LANGHAM
22.11 0935	YOUR TELEGRAM CONTRADICTORY STOP 0905 BBC REPORT OMALI SHOT DRIVING OWN CAR STOP IF ILL HOW DRIVING STOP TRUTH VITAL STOP YOUR ARTICLE DUE YESTERDAY STOP LANGHAM
22.11 1145	NO ARTICLE YET RECEIVED STOP NO EXCUSE STOP YOUR REPLACEMENT ARRIVING BA FLIGHT 209 STOP SAVE JOB MAYBE WITH 800 WORDS OMALIS FATE AND PROFILE NEW JUNTA STOP LANGHAM

Expanding notes

**We send telegrams when we are in a hurry, and
have no time to write a letter. The words are kept to
a minimum to save money. Compare the telegram
and the letter here on a similar subject.**

MUST CANCEL VISIT
SEVENTEENTH. IMPOSSIBLE
OBTAIN FLIGHT. BOOKED
FOLLOWING DAY. ARRIVE
AIRPORT ELEVEN MORNING.
SORRY UPSET PLANS. PLEASE
MEET. ROBERTO.

Dear Sarah,

It was a great pleasure to receive your letter confirming the dates of my stay. Unfortunately, I have discovered that the flight on the 17th is fully booked and the waiting list is closed, so I have booked on the first flight on the next day, which arrives at Heathrow at 11.00. I am sorry if this upsets your plans in any way, but I hope you will be able to meet me the following day, as planned. If you cannot do so, perhaps you could ring me and give me directions, so that I can make my own way to your house by taxi.

I look forward very much to seeing you. My kindest regards to your parents.

Sincerely, Roberto

Activity 1 – pair work

Read the following telegrams and write suitable letters for the same situations, assuming that the need to convey the information in each case is not so urgent. Remember to begin and end the letters appropriately, and take the content of the telegram into account to adopt a suitable tone (pleased, sorry, excited, etc.).

1 Tony sent this telegram to his parents, who live in France. The following week he wrote to his old friend, Andrew. Write Tony's letter, noting the time difference.
TERESA TWINS ROBERT AND EMILY. MOTHER BABIES DOING WELL. CENTRAL HOSPITAL. GO HOME THURSDAY. TERESA SENDS LOVE. TONY.

2 Sally sent this telegram to her brother, James, on holiday abroad.

Two days later she wrote to her cousin, Barbara, in Manchester to tell her her father was still seriously ill. Write Sally's letter to Barbara.
FATHER SERIOUSLY ILL HEART ATTACK. RUSHED HOSPITAL LAST NIGHT. CONDITION UNCHANGED. COME HOME IMMEDIATELY. SALLY.

3 An opera impresario sent this telegram to a famous singer because his leading tenor was ill. Imagine the illness was more serious but he had two months to find a substitute. Write his letter.
BRANQUIST ILL SEVERE COLD. UNABLE SING CARMEN SEVENTH. CAN YOU SUBSTITUTE TENOR ROLE? FLY TOMORROW. TWO DAYS REHEARSALS. ADVISE

ACCEPTANCE OR WILL CANCEL. LA SCALA OPERA.

4 A defence lawyer at a trial sent this telegram to Alan Murray, on holiday in the Bahamas, because he was a vital witness and the trial had been brought forward. Imagine that there was no hurry, and he wrote to Alan at home in the normal way a month beforehand. Write the lawyer's letter.
CANTWELL TRIAL ADVANCED TO THURSDAY NEXT. REQUIRE YOU AS KEY WITNESS. VITAL TO DEFENCE. CONTACT IMMEDIATELY TO DISCUSS EVIDENCE AND CONFIRM APPEARANCE. BARCLAY.

Newspaper reports

Telegrammatic reports to newspapers are often converted into short articles. Compare the report and the story below and notice where the writer of the news story has added or omitted anything. Note down any changes you would have made in your treatment of this report.

. . . DEEPDALE CIRCUS BLACK PANTHER REPORTED MISSING 0615 STOP CAGE DOOR BROKEN OPEN STOP ACCESS CAGES RESTRICTED CIRCUS STAFF STOP LOOKS LIKE INSIDE JOB SAY POLICE STOP SACKED CIRCUS HAND SUSPECTED STOP PANTHER LAST SEEN 0115 STOP FED BEFORE BUT PROBABLY HUNGRY NOW STOP TRAILED BY POLICE BELIEVED HEADING DARTINGTON AREA STOP POLICE WARNING ANIMAL DANGEROUS DO NOT APPROACH STOP . . .

The black panther reported missing from the Deepdale Circus early this morning has still not been found, despite police efforts to track down the animal. The panther, last seen by circus staff at 1.15 last night after it had been fed, was apparently let out of its cage intentionally by someone with inside knowledge of the circus, and police are looking for a sacked circus hand, who may have known how to get access to the cages. Latest news of the panther, from the police who are trying to trail it, is that it is believed to be heading for the Dartington area. A police spokesman warned the public that it will be hungry by now, may be dangerous, and should not be approached.

Activity 2 – group work

Study these messages and convert them into stories.

1. TURIN MILLIONAIRE GIACOMO LEONI KIDNAPPED EARLY THIS MORNING STOP FIRST NEWS OF DISAPPEARANCE 1015 STOP HIS WHITE MERCEDES FOUND IN MOTORWAY RESTAURANT CAR PARK NEAR BOLOGNA STOP MAFIA SUSPECTED STOP NOT FIRST TIME LEONI FAMILY IN KIDNAPPING STOP LAST YEAR GIACOMOS SON GIOVANNI KIDNAPPED FROM SWISS SCHOOL LAUSANNE BY TERRORIST GROUP BLUE HAND STOP SON LOCATED BY SWISS POLICE NO RANSOM PAID STOP LEONI ANTI-MAFIA REVENGE FEARED STOP . . .

2. PICASSO PAINTING LA DONA STOLEN MUNICH AUGUST LAST FOUND GARAGE PARIS UNDAMAGED AFTER ANONYMOUS PHONE CALL STOP VALUED TWO MILLION DOLLARS PROPERTY GERMAN INDUSTRIALIST FRITZ REDEL STOP FRENCH POLICE BELIEVE PAINTING DUMPED BECAUSE IMPOSSIBLE RESALE STOP

3. FIRE OUTBREAK WEST OF VALENCIA SPAIN UNCONTROLLED AFTER TWO DAYS STOP RAIN STORM HOPES IN AREA TONIGHT STOP LARGE AREA AFFECTED STOP FIREMEN FROM THREE PROVINCES THOUSANDS CIVILIAN HELPERS NOW REINFORCED BY MORE ARMY UNITS STOP FIREMEN SAY FIRE CAUSED BY CARELESS PICNICKERS STOP ABANDONED CAR SPOTTED BY AIR PATROL NEAR WHERE FIRE STARTED STOP NO VICTIMS YET REPORTED STOP

4. SAFARI PARK BUS CRASH TRENTHAM EARLY AFTERNOON STOP GENTLE COLLISION WITH UNEXPECTED ELEPHANT ON BEND STOP DRIVER UNHURT BUT FIFTEEN INJURED MAINLY SHOCK AND OR GLASS CUTS WHEN BUS OVERTURNED STOP ELEPHANT MILDLY ANNOYED BUT UNHURT STOP

Below you will find a list of expressions that might help you connect the various points to be made in the article.

in future	on the other hand
in the first place	on the contrary
secondly	in that case
thirdly	as for
lastly	on the whole
up to a point	above all
in fact	consequently
what makes it worse	

① BACKGROUND, (40 words) Following 17 year old rock fan Malcolm Truman's fatal fall at last Wed night's rock concert in Catford Stadium — some voices (15/36) raised in City Council meeting calling for TOTAL BAN on rock concerts.

② "BANNERS" 4 BASIC ARGUMENTS (±60 words). 1) "Rock causes violence".. 2) any more gatherings potentially dangerous... 3) traffic chaos before and after... 4) noise pollution rock music a health hazard.

③ ARE BANNERS' ARGUMENTS JUSTIFIED? (80 words) SOME justification (1) some violent incidents at rock concerts in recent years and a few groups provoke it deliberately [BUT] concerts serve purpose for young - ban Not a solution - might frustrate young enough to provoke violence elsewhere - where police would be less prepared...

④ CONCLUSION (70 words) traffic problems? No worse than football matches (which are potentially more violent)... Banning rock but not football would be seen as discrimination by rock fans (most too young to vote and can't express disagreement democratically).

Activity 3

Bill Caxton, a young reporter with the *Calford Courier*, has been given instructions by his editor to write a 250-word article on a campaign within the City Council to ban rock concerts from the city, following a fatal accident to a young rock fan. On the right you will see a page from Bill's notebook on which he has written a basic 4-paragraph plan for the article, with brief notes of what each paragraph may contain. He is just about to write the article when he is called away to cover an emergency, and you are left with the job of doing it with the deadline in 25 minutes.

Composition

1. Write a suitable letter or newspaper report based on any of the topics on pages 20–22, which you have not done in class.
2. Rewrite the story on this page, using the same paragraph organisation, but this time direct it at teenage readers.

Processes

Looking good, feeling fit

Look at the following information on proteins, vitamins and minerals and the chart showing the nutritional value of vegetarian foods. Then advise each of these five people on which vegetarian foods would improve their health.

1. a 75-year-old grandfather who says his teeth 'aren't what they were'
2. an overweight business person
3. a teenager with a skin problem
4. a working wife and mother
5. a young person who complains of lack of energy and of sleeping badly

Proteins
Good for keeping your body firm and in good working order.

Vitamins
Vitamin A: good for the skin, bright eyes; helps body build up resistance to illness.
Vitamin B family: help to stabilise the heart and nerves.
Vitamin C: helps to keep all parts of the body young and supple.
Vitamin D: helps keep teeth and bones straight, firm and strong; helps body relax by aiding in the body's efficient use of calcium.
Vitamin E: helps prevent 'old age' illnesses.

Minerals
Calcium/Phosphorus: give hardness to bones and teeth; especially important for older people.
Calcium (+ Vitamin D): calms and steadies the nerves; helps you sleep soundly.
Iron: regulates the progress of oxygen and carbon dioxide in the blood stream; builds energy; lack of iron causes anaemia.
Potassium: helps maintain pliability and suppleness and keep the blood pressure normal; helps treat fatigue, overweight and headaches.

VEGETARIAN FOODS	MAINLY USED AS A SOURCE OF: (x minor source, xx useful, xxx important source)			
	Prot.	Minerals	Vitamins	Cals.
MILK YOGURT (fresh and whole)	xxx	xxx Ca K P	xxx A B C D B_{12}	xxx
CHEESES (hard)	xxx	xxxx Ca K P	xxx A B D B_{12}	xxx
BUTTER			xx A D	xxx
EGGS (fresh, whole)	xxx	xx K P Fe	xx A B D B_{12}	x
WHOLE WHEAT	xx	xx P Mg K Ca Fe	xx B	xx
OATS, OATMEAL	xx	xx P Mg K Ca Fe	xx B	xx
BROWN RICE, MILLET, RYE, etc.	xx	xx P K Fe	xx B	x
MARGARINES, COOKING FAT			xx A D	xxx
COOKING OILS, OLIVE OIL			x A D	xxx
BRAZILS, WALNUTS, ALMONDS, HAZELS	xxx	xxx Ca K P Mg	xx B	xxx
PEANUTS	xxx	xx Ca K P Mg	x B	xxx
CASHEWS	xxx		x B	xxx
PEAS, BEANS (fresh, raw)	xxx	xxx Ca K P Fe	xx A B C	xx
LENTILS (uncooked)	xxx	xxx Ca K P Fe	xx B	xx
SOYA, TVP (the new protein food)	xxx	xxx Ca K P Fe	xx B	xx
ALL GREENS (raw)	x	xxx Ca K P	xxx A B C	x
ROOTS: CARROTS, POTATOES	x	xxx K P	xx B	xx
ONIONS, LEEKS (raw)		xxx K P	xx B C	x
MUSHROOMS (raw)	x	xx K P	xx B C	
LETTUCE, CRESS, ENDIVE, etc.	x	xxx K P	xxx A B C	x
TOMATOES (raw)		xxx K P	xxx A B C	
CUCUMBER, RADISHES and all salad stuff	x	xxx K P	xxx B C	x
CITRUS FRUIT		xxx Ca K P	xxx A B C	x
APPLES, PEARS		xxx K	xxx A B C	x
BANANAS		xxx K Mg P	xxx A B C	x
EXOTICS: Peaches, Avocado		xxx K P	xxx	x
DATES, Raisins, Figs	x	xxx Ca Mg K P	xx	x

FOODS ABOVE ARE ALL RAW, WHOLE
Ca calcium; Fe iron; Mg magnesium; K potassium; P phosphorus.

In the vitamin indications, B includes the B group, and only the main vitamins are mentioned.

Games

As in articles describing scientific processes, an article about a game can be built up in paragraphs depending primarily on   a) classification; b) a description of the process, in this case of how the game is played;   c) space and time relationships – here, references to the origins of the game and where it is played today.

Activity I

Read the following article on golf.
1   Find examples of the way golf is distinguished from other games played with sticks.
2   Describe what a good player would normally expect to do on a standard hole.

3   In the last paragraph, decide how the last sentence relates to the first and how it contrasts with the second to last sentence.

Golf is one of a number of games men have played with sticks since the earliest times; others are the different forms of hockey and polo, played on horseback. Unlike the others, however, golf is an 5 individual game, and its origins can be traced to one country, Scotland. Hockey, too, was played in Scotland in a rough form several hundred years ago and seems to have derived from the Irish game of hurling. Polo, on the other hand, is of Asian origin, 10 and something like it was played in Persia around 600 BC.

The modern game of golf is played by up to four players. Standard golf courses consist of eighteen holes of between 100 and 600 metres in length, the 15 object being to hit a small white ball into a hole in the fewest possible strokes. Courses are designed so that good players can normally complete a hole in four, and a round of eighteen holes in 72 strokes, but this is not just a matter of strength and 20 direction, since the average hole encloses various hazards – sand traps (called bunkers), trees, ponds and streams – to complicate the task. Golfers normally use woods (clubs with wooden heads) for their first shot, irons (with metal heads) for the 25 intermediate strokes, and a putter for the final strokes on the carefully tended greens, which are usually surrounded by bunkers.

Golf is mentioned in documents from the Scottish court as early as 1424, but it was not until 1744 30 that the first golf club was formed in Edinburgh, and not until 1860 that the first major championship, the British Open, was played. Since then golf has spread all over the world, above all to the United States, the former British dominions, Euro- 35 pean countries, South America, and in recent years to Japan and Southeast Asia. For most people, the game is still expensive. Apart from the cost of a set of clubs and the balls, the considerable space required for golf courses and the need to maintain 40 them in good condition has usually made it a rich man's sport. This is not the case, however, in its original home, Scotland, where boys and girls are taught to play from an early age on the many public courses where one can play for as little as £2 a 45 round.

Activity 2 – group work

Use the article on golf on the opposite page and the
information provided below to write a similar article about
tennis.

Other games played with racquets
Squash (walls, black ball, indoors); badminton (indoors, shuttle instead of ball); various forms of *pelota
vasca* (walls, hand, bat or *cestera*). All derived from ancient games (time of Alexander the Great) and
especially from Real (royal) tennis, popular above all in France in the Middle Ages and the sixteenth and
5 seventeenth centuries.

Rules
Tennis scoring similar to real tennis, different
from other games.
Players serve each game in turn, up to 2 serves
10 for each point (fault, double fault), beginning
from right-hand court.
Scoring: 15,30,40,game. 40–40 = deuce,
players must continue till one has advantage of
two points.
15   6 games = 1 set. At 5–5 players must continue
till one has advantage of two games, but in
modern professional matches, tie break is used
at 6–6 (first to win 7 points, or if 6–6, advantage
of two points).
20   Matches normally best of 3 sets (e.g. 2–0,
2–1), but in some matches best of 5.

Main historical events
Modern game based on rules patented by
Walter Wingfield (1874).
25 First All-England championships at Wimbledon
(1877).
Foundation of Lawn Tennis Association (1885).
First Davis Cup match (Great Britain v. USA,
1900).
30 Open tennis established in 1968, founding
modern professional circuit.

Social background
Originally popular as mixed sport at Victorian
garden parties, played on grass. Attraction: men
35 and women could play together. Once middle-
class game, but now spreading rapidly through
provision of public courts, especially in English
public parks. Surfaces: grass, clay, asphalt,
wood (indoors), new synthetic surfaces indoors.

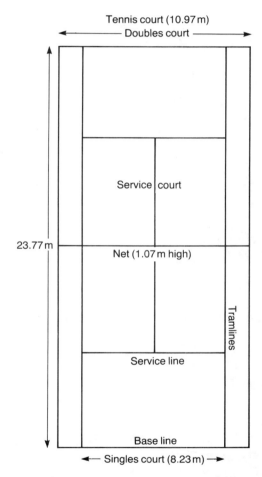

Tennis court (10.97 m)
Doubles court
23.77 m
Service court
Net (1.07 m high)
Tramlines
Service line
Base line
Singles court (8.23 m)

Saga of a film script

How the film world turned hope into despair . . . the progress of a brilliant young writer's exciting script through the machinery of the film industry.

1.

FILM DIRECTOR IRVING QUAKENBUSH INVITES RISING YOUNG SCREEN WRITER, NORMAN COLEMAN, TO LUNCH AT LONDON'S 'CHEZ GROPPI' TO DISCUSS COLEMAN'S ORIGINAL FILMSCRIPT AND THE FUTURE:

NORMAN I LOVE IT! IT'S A WONDERFUL SCRIPT.

GREAT! WHAT DO WE DO WITH IT?

THE EPPING GROUP. I SEE IT AS A VEHICLE FOR WAYNE COOPER.

2.

BUT WHEN QUAKENBUSH SUBMITS THE SCRIPT TO EPPING STUDIOS, EXECUTIVES STERLING STONE AND CLINTON BURKE HAVE OTHER IDEAS:

QUAKENBUSH IS THINKING ABOUT WAYNE COOPER. THAT MEANS A MILLION FOR 3 WEEK'S WORK!

WHY NOT GO WITH FRANK FELICIANO? HE'S STILL PROFITABLE.

BUT WHAT IF QUAKENBUSH DOESN'T WANT FELICIANO?

LET'S HAVE A MEETING WITH THE WRITER. AFTER ALL IT'S HIS PROPERTY.

3.

OVER COCKTAILS IN THE CUNARD LOUNGE, COLEMAN LEARNS THAT THE PROJECT HAS A NEW DIRECTOR, MERLIN SPIEGELEI.

WE'RE EXCITED! MERLIN HERE THINKS IT'S A PERFECT VEHICLE FOR FRANK FELICIANO.

NO PROBLEM FRANK, NORMAN IS READY TO GO TO WORK.

THE ENDING HAS GOT TO BE CHANGED. I SEE THIS MAN AS A TOUGH CHARACTER. HE'S GOT TO GO ON FIGHTING.

FROM HIS PENTHOUSE MOVIE STAR FRANK FELICIANO CALLS FOR A COMPLETE REWRITE

5.

COLEMAN REWRITES THE SCRIPT AND SUBMITS IT TO FELICIANO. HE HEARS NOTHING FOR WEEKS. FINALLY IN DESPERATION HE CALLS STERLING STONE AT EPPING STUDIOS

SORRY NORMAN BUT THERE'S NOTHING DEFINITE. WE HAVE IT UNDER REVIEW. LOOK, PERHAPS YOU COULD TRY CREATIVE.

6.

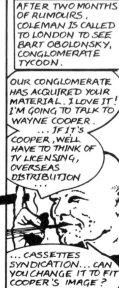

AFTER TWO MONTHS OF RUMOURS, COLEMAN IS CALLED TO LONDON TO SEE BART OBOLONSKY, CONGLOMERATE TYCOON.

OUR CONGLOMERATE HAS ACQUIRED YOUR MATERIAL. I LOVE IT! I'M GOING TO TALK TO WAYNE COOPER. ... IF IT'S COOPER, WELL HAVE TO THINK OF TV LICENSING, OVERSEAS DISTRIBUTION ...

... CASSETTES SYNDICATION... CAN YOU CHANGE IT TO FIT COOPER'S IMAGE?

Activity 3 – pair work

Work through the story picture by picture, making notes
for a step-by-step report on the process the script follows.
The questions below will serve as a basis. Finally compare
your notes with a partner's.

Picture	Question
1	Who had the script been shown to and why? Who would it be submitted to afterwards and why?
2	In what terms was it being discussed by Burke and Stone? In what ways would it be changed by their suggestions?
3	Since the situation in picture 2, what had happened to Quakenbush and why, and why had Spiegelei been brought in? In what way do you think the script would be changed by having Spiegelei as director instead of Quakenbush?
4	In what ways would the story be changed if Feliciano's demands were met? If the script were changed to meet those demands, how do you think Coleman might feel while doing it?
5	Since the situation in picture 4, what had been done with the script a) by Coleman and b) by the studio?

Picture	Question
6	In what ways would the script be improved by being taken over by Obolensky's conglomerate? In what ways would it have to be changed to 'fit Cooper's image'?
7	Since the situation in picture 6, what had been done to the script? If it needed a 'few changes' and 'a few *Generation* touches', how do you suppose it would have to be changed?
8	Why did Coleman feel it would be ruined by the new suggestions? In what way(s) could it have benefited from them?
9	Looking back at the story as a whole, do you think it is summarised in any way by the final picture?
10	Describe what really happened to the script in three or four sentences.

Active and passive

In the interests of giving importance to what *is done*, not who *does* it, the writers of scientific texts make frequent use of the Passive rather than the Active voice, thus giving the text an objective, impersonal ring.

Activity 4

Read the text below and then work through it, changing the Active verbs in italic into the Passive and making any other necessary changes.

Researchers (1) *are trying* combinations of attractants and poisons against several insect species. Government scientists (2) *have developed* an attractant called methyl angenol, which males of
5 the oriental fruit fly (3) *find* irresistible. They (4) *have combined* this with a poison in tests in the Bonin Islands, 450 miles south of Japan. They (5) *impregnated* small pieces of fibreboard with the chemicals and (6) *distributed* them by air over the
10 entire island chain to attract and kill the male flies. They (7) *began* this programme of 'male annihilation' in 1960: a year later the Agricultural Department estimated that it (8) *had eliminated* more than 99% of the fruit fly population. The
15 method scientists (9) *apply* here seems to have marked advantages over the conventional broadcasting of insecticides. They (10) *confine* the poison, an organic phosphorus chemical, to squares of fibreboard, which wildlife (11) *are*
20 *unlikely* to eat; the air, moreover, quickly (12) *dissipates* the residues, and so they are not potential contaminants of soil or water.

But not all communication in the insect world is by scents that lure or repel. Sound also may be a
25 warning or an attraction. What use, if any, (13) *can* scientists (13) *make* of this ability of the insect to detect and react to sound? As yet in the experimental stage, but none the less interesting, is the initial success scientists have had in attracting
30 male mosquitoes to playback recordings of the flight sound of the female. They (14) *lured* the males to a charged grid and so (15) *killed* them. Some scientists in Canada (16) *are testing* the repellent effect of bursts of ultrasonic sound against
35 cornborer and cutworm moths. Elsewhere others (17) *are also testing* sound as an agent of direct destruction. Ultrasonic sound (18) *will kill* all mosquito larvae in a laboratory tank; however, it (19) *kills* other aquatic organisms as well. In other
40 experiments, airborne ultrasonic sound (20) *has killed* blowflies, mealworms and yellow-fever mosquitoes in a matter of seconds.

From *Silent Spring* by Rachel Carson (adapted)

Composition

1 Describe a course of treatment for any common illness.
2 Describe how any product you know about is made.
3 Give an account of one of the main industries of your country, explaining where the products are made or grown, and where they are exported to.
4 Write a brief historical account of the development of any game or sport in your country.

The Press

News shorthand

Work in groups. Each group represents **one** of the following newspapers or magazines: a) a gossip magazine; b) a youth-oriented community newspaper; c) a 'quality' daily newspaper; d) *The Green File*, an ecological magazine; e) a 'popular' daily newspaper.

Look at the following five news agency extracts and decide which story you would feature as your main front-page item in the next edition and which other one you would include.

...17/10 1405 hrs...Dillingham school scandal latest. Headless body of missing headmaster Dr Trevor Sugden found in wood near school. Mrs Sugden attacked this morning by intruder. Ex-pupil of school suspected because killer apparently had inside information on school organisation. Sugden had many enemies but wife a saint, according to parent-teacher association. Police hoping to make arrest 'in near future'...

...17/10 1535 hrs...Former Arsenal and Scotland football star Steve Brayne has found woman of his life. Brayne, twice married, finished football career prematurely with alcohol scandal. Has given up drinking and gambling since meeting actress (latest Bond film) and former beauty queen Sally Anne Spokes. Said Ms Spokes, 'What Steve needs is to forget the past, and I'm going to help him make a new life. But he mustn't be jealous of my career; he knows that.' Said Brayne's former wife, Norma Braham, since remarried, 'I wish her the best of luck. I'm afraid she doesn't know what he's really like.'

...17/10 1555 hrs...Farmers in Australia want reduction country's estimated nine million kangaroo population by ten per cent. Farmers say official estimate nine million kangaroos ridiculously low. Really more like double. Kangas cause millions dollars worth damage to farming property every year...

...17/10 1845 hrs...New Liverpool firm Future Games has orders at least 100000 boxes new product, game called MANDALA. Game invented only a year ago. Till last August no money available to take game beyond prototype stage. £125000 backing now found from Midland Bank and ICFC. Ten school-leavers taken on and two unemployed teenagers. Six new ideas for games sent in by inventors and now being tested. At least one of six to be developed next year.

...17/10 1855 hrs...Emergency pollution teams fighting Humber estuary to prevent oil slick spread from damaged tanker. First beaches affected this afternoon. Tanker collision with dock Immingham yesterday. Load 104000 tons Nigerian crude. 3000 tons now in river. Only two tanks broken out of ten. Eight unloaded. Only one of two full oil but 9000 tons. Fight now stop remaining 6000 tons. 20000 birds at risk. Unemployed to help clear beaches.

Headlines

The following pages compare three newspapers, the *Daily Telegraph*, the *Guardian* and the *Sun*. When reading an English newspaper, it is important to know the sort of public it is written for and its political outlook. Keep the following information in mind in attempting the activities in this unit.

The *Daily Telegraph* (circulation 1,305,000) is the official newspaper of the Conservative party, though not owned by it. It is mainly read by business people and middle-class people with right-wing views.

The *Guardian* (circulation 420,000) appeals primarily to professional people and intellectuals of all types. Politically, it is left of centre, tending to favour the Liberal or Social Democrat options.

The *Sun* (circulation 4,077,000) is not aligned to any political party. It aims to provide entertainment for a predominantly working-class readership.

Headlines in English newspapers are often difficult to understand because their main purpose is to attract attention. The first paragraph usually paraphrases them in clearer language.

Turks reject generals

Besieged Arafat is defiant

Joan's new love is on the run

The beleaguered forces of PLO chairman, Mr Yasser Arafat, were pushed back to their final stronghold outside this northern Lebanese city yesterday after Syria had reinforced its 12,000 troops with an armoured brigade and the four-day-old battle threatened to spill into the streets of Tripoli.

Private hospitals and clinics are to be charged for blood supplied by the National Health Service. Supplies have previously been provided free by the blood transfusion service.

PACKAGE HOLIDAY firms erupted in fury last night over a sunshine flights 'hijack' by Spain.

The bombshell move, which would FORCE Britons to use Spanish airlines, will send holiday prices soaring.

At present, only 20 per cent of the three million Britons who go to Spain every year fly there in Spanish planes.

Activity I

1 Match these headlines with the news stories below them. (These were the main news stories selected by the three newspapers on Monday, 7th November 1983.)
2 Two of the main news stories of the day were covered by both the *Daily Telegraph* and the *Guardian* (as first and third in importance on the front page). Identify these stories and the headlines that go with them.
3 Which three stories came from the *Sun*, in your opinion, bearing in mind its readership? If in doubt, look for sensational adjectives.

ARAFAT RETREATS TO HIS LAST BASE

OZAL AHEAD IN TURKEY POLL RACE

Dublin riot jail warders 'irresponsible'

SCARGILL MAY RUN LABOUR FINANCE

NHS to charge private clinics for blood

Spain bid to hijack holiday flights

Both the United States and Israel were reported yesterday to be planning attacks on Lebanese extremist groups while the Syrians and rebel Palestinians besieged Yasser Arafat in his last stronghold in the embattled country.

Striking prison officers were sent home yesterday when they made a second attempt to return to work following serious rioting at Dublin's Mountjoy jail.

Mr Michael Noonan, Justice Minister, branded the warders as irresponsible. 'They could not be trusted,' he said.

HARD-LINE Left-wingers want militant miners' leader Arthur Scargill as Labour Party treasurer.

TURGUT OZAL, the monetarist former deputy prime minister who masterminded the country's economic recovery after the 1980 coup, appeared yesterday to be heading for a resounding triumph in Turkey's general election.

THE MAN superstar Joan Collins is madly in love with is on the run from police on a diamond-smuggling charge.

Turkish voters seemed last night to be overwhelmingly rejecting the generals who have ruled the country for the past three years.

Editorials

Activity 2

The three editorials reproduced on these two pages appeared in the three newspapers on Monday, 8th November, 1983. Decide from the content and layout which came from which newspaper. Then answer the questions on each of the three editorials.

Let's open Buck House!

THE QUEEN'S pay is being reviewed but the outcome will not be known for a year.

One thing is already clear: There can be no justification for a large increase.

5 Of course the Royal Family's costs have grown, but so has the taxpayers' handout to them known as the Civil List.

This stands at £4.5 million a year, four times the sum the Queen received in the early
10 Seventies.

The fact is the Queen is the wealthiest woman in the world.

She has palaces galore, travels free, and her children are amply provided for.

15 The Royal Yacht Britannia is costing the nation £3 million a year and is about to get a £5 million refit at our expense.

At a time when all public spending is supposed to be curbed, there must be no sugges-
20 *tion of exempting the super-rich royals.*

But the Sun has two suggestions for helping the Queen make ends meet:

● **SCRAP** the Royal Yacht at once;
● **THROW** open Buckingham Palace to the
25 public.

With all its historical treasures the public would queue round the block to pay, say, £1 a time for a look at history.

And all the money at the 'gate' could go
30 **into the royal coffers.**

THE NEWEST PROFESSION

A REPORT on Saturday by our Local Government Correspondent about a number of well-paid public service jobs, often newly created for the purpose, which have been given to Left-
5 wing activists may have shocked many readers but should come as no surprise. Though spoken of with bated breath, by many people who should know better, as 'local self-government' or 'local democracy,' local government, particu-
10 larly in urban areas, has largely become the preserve of small self-perpetuating cliques of political activists, using patronage from the public purse to buy political support.

Their political constituency includes fami-
15 lies living on welfare, exempt from rates thanks to the rate-rebate system and largely exempt from paying council rents, thanks to the new permissive attitudes towards rent arrears. It also includes employees in new non-jobs like
20 community workers, race-relations advisers, members of local enterprise boards (an extension of class war by other means) and those in highly-professionalised 'voluntary bodies,' many wholly dependent on State funding, some
25 doing useful work, but many simply Left-wing pressure groups run by unelected professional politicians. Socialism has become the newest profession.

It might be argued that this merely con-
30 tinues the professionalisation of politics and rewards for political careers which has existed since parliamentary government began. Even before the 1914–18 war, ROBERT MICHELS, in his 'Iron Laws of Bureaucracy', demonstrated how
35 socialist movements became bureaucratised and professionalised till **place** excluded socialism as the main objective. But 'careerism', as the Left called it, acted to mollify socialist fanaticism, to encourage 'reformism', creating a common lan-
40 guage between supporters of the status quo and those who, having fought their way into it, were prepared to linger and enjoy its fruits before pressing change further. Now, a new breed of professional revolutionaries, convinced that
45 they will be able to enjoy their privileges in the ruins of our society, is evident in local authorities, voluntary organisations and quangos. It is time the Government took note.

place: obtaining a political position

An Oxbridge hurdle goes

For Oxford and Cambridge, this is a time of small changes which may have large social consequences, though not of the commonly expected kind. Both of our oldest universities have decided
5 to abolish general scholarships and exhibitions. More radically, Oxford has agreed to end the post-A-level entrance examination which has traditionally been the most important element in its selection process. It was also the element most
10 likely to favour applicants from public schools, since the state sector rarely had the resources to teach such a small number of pupils for an extra term after A-levels. As a result, some people will jump to the premature conclusion that Oxford has
15 at long last struck a blow for egalitarianism, while on past form others will no doubt bemoan the passing of a test that the *Daily Telegraph* recently described as 'among the finest exams ever devised'. This would, however, entirely miss the
20 point.
Until very recently, the debate in the Oxbridge senior common rooms was divided neatly between those who argued that the entrance exam should be abolished because it was instrumental in
25 securing some half of the places for pupils from public schools – with the implication that we could hang the academic consequences since fairness was more important – and those who maintained that excellence would suffer and should come first.
30 That, though, was before some rather riveting research by Dr Paul Collier and Dr Colin Mayer. According to Mayer and Collier, the bias to comprehensives in the selection process was clear but not marked enough. Comprehensive school
35 students tended to do better than public school students for any given A- and O-level grades.
Both Oxford and Cambridge have inevitably lost some of their previous dominance with the expansion of higher education and the high quality
40 of much research and teaching elsewhere. Their graduates now have a higher unemployment rate than many other universities. If Oxford – and maybe later Cambridge – now succeed in creaming off more successfully the students with the greatest
45 academic potential, they may also be able to claw back, maintain or reinforce their pre-eminence, depending on where you think they rank now. Another implication is that the return on parents' investment in private education is going to slip
50 badly, as the Oxbridge elites will be increasingly drawn from the maintained schools. That in itself would represent a considerable advance, since meritocracy is surely to be preferred to the power of a parental purse.

Let's open Buck House

1 Why do you think this editorial might appeal to working-class sentiments?
2 In what ways does the layout of this editorial differ from that of the others?
3 What do you notice about the length of the sentences and paragraphs and the typeface used?
4 Compare this editorial to the advice given on paragraphing on page 14. How far does it follow the advice? Assuming it is deliberate, why do you think the paragraphs are organised in this way?

The newest profession

1 Which attitudes in the editorial clearly indicate the newspaper's political position? Find a phrase describing its opponents in the first paragraph and compare it with an even less flattering phrase in the last.
2 What are meant by 'non-jobs' (line 19) and why is this phrase used?
3 Why is 'voluntary bodies' (line 23) printed in inverted commas?
4 What is 'the newest profession' referred to?
5 How does the editorial differentiate between the old type of socialist and the new in the last paragraph? How would its description of the new type's aims differ from their own statement of them?
6 The second paragraph is a continuation of the first. Does it work by means of examples, comparison, or contrast?
7 One of the most powerful weapons in argument is to appear to justify one's opponent's case, and then to destroy it. Find an example of this. Is the destruction based on evidence, or a statement of opinion?

An Oxbridge hurdle goes

1 What do you imagine this newspaper's attitude towards Oxford and Cambridge has been up to now, and why?
2 What is the paper's attitude to private education? How is it likely to view its decline? Why?
3 In what way has Mayer and Collier's research apparently altered the debate at Oxford and Cambridge?
4 How does the last sentence of the first paragraph link what is said before to what is said afterwards? What is 'the point' that may be missed? If Collier and Mayer's research is reliable – it was, in fact, based on very limited evidence – what does the paper think is Oxbridge's real motive for the change?

Main news

One of the main news items of Tuesday,
8th November, 1983, reported by all three
newspapers, was an interview between the Prime
Minister, Mrs Thatcher, and the United States
Deputy Secretary of State.

Activity 3

1 Decide which newspaper printed which story.
2 What do the differences in point of view tell us about
the attitude of each newspaper towards   a) Mrs
Thatcher;   b) the USA and its action in Grenada;
c) the USA's proposed action in the Lebanon;
d) American plans to start selling arms to Argentina
again?

Envoy at Chequers

By DAVID ADAMSON Diplomatic Correspondent

THE danger of a new Anglo-American policy rift, this time in the Middle East, surfaced yesterday at a Chequers breakfast meeting between Mrs Thatcher and a senior American official, Mr Kenneth Dam.

Mrs Thatcher, backed by Sir Geoffrey Howe, emphasised that Britain would not support American strikes against Syrian targets to avenge the slaughter of American marines in Beirut.

American naval movements which will place three aircraft carriers in the vicinity of Lebanon have heightened British concern about American intentions.

It is recognised that there may well be links between the Syrians, who have troops in Lebanon, and the perpetrators of the bombing attacks which killed nearly 300 American and French troops.

But the British view is that retaliation should be limited to the perpetrators and not extended to their backers.

Maggie in new blast at Reagan

By TREVOR KAVANAGH
Political Editor

PREMIER Margaret Thatcher waded into President Reagan yesterday with a 'keep out' warning on two fronts.

She told him: DON'T carry out revenge raids on the suicide bombers in Lebanon; and DON'T resume arms sales to Argentina.

Mrs Thatcher's 'cool it' call was delivered over a bacon-and-eggs breakfast with the U.S. Deputy Secretary of State Kenneth Dam at Chequers.

Flashpoint

He was supposed to mend the rift with Mrs Thatcher over the Grenada Invasion – but she sent him away with a flea in his ear.

PM is snubbed over US retaliation

By Hella Pick

Mrs Thatcher failed yesterday to secure assurances that the United States will refrain from retaliation against the instigators of last month's bomb explosions at the headquarters of the US marines peace-keeping force in Beirut.

A senior US official emphasised that each of the four peace-keeping forces – from the US, Britain, France, and Italy – was under separate command, and that the US saw no need to reach a consensus before taking action 'in defence of its own men in Lebanon.'

The Prime Minister, during a breakfast meeting at Chequers with the US Deputy Secretary of State, Mr Kenneth Dam, seems to have been equally unsuccessful in her search for a firm US undertaking to maintain the arms embargo against Argentina, even though she apparently left no doubt that a renewal of US arms sales would damage the Anglo-American relationship far more grievously than the US invasion of Grenada.

Sports news

On the sports pages the same day, the three newspapers commented on a forthcoming tennis match.

Activity 4

1 Decide which newspaper printed which report; bear in mind the use of sensational language (the *Sun*) and of longer sentences (the *Guardian*).
2 Do you see anything in common between the way in which each of the newspapers approaches politics and an international tennis match?
3 Compare the articles from each newspaper in terms of nationalism.
4 In considering all the articles reproduced from the three newspapers, how would you recognise that they were written for the kind of readership described on page 30?

David Irvine on the Wembley draw

McEnroe return ordeal for Lloyd

As in 1979, when he last competed in the tournament, John Lloyd – one of only two British players in a strong field of 32 – will again meet the holder John McEnroe, who has just ended a 21-day suspension, in the opening round of the £195,000 Benson and Hedges championship which begins at the Wembley arena today.

Good performances at the United States Open, where he reached the last 16, and in the Davis Cup tie with Chile earned Lloyd an invitation but hopes of a favourable draw were dashed when he was paired with the man who has dropped sets to only two opponents in winning 24 of 25 singles in Wembley over the past five years.

Supermac won't frighten the new Lloyd

By HUGH JAMIESON

JOHN LLOYD jetted into London last night on Concorde hoping for a supersonic performance in the opening round of the £162,000 Benson and Hedges tournament at Wembley.

Lloyd, Britain's one-time 28-year-old golden boy, had drawn the short straw with tomorrow's clash against the holder and top seed John McEnroe.

McEnroe, the 24-year-old New York left-hander, is gunning for a second successive title as he bids to keep Czech Ivan Lendl at bay in the race for the world's top spot.

TENNIS

LLOYD TO MEET McENROE

By JOHN PARSONS

JOHN LLOYD has drawn John McEnroe, the Wimbledon champion, in the first round of the Benson and Hedges Championship starting at Wembley today – just as he did when he last had the chance to play in this major grand prix event four years ago.

Then Lloyd – who had been runner-up to Bjorn Borg, the then Wimbledon champion, in 1976 – was beaten 6-4, 6-1 and McEnroe went on to the second of his four Wembley titles in five years.

Lloyd, 29, has shown distinct signs in the last few months – particularly at the US Open and in Britain's Davis Cup tie against Chile – of rediscovering world class form. His ranking of 272 going into Flushing Meadow has improved accordingly to 155.

Equally, he must have hoped for something kinder from the draw for his wild card than simply a repeat of his 1979 wild card, especially as McEnroe should be well rested and doubly eager after three weeks away from competitive tennis while under suspension.

Discussion

Compare these newspapers with those of your own country from the point of view of content and presentation.

Composition

Using the facts given below, construct a news item for a quality newspaper. Write *three* paragraphs, following this order: TOPIC, EXPOSITION, CONCLUSION.

1 Scotland Yard detective to fly to Switzerland today to interview man in connection with blackmail threat to smuggle poisoned food and drink on to supermarket shelves.

2 Man caught yesterday entering Geneva bank, by Swiss Interpol officers acting on Scotland Yard instructions. Man from Bournemouth, Dorset.

3 British supermarket chains had agreed to pretend to play along with the threats. Suspect was expecting to be paid first down payment of £50,000 in bank. Further letters showed he hoped to go on and obtain hundreds of thousands of pounds.

4 Not first time supermarkets threatened like this. Two years ago a blackmailer tried to obtain £500,000 from the Safeways supermarket chain after planting three food jars containing weedkiller, paraquat, on shelves in different stores round the country. Though amounts found not lethal doses, stores' business hit for several weeks. Also, last Christmas, extremist animal liberation group claimed it had injected frozen Christmas turkeys with paraquat, but no traces found.

5 Police and supermarkets say these very rare cases. All such threats are taken seriously and immediately and exhaustively followed up.

Disasters and accidents

Quiz

A What do you imagine is the largest number of people to have died as a result of the following? Guess the nearest figure to the correct answer, choosing a), b) or c). The answers, and dates when the events took place, are given at the back of the book.

1 Aircraft accident: a) 300; b) 400; c) 500?
2 Avalanche: a) 1,000; b) 2,000; c) 5,000?
3 Earthquake: a) 100,000; b) 500,000; c) a million?
4 · Fire (in a building): a) 500; b) 1,000; c) 1,500?
5 Flood: a) 100,000; b) a million; c) 3 million?
6 Hurricane/tornado (i.e. wind alone) a) 500; b) 1,000; c) 1,500?
7 Railway accident: a) 500; b) 800; c) 1,000?
8 Road accident: a) 50; b) 100; c) 200?
9 Shipwreck: a) 1,000; b) 3,000; c) 5,000?
10 Tiger (man-eating): a) 50; b) 100; c) 500?

B Which of the following were or could have been the causes of the disasters listed above? Find one possible cause for each from the list below.

1 A lighted match.
2 A river bursting its banks.
3 A torpedo.
4 Atmospheric pressure.
5 A collision on the runway.
6 Brakes which failed.
7 The driver ignoring a signal.
8 Hunger.
9 Seismic movement.
10 Snow melting.

C How do you imagine the majority of the victims died in these disasters? Were they burnt, buried, drowned, eaten, killed by the impact?

In fact most of the victims of the fire probably choked or were trodden on. The victims of the road accident were drowned. Explain why you think this could have happened.

D In most of these cases, there is nothing people can do to avoid the disaster. What do you think would be the best course of action in the following cases?

1 If you were warned that an earthquake was likely, would you
a) stay at home?
b) go out into the nearest open space?
2 If the house was burning, but firemen were coming to rescue you, would you stay
a) in the middle of the room?
b) near the wall?
3 If your boat overturned in the English Channel five miles from the coast, would you
a) cling to the boat?
b) try to swim to shore?

Disaster at sea

The Titanic, at that time the most luxurious liner ever built, sank on its maiden voyage across the Atlantic in 1912. Read the account given below before answering the questions.

At 11.40, in **Lat.** 41° 46′ N. **Long.** 50° 14′ W. Frederick Fleet, the look-out in the crow's-nest, saw or sensed an iceberg ahead. The *Titanic* veered to **port**, so that it was her **starboard**
5 plates which were glanced open. The engines were stopped. There was a perfectly still atmosphere. It was a brilliantly starlit night but with no moon, so that there was little light that was of any use. She was a ship that had come quietly to
10 rest without any indication of disaster. No ice was visible: the iceberg had been glimpsed by the look-out and then gone. There was no hole in the ship's side through which water could be seen to be pouring, nothing out of place, no
15 sound of alarm, no panic, and no movement of anyone except at a walking pace.

Within ten minutes the water had risen fourteen feet inside the ship. Mail bags were floating about in the mail room. The passengers had no
20 idea of danger. Beesley, who was in bed, noticed no more than what he took to be the slightest extra heave of the engines. What most people noticed first was the sudden lack of engine vibration. This had been with them so constantly
25 for the four days of the voyage that they had ceased to be conscious of it, but when it stopped they noticed the supervening silence and stillness. The only passengers who saw an iceberg were a few still playing cards in the smoking
30 room. They idly discussed how high it might have been, settled on an estimate of 80 feet, and went back to their cards.

There was no panic because there was no awareness. The *Titanic* was assumed to be un-
35 sinkable. The shipbuilders had said so. Practically everyone believed she was as unsinkable as a railway station. A Rothschild, asked to put on his life jacket, said he did not think there was any occasion for it and walked leisurely away. Ste-
40 wards rode bicycles round and round in the gym. She was in fact sinking very fast, and by midnight was a quarter sunk already. There was something unusual about the stairs, a curious sense of something out of balance, a sense of not
45 being able to put one's foot down in the right place. The stairs were tilting forward and tended to throw your feet out of place. There was no visible slope, just something strange perceived by the sense of balance. The *Titanic* was **settling**
50 **by the head.**

From *The Liners* by Terry Coleman

Lat. = latitude; **Long.** = longitude.
Latitude measures distance in degrees north or south of the equator; longitude measures distance in degrees east or west of the 0° meridian. They are used to pinpoint an exact position on a map.
port and **starboard:** respectively, the left- and right-hand sides of a ship
settling by the head: sinking at the bows (the front part of the ship)

Activity 1

1 Which sentences or phrases in the first paragraph explain why the passengers were not at first aware of the disaster?
2 How did the passengers first realise that something was strange about the ship?
3 Find two examples in the third paragraph of the passengers and crew being unconcerned by the situation.
4 What would an experienced sailor have realised when he was on the stairs?
5 How does the writer build up the impression of disaster being imminent, and why is it particularly horrifying? Consider the use of contrast throughout the passage.

Rail and road accidents

While travelling on the Trans-Siberian Luxury Express across Russia in the 1930s, the writer suddenly woke up when his case fell on top of him and he discovered that the train had gone off the rails.

It would be difficult to imagine a nicer sort of railway accident. The weather was ideal. No one was badly hurt. And the whole thing was done in just the right **Drury Lane** manner, with lots of
5 twisted steel and splintered woodwork and turf scarred deeply with demoniac force. For once the Russians had **carried something off**.

The air was full of agonising groans and the sound of breaking glass, the first supplied by two
10 attendants who had been winded, the second by passengers escaping from a coach in which both the doors had jammed. The sun shone brightly. I began to take photographs as fast as I could. This is strictly forbidden on Soviet territory, but the of-
15 ficials had their hands full and were too upset to notice.

The staff of the train were scattered about the wreckage, writing contradictory reports with trembling hands. A charming German consul and
20 his family — the only other foreigners on the train — had been in the last coach and were unscathed. Their small daughter, aged six, was delighted with the whole affair, which she regarded as having been arranged specially for her entertainment; I am
25 afraid she will grow up to expect too much from trains.

Gradually I discovered what had happened, or at least what was thought to have happened. As a rule the Trans-Siberian Expresses have no great turn of
30 speed, but ours, at the time when disaster overtook her, had been on top of her form. She had a long, steep hill behind her, and also a following wind: she was giving of her best. But, alas, at the bottom of that long, steep hill the signals were against her, a
35 fact which the driver noticed in the course of time. He put on his brakes. Nothing happened. He put on his emergency brakes. Still nothing happened. Slightly less rapidly than before, but still at a very creditable speed, the train went charging down the
40 long, steep hill.

The line at this point is single track, but at the foot of the hill there is a little halt, where a train may stand and let another pass. Our train, however, was in no mood for stopping: it looked as if she was
45 going to ignore the signals and try conclusions with a westbound train, head on. In this she was thwarted by a pointsman at the little halt, who summed up the situation and switched the runaway neatly into a siding. It was a long, curved siding,
50 and to my layman's eye appeared to have been designed for the sole purpose of receiving trains which got out of control on the hill above it. But for whatever purpose it was designed, it was designed a very long time ago.
55 We were altogether too much for the siding. We made matchwood of its rotten sleepers and flung ourselves dramatically down the embankment.

From *One's Company* by Peter Fleming

Drury Lane: home of the oldest theatre in London, the Theatre Royal, and so, in a theatrical manner
carried something off: done something in a spectacular way

Activity 2

1 This passage is written in a very different tone from that on the *Titanic*. How does the writer indicate that the passage is amusing and ironic from the beginning, and how does he justify this amusement?

2 The first sentence of the second paragraph is an example of irony. Why is the use of 'agonising groans' ironic in the context? Find other examples of irony in the third paragraph.

3 How does the writer suggest to us that the train had a will of its own? How does he suggest that the driver, and the railway system in general, were inefficient?

4 Now compare this passage with the one opposite. They begin in the same way with the accident taking place but are afterwards different in the way they tell the story, as well as the tone. How, and why? Consider who is telling the story, what happened, and how much he knew about it at the time.

Activity 3 – pair work

Fortunately, not all accidents are serious. Read these accounts of accidents and then draw diagrams to show how they took place. Note that in all cases, the drivers were in cars with left-hand drives, driving on the right-hand side of the road. In the first case, the witness was a passenger in a car, in the others he was on foot.

1 My wife was driving along a dual carriageway which had parallel intersections allowing traffic to cross from one side to the other. As we approached one of these, a big Ford came out of a narrow side road and stopped halfway across our side of the carriageway. The driver was looking in the opposite direction. He was asking the girl beside him whether he should cross the carriageway or turn right. My wife accelerated to pass the stationary car but just before we reached it, the man turned towards the right in our lane. My wife braked but a collision was inevitable.

2 A woman backed out of her garage, narrowly missing me on the pavement, and reversed rapidly across the road to station herself behind the line of waiting cars in the middle lane of a one-way street, about twenty metres from the traffic lights. Then she suddenly noticed that there were fewer cars in the right-hand lane and moved into it just in time to collide with a taxi racing down it from behind.

3 Two cars were converging on each other very slowly at right angles along narrow one-way streets. Either driver could have stopped at any moment up to the point of impact, but neither would give way, so their front wheels met with a gentle thud in the middle of the intersection. The two men leapt out of their cars and began insulting each other at the tops of their voices.

4 A woman was driving slowly along a narrow road while a line of cars breathed down her neck, itching to pass her as soon as the road widened ahead. There was a hill to the right a few metres before the road opened out and, without signalling her intentions, she slowed almost to a standstill to turn. The driver behind slammed on his brakes, but, unfortunately for him, the next six cars piled into the back of him. The woman completed her turn and drove up the hill in the same stately manner, leaving the others to sort out the mess.

Who do you think was really to blame for the accident in each case, and who is legally to blame (according to the traffic regulations in your country)? (Answers at the back)

40

Fire!

Activity 4 – group work

The following account of a fire has been printed with the sentences and paragraphs out of order, except that the first sentence of each paragraph is in the correct position. Use the connecting words and phrases and the linking references printed in italic to decide on the correct order of the paragraphs and of the sentences in each paragraph.

1 People often pass banks and shops on their way to work in the morning, hear bells ringing, and take no notice because they assume that someone has set them off by accident.   **a)** All down the corridor men and women in dressing gowns stood gazing, as if mesmerised, at *a light flashing on the wall* opposite.   **b)** *Consequently*, I went on shaving, though it was surprising, *all the same*, that in such a big hotel there was no one around to turn this one off.   **c)** *In spite of that* no one moved, until one of the staff came hurrying past and *told us to leave the hotel immediately*.   **d)** *Eventually*, curiosity got the better of my laziness and I went out to see *what was happening*.

2 The groups of people shivering in the courtyard below clearly thought so, *too*, until three or four fire engines arrived and ranged themselves outside the hotel.   **a)** A little smoke would *at least* have added excitement to the proceedings and helped us to forget the cold.   **b)** Everyone looked up, *no doubt* expecting to see flames shooting from the upstairs windows, but there was *not even a sign of smoke*.

3 It was eight o'clock in the morning, our first morning in the hotel.   **a)** *Instead of that, however*, we heard a monotonous sound like *an alarm bell ringing*.   **b)** I had put a card outside the night before, ordering breakfast from Room Service at 8.00, and we expected to hear the waiter's sharp tap on the door *at any moment*.   **c)** *While* I shaved I could hear my wife commenting on the beautiful view of the castle she could see from our fourth-floor window.

4 A few minutes later we were told we could go back upstairs.   **a)** *As* I opened the bedroom door, my teeth chattering, he poked his head out and said, 'What was all that damned noise about?'   **b)** *On the whole, this seemed wise* but I could not help envying *the old man in the room next to us*.   **c)** It turned out that there had been a small fire on the top floor but the staff had put it out themselves and had only called the fire brigade *as a precaution*.

5 I told my wife and ran along the corridor to my son's room.   **a)** *In the end*, we grabbed our passports, traveller's cheques, money and a few things of sentimental value and ran to the fire escape.   **b)** *Once* we were in the cold air outside, we realised it would have been wiser to have brought our overcoats, but we still believed that it was surely *a fuss about nothing*.   **c)** *As* we dressed quickly, we wondered what to take and what to leave behind.

Activity 5 – group work

1 Look at the fire prevention poster below. First, narrate the story of the fire, following the sequence of the pictures.

2 Tell the story from the point of view of: a) a member of the family that caused it;   b) one of the firemen;   c) a picnicker who helped fight the fire;   d) an occupant of the burnt house;   e) an ambulance driver;   f) one of the foresters.

ONE PICNIC LUNCH CAN COST MILLIONS ∘ DON'T PLAY WITH FIRE

Composition

1 Describe an accident you have witnessed or been involved in.

2 Describe any natural disaster you have witnessed or read about.

Timetables and programmes

Deciphering timetables

You are the secretary to the head of an international company based in Malaga, Spain. Your boss must attend an important conference in Denver, Colorado, from next Wednesday, beginning at 6.00 p.m., until the following Sunday afternoon. Consult the data in your timetable to decide on the most satisfactory route to Denver and the most satisfactory return journey, but

allow at least an hour between the arrival and departure of connecting flights. Remember to check the days of the flights as well as the times. List all the details for the outward and return journeys, giving departure and arrival times, changes to connecting flights and/or stopovers in hotels.

DAYS	DEPARTURE	FLIGHT	ARRIVAL	VIA	DEPARTURE	FLIGHT	ARRIVAL
From	**MALAGA**	To	**CHICAGO**				
1,3	1640	IB959	1830	JFK	2100	AA571	2228
2,5	0830	IB655	1025	LGA	1345	UA518	1525
From	**CHICAGO**	To	**DENVER**				
12467	0700	AA519	1000				
13456	1215	UA721	1515				
12345	1835	AA604	2225				
12345	2045	UA293	2350				
From	**MALAGA**	To	**HOUSTON**				
2,5	0845	IB908	1035	M	1700	UA613	1835
1	1900	IB711	2105	M	2245	AA901	0025
From	**HOUSTON**	To	**DENVER**				
12345	1555	AA228	1905				
2467	1855	AA477	2205				
From	**DENVER**	To	**LISBON**				
356	1945	TP818	1640				
147	2155	TP900	1850				
From	**LISBON**	To	**MADRID**				
1234	0940	TP700	1140				
246	1045	IB076	1245				
357	1420	TP708	1620				
1457	1700	IB072	1900				
From	**MADRID**	To	**MALAGA**				
357	1155	IB119	1255				
12345	1205	IB363	1305				
12345	1305	IB365	1405				

Notes

Days:	1 = Monday, 2 = Tuesday, 3 = Wednesday, etc.
Via:	JFK = J.F. Kennedy airport, New York; LGA = La Guardia airport, New York; M = Miami.
Airlines:	UA = United; AA = American Airlines; TAP = Portuguese Airlines; IB = Iberia.

Social programmes

**The following is the programme of a social club
Lynne Edwards belongs to in a small town in
England. Lynne is the secretary, so she had to write
an account of these activities for the local paper,
mainly to attract prospective new members.
Study the way in which the events are presented in
her account.**

Monday, 12th: 8.00 p.m. Discussion on the environment. Speakers: Desmond Wheeler (ecologist), J. H. Hammond (Town Councillor), P. Croft (university student). Open meeting. All welcome.

Tuesday, 13th: 7.00–10.00 p.m.. Painting Group. Meet at 17 Wilson Street. Prospective members apply to club.

Wednesday, 14th: Film session 8.00 p.m. *Stagecoach* (John Ford). Club members free. General public 75p (pay at entrance).

Friday, 16th: Dance 8.00 p.m. Bar and refreshments. Bar open till 12.00 p.m. Tickets from Club Secretary (£1).

Saturday, 17th: 3.00 p.m. Football. St. Mary's Athletic. (Club ground, Allan Road). Entrance free.

Sunday, 18th: All-day ramble to Cheston Hills, Prospective members welcome. Meet at club premises, 9.30 a.m.

Farley Social Club have a full programme of events this coming week, almost all of which are open to non-
5 members. On Monday evening at 8.00 p.m. we have what promises to be a very interesting discussion on the environment, focusing on local
10 issues. The Town Council's point of view will be expressed by Cllr. J.H. Hammond, and he will be joined on the platform by Desmond Wheeler, the well-
15 known ecologist, and Peter Croft, a Farley man studying geography at Sheffield University. This meeting is open to the general public. All
20 are welcome and no charge will be made.

Regular events are featured on Tuesday and Wednesday. The Painting Group will meet at
25 17 Wilson Street from 7.00 to 10.00 on Tuesday evening; non-members interested in joining should apply in the first instance to the club for further details.
30 Our Wednesday film this week, at 8 o'clock, is John Ford's classic Western, *Stagecoach*. The sessions are open to the public; tickets, at 75p each, can
35 be obtained from the club premises on the night. Tickets (£1) are also available from the Club Secretary for our Friday night dance, which begins at
40 8.00. The bar will be open until midnight, and refreshments will

also be served at reasonable prices.

Our football team is doing
45 well in the Farley League this year, and this week's top of the table clash with St. Mary's Athletic at our ground in Allan Road should provide excellent
50 free entertainment. The kick-off is at 3.00. Those who are fond of the outdoor life can take advantage of the all-day ramble to Cheston Hills on Sunday.
55 Anyone thinking of joining the club will find this a perfect opportunity to get to know members in a relaxed atmosphere.

Activity I

Here is part of another list of events, for a language school in Oxford. Write a newsletter article, similar to the article opposite, to make the social programme more attractive to new arrivals.

Sunday, 11th:	8.00 p.m.	Welcoming speech by Principal. Introductions to staff. Disco dance – free.
Monday, 12th:	2.30 p.m.	Tour of the colleges. Coach from school £2.
	7.00 p.m.	Talk on history of Oxford by Prof. Geoffrey Guntrip. Illustrated. School lecture room.
Tuesday, 13th:	2.30 p.m.	Football match, Marston Road ground. Students v. staff. Interested players contact Mario Gentile.
	7.00 p.m.	Lecture: *Hamlet*, by Malcolm Macdonald, actor in the Royal Shakespeare Company.
Wednesday, 14th:	2.30 p.m.	Trip to Stratford to see *Hamlet*, return 12.00 midnight. (Price £10, including theatre ticket) *or* tour of the Cotswold villages, back 7.00 p.m., price £3.

Press release

Jonathan Bird is Press Officer to Marchester City Council. Having worked out a programme of events for the visit of a delegation of art experts from Ruritania interested in the Roman remains in the city, he has to inform the press, basing his press release on the timetable.
Compare the timetable with the press release on the next page.

TIMETABLE: Visit of HE the Ruritanian Minister for Arts and Culture, June 10th, 1984

- 10.45   Lord Mayor and Mayoress, Councillors and Curator assemble at Marchester station.
- 11.00   Arrival of Minister's train.
- 11.05   Mayor and Mayoress accompany Minister to Marchester Museum.
- 11.15   Conducted tour of Museum.
- 11.45   Presentation to Minister.
- 12.00   Party return to Marchester City Hall for reception.
- 12.10   Reception. Drinks, refreshments.
- 1.00   Lunch, Boar's Hotel, Tavistock Street.
- 2.15   Speeches: His Worship the Lord Mayor.
    - HE the Ruritanian Minister for Arts and Culture.
    - H. Curtis, Curator of the Marchester Museum and Art Gallery.
    - V. Klob, Cultural Attaché, Ruritanian Embassy.
- 3.20   Cars ready to escort party to Marchester station.
- 3.48   Train departs for London.

Marchester City Council

PRESS RELEASE

Arrangements for the Visit of His Excellency, the Ruritanian Minister for Arts and Culture, to Marchester, June 10th, 1984

The Minister's train will arrive at Marchester station at 11.00 a.m. The Minister, who will be accompanied by a party of art experts from Ruritania and officials from the Ruritanian Embassy, will be met by His Worship the Mayor, Mr R. G. Smith, the Mayoress, members of the City Council, and the Curator of Marchester Museum and Art Gallery.

The Minister will be driven in company with the Mayor and Mayoress to the Museum, where there will be a short conducted tour, followed by the presentation to the Minister of a souvenir marking his visit.

The party will return by car to the City Hall. Drinks and refreshments will be served at a reception to which the Press and representatives of the other communications media are cordially invited. Afterwards the party will lunch at the Boar's Hotel, Tavistock Street, where the speakers will be: His Worship the Mayor, welcoming the distinguished guests; His Excellency, the Ruritanian Minister for Arts and Culture, replying; Mr Harold Curtis, Curator of the Marchester Museum and Art Gallery, who will announce recent findings of the archaeologists working on Roman remains in Marchester; and Mr Vladislav Klob, Cultural Attaché to the Ruritanian Embassy, who will reply on behalf of the guests, referring to plans for closer cultural links between Ruritania and Great Britain.

Note: Copies of the Mayor's speech will be made available to the Press at the reception preceding the lunch. Members of the Press wishing to reserve places at the Press Table during the lunch should contact this office not later than Wednesday, June 3rd, otherwise places cannot be guaranteed.

The function is expected to end about 3.15 p.m. The Mayor and Mayoress will escort the Minister and his party to Marchester station, where they will catch the 3.48 train to London.

> JONATHAN BIRD
> Press Officer, City Hall

Activity 2 – pair work

Draw up a programme for the visit of a party of foreigners to your town, school or university. Write out a timetable for a one-day visit, including enough detail to indicate to your colleagues what is planned and what their responsibilities will be.

Irene Matthews is personal secretary to Jerome S. Buck, President of a multinational company called Skarneck International, based in Toronto. Mr Buck is telling her about his forthcoming trip to Europe.

BUCK	I think we'd better go over my schedule, Irene. I'm going to have a look at our European operation, as you know, and as I'll be visiting a number of countries, I'd like you to make the bookings.
IRENE	Right, Mr Buck. I'll take down the details.
BUCK	Well, I'm leaving on Tuesday, April 15th, for London. I'm going to attend a sales conference for our British representatives. That runs through Wednesday and Thursday, and then there's a reception at Canada House on the Thursday evening.
IRENE	Are you going to meet the Ambassador, then?
BUCK	I guess so. But the main thing is that on Friday morning, I have a meeting with the British Minister of Trade and Industry. We're going to discuss the site of our new plant in Scotland.
IRENE	So when are you leaving for Paris?
BUCK	First flight on Saturday morning. I'm planning to meet my wife there. She's going to fly over direct, arriving in the afternoon. Then we'll have a relaxed weekend before I see M. Chambery, the European Manager, on Monday. So from Paris on, I'll need a double room.
IRENE	How long are you going to stay in Paris, Mr Buck?
BUCK	Only till Monday evening. I'm going to Rome to see our plant there on Tuesday, and on Wednesday I'm due in Madrid to inspect the new factory.
IRENE	And that's the last item on the agenda. So when are you coming back? Are you going to fly from Madrid?
BUCK	Yes, on the first plane out on Thursday. We must be back for Friday, the 25th. It's our daughter Sharon's birthday.

Activity 3

Below is the first part of a press release issued to mark Mr Buck's visit. Complete it, noting that the **going to** form of personal intention will change to the more formal **will**, and that not everything Mr Buck is planning to do is of interest to the press. Invent any names needed.

Composition

1 Write a formal account, for insertion in a newspaper, describing the preparations for the foreigners' visit (Activity 2).
2 Write an article like that on page 44 about the social activities planned at your school or university or a club you belong to.

Mr Jerome S. Buck, President of Skarneck International, will visit Europe from April 15–24, to inspect Skarneck's European operation. On the day following his arrival, Wednesday, April 16, he will attend a sales conference for the company's British representatives, chaired by the British Group Manager, Mr Ian Leppard. On the evening of Thursday, 17 . . .

Cities

Around the world

Here are six maps of famous cities of the world. Match each city map with its description below, then compare your notes with a partner. (The answers are at the back of the book.)

1 Population 7,800,000. Not capital but very large seaport, cultural, commercial and financial centre. At the mouth of important river, sheltered from sea. Exports and industries: numerous. Original name was different from present one. Founded 1624. Changed hands and given present name in second half of seventeenth century. Capital 1789–1790.

2 Population 675,000. Capital. Till 1861, small port. Then occupied and developed by foreign power. Industries: textiles, food products, and furniture. Located at W. end of island in lagoon opposite mouth of river. Linked by road-bridge to mainland.

3 Population 3,640,000. Not capital now, but was founded as one in 1703 and originally given name of founder. Now 400 miles NW of capital. Industries: numerous. Located on banks of river. Important port, easy links with Europe, but port free from ice April–November only. Present name given in 1924.

4 Population 850,000. Capital. On N. shore of long river, where estuary narrows before river flows into ocean. Founded by Phoenicians. In 716 captured by Moslems. Moslem till 1147. Earthquake 1755, caused terrible destruction, but city rebuilt on modern plan. Great port. Joined by famous road-bridge to industrial suburbs across estuary.

5 Population 11,000,000. Very large city on SE coast of large island. Extends on both sides of river. Originally had other name. Present name given in 1868, when it became capital. Earthquake 1923, caused terrible destruction. Very large port.

6 Population 2,500,000. Two capitals in one. Traditional date for foundation 753 BC. Built on seven hills. Great fire of AD 64. watched by notorious politician/musician. Sacked by Vandals in 455.

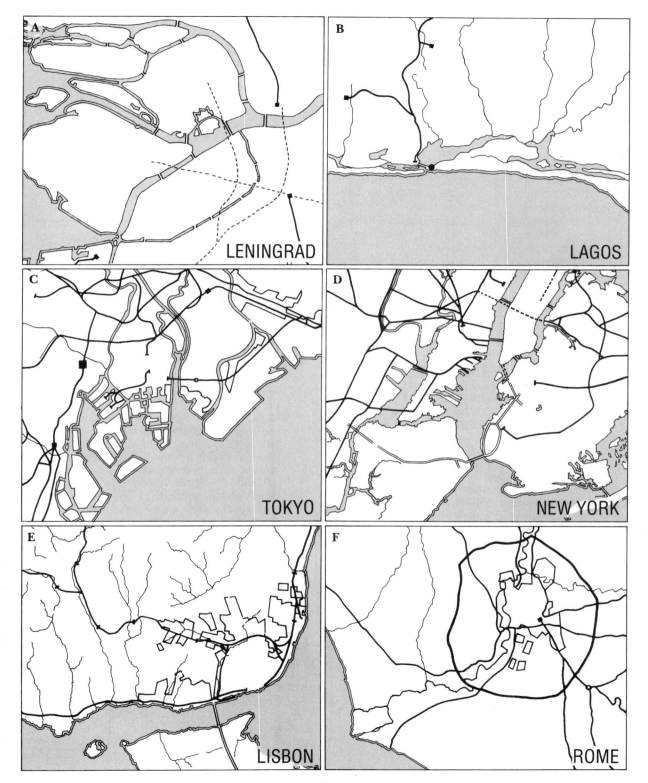

A LENINGRAD

B LAGOS

C TOKYO

D NEW YORK

E LISBON

F ROME

Cambridge

Activity 1 – group work

1 Look at the five types of publication listed on the left, and decide which features of content and style, listed on the right, would be likely to appear in such publications.

1) an autobiography for general readers
2) a city history for general readers
3) a publicity leaflet trying to attract tourists
4) a tourist guide conveying general information
5) a specialist guide for readers with specific interests

a) tabulated information
b) superfluous adjectives
c) use of the first person in narrative
d) content unlikely to mean much to the average reader
e) chronological presentation

2 Read the texts on Cambridge on these two pages and decide which of the five types of publication each was taken from, and what sort of reader each was intended for.

3 Reread the tourist guide text and make notes for a similar guide to your own city or town.

A

The history of Cambridge began many hundreds of years before the first college, Peterhouse, was founded in 1284 by Hugh de Balsham, Bishop of ELY. In the century preceding
5 the Roman Conquest a Celtic settlement had arisen on what is known as Castle Hill, lying between Castle Street and Chesterton Road to the N. of the town. At the foot of the hill was a ford across the River Cam, and successive Roman
10 developments probably included the building of a bridge at this point. This bridge became the only one to have given its name to an English county. Its location was of great importance as marking the place where the Roman roads, in particular the *Via*
15 *Devana* from COLCHESTER to CHESTER, converged with the system of rivers and canals. As the northernmost point before reaching the fens such a site was of great strategic and commercial importance.
20 With the departure of the Romans the town continued to spread to its present position on the East Anglian side of the river. The Normans, however, rebuilt the castle and moved over to the opposite bank of the Cam. Nothing remains of the
25 castle today but the mound. The thirteenth century saw the founding of the first Cambridge college and the consequent increase in the importance of the city as a seat of learning and a centre of communal life.

B

Then, Cambridge. I know Cambridge well enough, having spent three years there, and many an odd day or two since. A lovely old place, far lovelier now than Oxford. But either
5 you are completely and happily at home there or are always faintly uncomfortable, longing to escape from Kings Parade and the Trumpington Road. I was always faintly uncomfortable, being compelled to feel – and quite rightly too –
10 a bit of a lout and a bit of a mountebank. I am not pleased with myself about this discomfort of mine at Cambridge. Probably it is because they *know*, whereas I am always only guessing. But wistfully, as a self-condemned lout and
15 mountebank, I wish Cambridge did not tend to take every advantage of the fact that it knows more than anybody else about seventeenth-century prose or electrons or the foreign policy of Choiseul or Vitamin E. I wish it were not so
20 primly pleased with itself, as if it were a hard-working charitable spinster and the Absolute its delighted vicar. I wish that somebody, one day, would rise in the Senate and begin: 'Look here, we're a conceited parochial gang . . .' It would
25 not be true, but I cannot help feeling that the resulting shock would be of some benefit.

C

Cambridge, the county town, a city of 95,400 inhabitants, situated on the river *Cam* (known also as the *Granta* above Silver Street Bridge), in a flat but not unpleasing district, is the seat of
5 one of the two great and ancient English universities, and, thanks to its freedom from industry, has some claim to be considered the only true university town in the country. Its college architecture is delightful, and King's
10 College Chapel is unique, while in the Backs (see p. 197) it possesses a charm peculiar to itself.

HOTELS. *University Arms*[1] (u. E 4), 126 R.; *Garden House*[1] (g. C 4), 80 R.; *Blue Boar*[1] (b, C 2, 3), TH, 47 R.; *West House*[1]
15 (w, B 4), 13 R.; *Royal*[2] (r, D 5), 60 R.; *Station*[2], 16 R.; *Windsor*[2], unlic., near the station, 11 R.; etc. – RESTAURANTS. *Arts Theatre* (see below); *K.P., Miller's Wine Parlour*, both in King's Parade; *Le Jardin*, 17 Hills Rd; *Turk's Head Grill*, 14 Trinity St. (C 3); etc.
RAILWAY STATION, 1½ m. from the city centre (beyond E 5). – CAR
20 PARK (multi-storeyed), Park St. (D 3).
TRAVEL AGENTS. *Cook's*, 5 Market Hill (CD 3); *Lunn's*, 6 King's Parade.
THEATRE. *Arts Theatre* (C 3), Peas Hill.
BOATING. Punts and canoes may be hired at Great Bridge (C 1, 2),
25 Garret Hostel Bridge (B 3), or the Mill Pool (C 4), for the Backs and the pretty Upper River. The Lower River (E–G 1) is mostly used by racing craft. The Lent and May bumping races are rowed between the Pike & Eel and Baitsbite. – SWIMMING POOL (covered), Donkey's Common (F 4).
30 CHIEF SIGHTS. For a first visit the most attractive colleges are King's, Queens', St John's, Trinity, and Jesus, and then Clare, Caius, Magdalene, and Peterhouse. Visitors may stroll at their pleasure through the courts. If the hall, chapel, or library is closed, admission is usually obtainable on application at the porter's lodge. A visit to the *Backs,
35 i.e. the gardens on either bank of the river at the back of the colleges, is an essential part of even the briefest stay in Cambridge, and, if possible, a visit to the Fitzwilliam Museum and attendance at a chapel service at King's, St Johns, or Trinity should be contrived. Nor should the interesting post-war college buildings be disregarded.

D

A small city, beautiful, well preserved and without industry. The university controls the city and owns most of it, carrying on like a feudal landowner – still holding grand
5 banquets and paying subsistence wages to its loyal servants who live in tied cottages.

In term-time there are a lot of stimulating things going on as the town is dominated by students – but in the summer it changes into
10 a tourist centre.

Contact. Two good alternative bookshops – Cockagne and Last Exit – can put you in touch particularly with political activities.
15 Arjuna, the wholefood shop, has notices and would know of anything in the self-development direction. A meeting place is Romsey Town cafe. Most colleges have a notice-board just inside the entrance which
20 will tell you what's happening. Bookshops: p. 132; Arjuna p. 75 and cafe p. 70.

E

One of Britain's twin academic highspots, Cambridge is a must for the admirer of educational achievement. The elegant courts of the famed river colleges, many of them
5 hundreds of years old, overlook the Cam, where today's students (or undergraduates) punt their friends over the still, tree-fringed waters. Rich in tradition, Cambridge offers the unparalleled splendour of King's
10 College Chapel, a fifteenth century Gothic masterpiece, the magnificent gateway of Christ's, where Puritan poet John Milton prepared himself for the labours of his immortal *Paradise Lost*, and Trinity, attended
15 by poets William Wordsworth, Alfred, Lord Tennyson, and the present Prince of Wales. A visit to Cambridge takes you deep into the heart of England's heritage, a panoramic view of civilisation ranging from
20 Trumpington, where Chaucer's students seduced the local miller's wife and daughter, to the Cavendish laboratories, where Rutherford first split the atom.

Lyons

The passages on Cambridge on pages 50–51 reflected different styles and different forms of information aimed at various sections of the reading public. The passage below is an artist's impression of a city, but it also includes a great deal of information. Read it, and then answer the questions opposite.

It is at Lyons that the Rhône comes of age, so to speak: has its first real love affair with the quiet-flowing Saône, a river almost as wide but only half as swift. But the two rivers at their junction are
5 really responsible for the character of this great industrial city. Lyons has always been the hinge between the two climates and the two cultures of France, and while the ebb and flow of history has changed the disposition and architecture of the town
10 over and over again, nothing has ever managed to alter its influence as a catalyst, a transformer between the hot-blooded southern Frenchman and his more reserved northern brother. Even in Roman times, as today, Lyons was the natural axis of the European
15 road system in an age when it took one thirty days to traverse Gaul from the Pas de Calais to Marseilles. Today the axis still holds good for the modern road and rail system which nets eastern France. All roads lead to Lyons, and no wise traveller will complain
20 for this great city is also the axis of good eating – the very midriff of *haute cuisine*, as it were. Opinions have always differed about the climate of Lyons, yes; even among Frenchmen. But . . . you will not find a *gourmet* in France who has not made the sacred
25 pilgrimage called the *Circuit du Beaujolais*, for the wine-country of that famous name lies just north of Lyons, and is easily visited by the ardent wine-prover.

As for Lyons itself, the second city of France,
30 despite the splendour of its historic monuments, its great picture gallery, its magnificent squares and bridges, there is something not very inspiriting about its atmosphere. This is perhaps due to the

river-mist which so often seems to hang over it,
35 hazing up its sharp outlines. Despite the excellence of its *cuisine*. Myself I have always remembered the description of Daudet and found it not inapt. 'Strange town!' he writes. 'I remember a low-hanging sky the colour of soot, a perpetual mist
40 rising from the two rivers. It never seems to actually rain. It mists over; and in the flatness of this wet atmosphere the walls weep, the pavements sweat, the balustrades of the staircases stick to one's fingers. The people, too, in their way seem to reflect this
45 grey humidity . . .' No traveller will repeat these words to a Lyonnais without provoking the passionate cry: 'Unjust! Daudet was a blasted southerner. How could he appreciate our city?'

But there is much to reconcile one apart from the
50 food, and the industrious and inventive people of Lyons are right not to pay too much attention to sun-drunk southerners. The history of the town has laid its mark upon so many arts and industries – from fine printing to silk – that really it should be
55 exonerated for its sad climate. Here, after all, in some little bookshop you might actually stumble upon a bundle of medieval almanacs which provided Rabelais with an immortal pattern for his book! Or better still, if you find yourself on the banks of the
60 Saône at dusk, hunt out the little marionette theatre (30 du Quai Saint Antoine) and spend an evening watching the exquisite *Théâtre Guignol* at work! This famous local Punch and Judy show dates from 1808. Yes, Lyons has its charms. It has in fact always been a
65 favoured town owing to its unique location.

From Spirit of Place by Lawrence Durrell (abridged)

Activity 2

1 Before answering the detailed questions below, what overall impression do you get of the following features of Lyons: a) its size; b) its geographical position; c) its climate; d) its industries; e) its food; f) its people; g) its attraction for visitors?
Now find evidence in the text for the writer's opinions on all these subjects.

2 Study the construction of the first paragraph. In what way is the second sentence the point of development for the sentences that follow?

3 What appears to be the writer's principal interest in the city, and how does he provide the transition from the previous topic to this interest, which forms the conclusion?

4 Which phrase in the first clause prepares for the idea of a 'love affair' between rivers in the first sentence?

5 In what three ways is Lyons presented as an **axis**? Why is the word **midriff** an appropriate alternative to **axis** in lines 20–1?

6 Does the writer appear to agree with Daudet's opinion of Lyons? What would be particularly offensive in quoting Daudet to a Lyonnais?

7 Study the construction of the third paragraph. How is it developed from the topic sentence? In what way does the conclusion summarise the topic sentence and contradict the impression created by the second paragraph?

Getting away

The text below is taken from a travel agency
brochure. Study it critically and decide what effect
it intends to make, before working on Activity 3.

STUCK IN AN ENGLISH WINTER? SNOW OUTSIDE? ICE AND SLUSH ON THE
ROADS? READY FOR A WINTER HOLIDAY? SOMEWHERE TO CHASE THOSE
WINTER BLUES AWAY? How about CAPO BUONO on the southern Adriatic? It may be
January, but the skies there are blue and the sea warm and inviting. CAPO BUONO has
everything – beautiful spacious sandy beaches, charming little coves and islands to explore,
fine wines to savour and delicious local and international cuisine to delight the palate,
first-class shops, magnificent super-modern hotels and apartments with all the amenities
the most demanding traveller could ask for. So many things to do, too. Treat your chilled
body to a morning bathe in the gentle sea. Stretch out and tan on the sun-kissed beaches.
Breathe the clear air the warm south wind blows across from Africa. Wander in the
picturesque, quaint narrow cobbled streets of the old fishing village from which modern
Capo Buono grew. Eat in the colourful local restaurants and dance the night away in one of
Capo Buono's ultra-modern discos. Watch from the Roman harbour wall as the sardine
boats chug out on their nightly odyssey towards the flames of the setting sun. And when
dawn comes, climb the ancient winding Roman steps to St Bernard's fountain and make a
wish. If you're a gambler, there's the Golden Nugget Casino and four Bingo centres. And if
it's sport you're after, Capo Buono has all the sports facilities you could possibly ask for.
Yes, Capo Buono has everything and best of all, it has its people – warm, hospitable,
generous people who really **want** you to have a good time and go back time and time again
– people who care.
       IF CAPO BUONO SOUNDS YOUR KIND OF PLACE, READ ON . . . .

Activity 3 – pair work

1 List the attractions Capo Buono would have for the
   tourist.
2 List all the adjectives. Remove them to see what
   difference this makes to the text. What feelings are
   exploited by these adjectives?
3 Consider the following words and phrases and decide
   what emotions are excited by them: **stuck in an English
   winter, those winter blues, fine wines to savour,
   delight the palate, treat your chilled body, breathe the
   clear air, dance the night away, make a wish, people
   who care**.
4 Summarise what is said here, excluding all emotional
   language. Begin: *Capo Buono is a tourist resort on the
   southern Adriatic. The weather is good in winter . . .*

Composition

1 Write an account of your native city or a city you have
   visited for a tourist guide conveying general information.
2 Give an account of the history of your native city, or of
   one you know well.
3 Describe your experiences on visiting a city for the first
   time.

Journeys

Where to go?

**Tim and Barbara Carrington spent three days in
York last summer. Tim is interested in historic
houses, castles and ruins while Barbara is fond of
animals and the countryside.**

Study the map and the symbols and work out an
interesting route, including lunch stops, that Tim and
Barbara could have taken for each of the three days. On
the first day they drove north-east out of York, and on
the second day north. On the third day Barbara wanted
to spend the afternoon at Thirsk races, but they still
found two places of interest to Tim. There are several
possibilities.

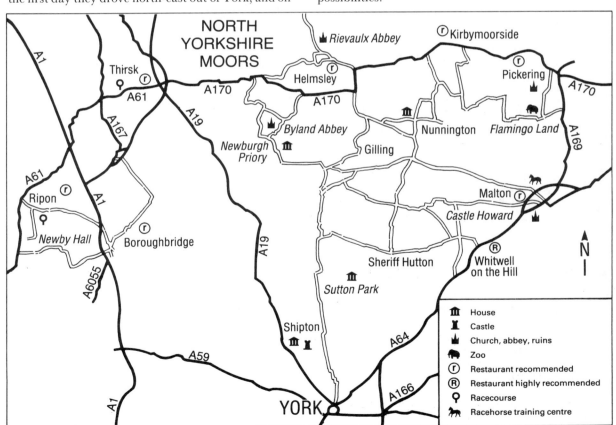

Abandoned ... stranded ... lost

It was 10.00 p.m. and, in the drowsy warmth of the train from Stockholm, 44-year-old Mrs Karin Edholm sleepily opened her eyes as the train began to slow down.

5   She must be nearing home at last. The 700-mile journey to Murjek, in Lapland near the Arctic Circle, had taken hours. Then the train suddenly jolted to a stop. 'Is this Murjek?' she asked a fellow passenger. He nodded and, grabbing her handbag,
10 Mrs Edholm hastily opened the compartment door, stepped out and found herself falling.

   Thick snow broke her fall. As she got to her feet, she looked around in alarm. There was no platform, no station, no lights and not a sign of anybody in
15 sight.

   She was in the middle of nowhere, her teeth already chattering in the bitter temperature of 27 degrees below freezing. As she turned to try to climb back on board the train started to move off.
20   She stumbled alongside for a few feet screaming, 'Stop, stop. For God's sake stop.' But nobody answered and nothing happened. She stood there shivering as she watched the lights of the train disappear in the distance.
25   And she was still in summer clothes. For she and her husband had arrived back from a six-week holiday in the heat of Sri Lanka. At Stockholm she had decided to return home by train rather than face the tiring journey by car. Her husband would still
30 be on the road somewhere miles away to the south.

   Now there was only one thing for her to do ... walk and follow the rail tracks to Murjek. She began to stumble along, jumping up and down, flapping her arms and holding her breath in a bid to beat the
35 bitter cold.

   The country was in the grip of the fiercest winter for 100 years and, as she slipped and fell, losing her shoes at one point, she became convinced she would just freeze to death.
40   But she was still alive after half an hour and she leapt with joy when she heard another train rumbling towards her. She waved and shouted. But nobody saw her and, with sinking heart, she watched the train thunder past.
45   An hour later she was almost unconscious on her feet. But she still managed to drag one foot after the other even though her clothes were now stiff with ice.

   Then a breakdown trolley came clattering along
50 the line on the way to thaw out a frozen set of points. This time she was spotted and the railway workers wrapped her in coats and took her to Murjek where she was immediately taken to hospital.
55   Doctors there said, 'She would not have lasted another thirty minutes.'

   Now reunited with her husband, who had arrived home to find the house empty and had then gone to the police, Mrs Edholm is wondering why her
60 fellow passenger told her that the train had stopped at Murjek?

   Was it an honest mistake? Or had she been the victim of a callous sense of humour?

From an article by Terry Greenwood in the *Sunday Express*

Activity 1

This story is told almost in chronological order.

1 How does the writer immediately give us the sense of time and place?

2 Find examples of direct speech to attract our attention at crucial points in the story.

3 Find two examples of the writer referring back to something that had happened previously. Why does he do this?

4 Find examples of repeated negatives (**no, nobody,** etc.). What is the effect of these?

The writer of this passage also describes an interrupted journey, but the effect is very different from that of the previous passage.

At Sirpur, just over the border of Andhra Pradesh, the train ground to a halt. Twenty minutes later we were still there. Sirpur is insignificant: the platform is uncovered, the station
5 has two rooms, and there are cows on the verandah. Grass tufts grow out of the ledge of the booking-office window. It smelled of rain and wood smoke and cow dung; it was little more than a hut, dignified with the usual railway signs, of
10 which the most hopeful was TRAINS RUNNING LATE ARE LIKELY TO MAKE UP TIME. Passengers on the Grand Trunk Express began to get out. They promenaded, grateful for the exercise.

'The engine has packed up,' one man told me.
15 'They are sending for new one. Delay of two hours.'

Another man said, 'If there was a cabinet minister on this train they would have an engine in ten minutes' time.'
20 I decided to look for a beer, but just outside the station I was in darkness so complete I had second thoughts. The smell of rain on the vegetation gave a humid richness to the air that was almost sweet. There were cows lying on the road: they were
25 white; I could see them clearly. Using the cows as road markers I walked along until I saw a small orange light about 50 yards away. I headed towards it and came to a little hut, a low poky shack with mud walls and a canvas roof. There was
30 a kerosene lantern on the doorway and another inside lighting the surprised faces of a half a dozen tea-drinkers, two of whom recognised me from the train.

'What do you want?' one said. 'I will ask for it.'
35 'Can I buy a bottle of beer here?'

This was translated. There was laughter. I knew the answer.

'About two kilometres down the road' – the man pointed into the blackness – 'there is a bar. You can
40 get beer there.'

'How will I find it?'

'A car,' he said. He spoke again to the man serving tea. 'But there is no car here. Have some tea.'
45 We stood in the hut, drinking milky tea out of cracked glasses. A joss stick was lit. No one said a word. The train passengers looked at the villagers; the villagers averted their eyes.

The Indian who had translated my question said
50 under his breath, 'This is the real India!'

From *The Great Railway Bazaar* by Paul Theroux

Activity 2

1 Find reference to time and place.
2 Explain why the writer uses direct speech in some places.
3 Find a reference to a previous event.
4 Find phrases that link together:
   a) the station and the countryside round it;
   b) the delay on the journey and the writer's search
   for refreshment.
5 What impression do you gain of India, judging from the final remark?

Activity 3 – group work

The account of a journey below has been printed with the sentences and paragraphs out of order, except that the first sentence of each paragraph is in the correct position. Use the time and place references in italic as a guide to decide on the correct order of the paragraphs and of the sentences in each paragraph.

1 I was staying less than 100 km from the French border so I decided that instead of going to Barcelona to catch the express I would pick it up at Port Bou on the frontier. **a)** It was the express and I had missed it. **b)** *It was not until we were a few kilometres from Port Bou* that I began to worry, when I saw a gleaming modern train sweep past us and disappear into the distance. **c)** The local train arrived on time *about 11.00 in the morning, and for some time* I enjoyed the scenery as we trundled gently along.

2 *At this moment* I suddenly remembered that I had not got her address and I did not know the name of my hotel, either. **a)** We drove *towards the village* and *eventually reached the house*; the taxi driver *had stopped* at a police station on the way to ask where Dr Schiller lived. **b)** She told me where the hotel was and we arranged to meet the next day. **c)** All I knew was that she was living at *the house of a Dr Schiller in a village near the city.* **d)** Anneliese came to *the door,* half asleep, but pleased to see me. **e)** I got a taxi and explained the situation to the driver, who was not in the least put out.

3 The most complicated journey I have ever made was one I did not expect would prove very difficult. **a)** *Earlier that summer,* I had met a German girl and we had been writing to each other *since she had returned home.* **b)** She could not invite me to *the house where she was living* but she said she would meet the express train from Barcelona to Geneva and book me into a hotel in the city. **c)** *At the time* I was still a student, *on holiday on the Costa Brava.* **d)** I had some days to spare *before I had to be back at the university* so I arranged to visit her *there.* **e)** *At the end of August,* I had had a letter from her, telling me that she had taken a job as an au pair *in Switzerland.*

4 As I *soon* discovered, however, my troubles were not yet over. **a)** He gave the clerk a passionate lecture on Swiss hospitality and insisted that he should find me *another hotel.* **b)** *At the hotel,* the supercilious clerk told me I had not arrived *in time to take up my room,* and it had been given to someone else. **c)** He must have carried the figures for the daily exchange rates in his head! **d)** *When we got to the other hotel,* I realised that I had no Swiss francs, but the taxi driver shrugged aside my embarrassment and cheerfully *went off into the night* with a handful of French francs and pesetas. **e)** I was too tired to argue *by this time,* but the taxi driver suddenly went mad.

5 *When I got to Port Bou,* the express had already left, but I was told I could reach Geneva a few hours later if I took four trains, to Narbonne, Avignon, Lyons and finally Geneva. **a)** There was no sign of Anneliese *at the station* and I imagined she had obviously given up hope of my arrival. **b)** Incredibly, this proved to be true and I arrived *in Geneva at 1.00 in the morning.*

Composition

Describe a journey you have made, concentrating on one of the following: a) the difficulties you encountered; b) the people you met; c) the interesting things you saw.

Women in society

Questionnaire

Complete the following questionnaire. Do not think for more than a few seconds about your answers. In each case, you should mark the appropriate column with a cross. Compare your answers with those of your partner. Where you disagree with one another, discuss your reasons.

++   I agree entirely with this statement.
+   In general terms, I agree.
o   You have no opinion, or you think the statement is vague and the real problem is rather different.
—   On the whole, I am not in favour of this.
=   I strongly disagree.

	++	+	o	—	=
1 A woman should be able to change a wheel on a car.					
2 A man should be able to sew and knit.					
3 Schoolgirls should be given career guidance like boys, on the assumption that they will go to work.					
4 The use of Mrs and Miss should be replaced by Ms.					
5 Children should not automatically be given their father's surname.					
6 In Britain, families with children pay less tax. Instead, the State should pay money direct to the mother.					
7 Men are not necessary to women's happiness.					
8 Men and women should get equal pay for equal work.					
9 Beauty contests should be banned because they are an insult to women.					
10 The state should pay wages for housework.					

The historical background

It would be an endless task to trace the variety of meannesses, cares, and sorrows, into which women are plunged by the prevailing opinion, that they were created rather to feel than reason, and that all the power they obtain, must be obtained by their charms and weakness.

Fragile in every sense of the word, they are obliged to look up to man for every comfort. In the most trifling dangers they cling to their support, with parasitical tenacity, piteously demanding succour; and their *natural* protector extends his arm, or lifts up his voice, to guard the lovely trembler – from what? Perhaps the frown of an old cow, or the jump of a mouse; a rat, would be a serious danger. In the name of reason, and even common sense, what can save such beings from contempt; even though they be soft and fair?

I am fully persuaded that we should hear of none of these **infantine** airs, if girls were allowed to take sufficient exercise, and not confined in close rooms till their muscles are relaxed, and their powers of digestion destroyed. To carry the remark still further, if fear in girls, instead of being cherished, perhaps created, was treated in the same manner as cowardice in boys, we should quickly see women with more dignified aspects.

'Educate women like men,' says Rousseau, 'and the more they resemble our sex the less power will they have over us.' This is the very point I aim at. I do not wish them to have power over men; but over themselves.

From *A Vindication of the Rights of Woman* (1792) by Mary Wollstonecraft

infantine: in modern English, infantile

Without telling her husband, Dr Lydgate, Rosamond has written to his rich relations begging for money. They assume that he told her to do it because he was too cowardly to ask himself and they despise him as a result.

'You have not made my life pleasant to me of late' – 'the hardships which our marriage has brought on me' – these words were stinging his imagination as a pain makes an exaggerated dream.

'Rosamond', he said, turning his eyes on her with a melancholy look, 'you should allow for a man's words when he is disappointed and provoked. When I hurt you, I hurt part of my own life. I should never be angry with you if you would be quite open with me.'

'I have only wished to prevent you from hurrying us into wretchedness without any necessity,' said Rosamond, the tears coming again from a softened feeling now that her husband had softened. 'It is so very hard to be disgraced here among all the people we know, and to live in such a miserable way. I wish I had died with the baby.'

She spoke and wept with that gentleness which makes such words and tears omnipotent over a loving-hearted man. Lydgate drew his chair near to hers and pressed her delicate head against his cheek with his powerful tender hand. He only caressed her; he did not say anything; for what was there to say? He could not promise to shield her from the dreaded wretchedness, for he could see no sure means of doing so. When he left her to go out again, he told himself that it was ten times harder for her than for him: he had a life away from home, and constant appeals to his activity on behalf of others. He wished to excuse everything in her if he could – but it was inevitable that in that excusing mood he should think of her as if she were an animal of another and feebler species. Nevertheless she had mastered him.

From *Middlemarch: a Study of Provincial Life* (1872) by George Eliot (Mary Ann Evans)

If I have laid stress upon these professional experiences of mine, it is because I believe that they are, though in different forms, yours also. Even when the path is nominally open – when there is nothing to prevent a woman from being a doctor, a lawyer, a
5 civil servant – there are many phantoms and obstacles, as I believe, looming in her way. To discuss and define them is I think of great value and importance; for thus only can the labour be shared, the difficulties be solved. But besides this, it is necessary also to discuss the ends and the aims for which we are fighting,
10 for which we are doing battle with these formidable obstacles. Those aims cannot be taken for granted; they must be perpetually questioned and examined. The whole position, as I see it – here in this hall surrounded by women practising for the first time in history I know not how many different professions – is one of
15 extraordinary interest and importance. You have won rooms of your own in the house hitherto exclusively owned by men. You are able, though not without great labour and effort, to pay the rent. You are earning your £500 a year. But this freedom is only a beginning; the room is your own, but it is still bare. It has to be
20 furnished; it has to be decorated; it has to be shared. How are you going to furnish it, how are you going to decorate it? With whom are you going to share it, and upon what terms? These, I think are questions of the utmost importance and interest. For the first time in history you are able to ask them; for the first time you are able
25 to decide for yourselves what the answers should be.

From *Professions for Women*, address to the Women's Service League,
by Virginia Woolf (published in *The Death of the Moth*, 1942)

When I was seventeen feminism meant to me shadowy figures in long old-fashioned clothes . . . From dim childhood memories I had a stereotype of emancipated women: frightening people in tweed suits and horn-rimmed glasses with stern buns at the backs
5 of their heads . . . Feminism seemed the very antithesis of the freedom I connected with getting away from home and school . . . My recognition of women as a group was as creatures sunk into the very deadening circumstances from which I was determined to escape. . . .
10 On the other hand, the 'mystique' was very much part of my own life. There was pop music for example. My own sense of myself as a person directly conflicted with the kind of girl who was sung about in pop songs. When I was sixteen I remember feeling really angry about 'Living Doll' ('I got myself a sleeping,
15 walking, crying, talking, Living Doll' – Cliff Richard, 1959) because it cut away from all my inside efforts towards any identity. It hurt me particularly because when I tried to argue about it with a boy I really liked I felt terribly constrained by his contempt when he said that was how he liked girls.

From *Woman's Consciousness, Man's World* (1973) by Sheila Rowbotham

Activity 1

1 Why do you think the author of the first passage on the opposite page emphasised the word **natural** (line 12)?
2 In what way is the second passage opposite an illustration of the first paragraph?
3 In what way is Lydgate's opinion of his wife a confirmation of the second paragraph of the first passage?
4 How far does Rosamond fulfil Mary Wollstonecraft's idea of what a woman should be?
5 'George Eliot', the author of the second passage, was really a woman. How does her last sentence contradict the general impression given by Mary Wollstonecraft? Do you think she sympathises with Lydgate or with Rosamond?

Activity 2

1 In the first passage above, the writer is attempting to define the position of professionally qualified women in society. How far do her aims resemble those of Mary Wollstonecraft?
2 What does she mean by 'rooms of your own' in this context (lines 15–16)?
3 Why would the question 'With whom are you going to share it?' (lines 21–22) have seemed strange to women like Rosamond?
4 What impression did the writer of the second passage, here, have of women of her grandmother's generation like those Virginia Woolf was addressing? Why did it confuse her?
5 Can you see anything in common between the attitude of men expressed in the two passages on page 60 and the lyrics of the song 'Living Doll'?

Two modern views

Activity 3 – pair work

Part 1: Study the following two texts together, paying particular attention to the sentences in italic. First, read them alone and note down your personal reactions; then compare notes with a partner. Make your notes under the list of possible headings below and add some of your own.

1 Are they writing about the same subject?
2 What sort of reader is each writing for?
3 What is 'a complete person' (Greer) and a 'total woman' (Morgan)?
4 If the two writers met in a debate, where do you think they might agree and disagree?
5 What risks and sacrifices might accompany any woman following either writer's view? What are each writer's *presuppositions* about women?

Loneliness is never more cruel than when it is felt in close propinquity with someone who has ceased to communicate. Many a housewife staring at the back of her husband's newspaper, or listening to his breathing
5 in bed is lonelier than any spinster in a rented room. *Much of the loneliness of lonely people springs from distrust and egotism, not from their having failed to set themselves up in a conjugal arrangement.* The marriage bargain offers what cannot be delivered if it is
10 thought to offer emotional security, *for such security is the achievement of the individual.* Possessive love, for all its seductiveness, breaks down that personal poise and leaves its victims newly vulnerable. Those miserable women who blame the men who LET THEM
15 DOWN for their misery and isolation enact every day the initial mistake of *sacrificing their personal responsibility for themselves. They would not have been any happier if they had remained married.*
   When a man woos a woman he strives to make
20 himself as indispensable as any woman is to any man: he may even determine to break down her self-sufficiency. *In the struggle to remain a complete person and to love from her fullness instead of from her inadequacy a woman may appear hard.* She may
25 feel her early conditioning tugging her in the direction of surrender, but she ought to remember that she was originally loved for herself; she ought to hang on to herself and not find herself nagging, helpless, irritable and trapped.
30 *Perhaps I am not old enough (at 30) yet to promise that the self-reliant woman is always loved,* that she cannot be lonely as long as there are people in the world who need her joy and strength, but certainly in my experience it has always been so. Lovers who are
35 free to go when they are restless always come back; lovers who are free to change remain interesting. *The bitter animosity and obscenity of divorce is unknown where individuals have not become Siamese twins.*

From *The Female Eunuch* (1970) by Germaine Greer

A total woman is not a slave. She graciously chooses to adapt to her husband's way, even though at times she desperately may not want to. He in turn will gratefully respond by trying to make it up to her and grant her
5 desires. He may even want to spoil her with goodies.
   Marriage has also been likened to a monarchy, where the husband is king, and his wife is queen. In a royal marriage, the king's decision is the final word, for his country and his queen alike. *The queen is certainly*
10 *not his slave, for she knows where her powers lie.* She is queen. She, too, sits on a throne. She has the right, and in fact the responsibility, to express her feelings, but of course, she does so in a regal way. *Though the king relies heavily on her judgement, if there is a*
15 *difference of opinion, it is the king who makes the final decision.*
   Now, hold on, I know just what you're thinking; remember, I've been through all of this too. What if the king makes the wrong decision? Oh, that's a hard one,
20 especially when you know you're right, and there are times when that is the case. The queen is to follow him forthwith. A queen shall not nag or **buck** her king's **decision** after it is decreed.
   In so many marriages today, the woman rules the
25 roost. In others, there are two co-equal rulers, whose decisions often clash. In still others, only the fittest survive. *None of these cases enhances romance. Emotions are sent plummeting to zero, and the husband is left wondering, 'How did I get into this mess?'*
30 I would like to say right here that in the beginning I was as dubious as anyone about *adapting.* But wow, has my thinking changed! I see now that *a man does not want a nagging wife, nor does he want a doormat. He wants one with dignity and opinions and* **spunk,** *but one*
35 *who will leave the final decision to him.*

From *The Total Woman* (1973) by Marabel Morgan

buck a decision (US): challenge/try to throw out
spunk: courage

Part 2:

1 How is the first paragraph in the first passage built up?
   Find three examples of the writer anticipating possible
   counter-arguments in paragraphs 2 and 3. What
   questions is she answering in advance?

2 How does the second writer develop her argument in
   the second paragraph? Find two examples further on of
   her anticipating counter-arguments.

3 Which text do you find more convincing in terms of
   argument? Do you consider the technique successful in
   both cases?

For or against

Activity 4 – pair work

You are journalists working for the Camford Courier.
Recently there has been a national campaign for housework
to be paid for by the State, and you have been asked by
your editor to write an 'opinion' article of 350 words
maximum. You feel the idea is impracticable, but consult
various people. Irrespective of sex and occupation, most
people agree with you.

Follow the pattern below in writing the article. On page
64 you will find a list of the most useful opinions you got
from your consultations. Go through the list together and
decide which ones will be useful in the article, and in which
paragraph. (w = a woman's opinion; м = a man's.)

One of you write paragraph 2, the other, paragraph 3,
and work together to write paragraphs 1 and 4.

1	TOPIC PARAGRAPH	Explain what the campaign is trying to do.
	about 60 words	

2	EXPLANATION OF THE CONSENSUS OPINION IN CAMFORD/WHAT THE MAJORITY FEEL	Set down the majority arguments one by one, keeping the best till the last.
	about 100 words	

3	WHAT THE MINORITY FEEL/ OPPOSITION ARGUMENTS WHICH YOU STATE AND THEN COUNTER	Set down the opposition arguments one by one and find what is wrong with each, but take them seriously if they deserve it.
	about 100 words	

4	CONCLUSION/HOW MOST CAMFORD PEOPLE WOULD ANSWER THE QUESTION	Make a brief synthesis, on the basis 'in spite of the points made in 3, the consensus view is…'
	about 50/60 words	

FOR

w It's very hard work and I don't see why it shouldn't be paid.

w I for one would give up my outside job if they paid me. I think a lot of people would. And that would help unemployment.

M A good idea if it's realistic pay. I mean, it's been calculated that housewives work an 80-hour week.

AGAINST

M I think it's a stupid idea. You pay people for productive work, where you can see the results, and I don't see why the State should pay for something that may or may not be done.

M I'm against. They'll only raise the taxes to pay for it.

M I think the housewife, sorry, houseperson, has a very good time of it already.

w It's still based on the idea that one person is responsible for the housework, normally we women. I think it'd be much more realistic and useful to make people aware that housework responsibilities should be shared.

w I personally believe that the women who want this are those who feel their work at home is taken for granted, undervalued. Asking to be paid is another way of asking for recognition.

w You can't keep both a job outside and a home going, not properly. If you take a job outside you've got to get a daily help, for the good of your health.

w A lot of women work because if they didn't their families would starve. I don't think the State would pay anything like enough.

M It's open to abuse, isn't it? There'll be a lot of people who pick up the money and do a job on the side.

M It's impracticable. How would they organise it? Allow families with a bona fide housewife to pay less tax?

Composition

Write an essay commenting on one of the following:
1 Men are not necessary to women's happiness.
2 Beauty contests should be banned because they are an insult to women.
3 What annoys men about feminists is that they do not seem to be feminine.

Dialogue and speeches

 ## To extend or not to extend

In the industrial city of Daffield, the city council has just voted in favour of extending the airport, and the decision has provoked a lively reaction from Daffield residents, who feel they were not adequately consulted. Radio Daffield has organised a phone-in programme in which residents can express their opinions, and you will hear an extract from it.
Below you will see a list of possible arguments for and against the decision. Listen to the tape and put a tick (√) against the arguments used by the three callers, then summarise the main reasons for their attitude in each case.

ARGUMENTS FOR

The larger airport will help relieve the city's unemployment problem.
It will attract attention to Daffield at national level.
It will make long-distance travel easier for Daffield residents.
It will bring Daffield into the twentieth century.
It will make Daffield more important than neighbouring Lambton.
It will attract outside investment for Daffield's industry.
It will benefit Daffield's tradespeople.
It will attract government subsidies for building much-needed new roads and transport links.
It will attract a lot of tourists to Daffield.

ARGUMENTS AGAINST

The larger airport will destroy the bird reserve.
People in areas disturbed by noise will have to be rehoused.
The decision was taken without sufficient consultation.
New road and rail links will spoil some open countryside.
It will be expensive for taxpayers to compensate home-owners whose property loses value because of the new airport.
There will not be as many new jobs as the airport's promoters claim.
The Turville old people's home and the main hospital will be inconvenienced by the noise.
The airport will cause insoluble traffic problems in Daffield.
The airport will cause pollution problems.

Summarising dialogue

Listen to this dialogue, and then study it, before answering the questions below.

SUSAN	I really can't see why children are forced to go through a system of exams at school. After all, *psychologists have shown that exams are not really a good guide to ability.*
HENRY	I don't think they've proved that. All they've proved is that exams are not as accurate as we would like them to be.
SUSAN	But that's very important. If students depend on them for their future careers, *a serious mistake on the examiners' part can ruin a person's whole life.*
HENRY	I still think they're necessary – a necessary evil, if you like. How else would you judge people's capabilities?
SUSAN	Well, *it would be fairer to base qualifications on teachers' assessments during the year. A good student may feel nervous on the day of the exam, and fail.*
HENRY	But not all teachers would apply the same standards or be equally competent to judge. As for feeling nervous on the day, in real life what matters is how we react when it's important, so it's a good test. Imagine a surgeon who knows all about the human body and has perfect technique, but whose hands shake when he actually has to operate!
SUSAN	That's an extreme case. What worries me most, I suppose, is that *many teachers are so obsessed by exams that they turn everything into a matter of memory, learning things by heart.* And *exams don't give much scope to people who have ideas of their own. Einstein wasn't much good at school,* apparently.
HENRY	There I agree with you. Doing exam papers is not the best way of preparing students for an exam, and exams themselves can easily be unimaginative. But then it's a matter of improving teaching methods and producing better exams, not of doing away with them altogether.

Activity I

Susan's arguments against examinations are indicated in italic, but a summary of her point of view would not necessarily follow the same order. Study the following summary, paying attention to the way in which the arguments are reordered and linked together. Then pick out the main points in Henry's argument and write a similar summary of his ideas.

Susan thinks that examinations are not really a good guide to ability. Outstanding individuals, like Einstein, for example, did not do very well in them because they do not give enough scope to people with ideas of their own. Apart from that, they may be inaccurate, and as a result, an examiner's mistake could ruin a person's career, or a good student could fail because he is nervous on the day of the examination, which is unfair. It would be fairer to base qualifications on teachers' assessments during the year. Above all, examinations have a bad effect on teaching, because teachers become obsessed by them and simply expect students to memorise facts.

Activity 2

Listen to this dialogue, in which two people are defending opposing points of view. Then study it and make notes on the points made by each speaker and write a summary of each person's views.

BOB	I really don't think you can deny that the microchip revolution is the greatest step forward, the greatest single advance the human race has ever made . . .
ALAN	Well, I would put it another way and say the microchip is not only a danger to the human race . . . it's also, potentially, unless we learn how to make sensible use of it, the greatest danger we've ever faced.
BOB	Oh come on, Alan, I think you're exaggerating there, you know. What about the bomb? Aren't you forgetting that?
ALAN	Yes, but the microchip is a much more real danger because it's affecting our lives *now*. It's changing the way we live. And it's highly dangerous precisely because it's a *peaceful* danger.
BOB	What you mean, surely, is that it's gradually, invisibly, taking a lot of the drudgery out of work, out of repetitive work, that is.
ALAN	The way I see it it's not taking the drudgery out of repetitive work . . . it's taking away the work altogether. If you give people the choice of a repetitive job or no job at all, I know which they'll choose.
BOB	But what you're seeing are the temporary negative effects of any technological step forward. That's the way human societies evolve, after all. Someone has a bright, new idea . . . that idea gets developed into a machine that does mechanical work twice as fast and twice as well as a human, and while the machine's working the human hands are free to do something else that a machine can't do, something involving thought or imagination . . . And of course human beings suffer, temporarily, but in the end it's good for them because they adapt to the new situation, they learn to do something new which a machine can't do, and in that way the machine has freed them too to make progress.
ALAN	I find that totally inhuman. What's happening now all over the world is that active working people are being told that their jobs are being taken over by machines, and that they're no use any more. How would you like someone to say that to you?
BOB	But you're taking this at a personal level. I'm trying to look at the world from outer space and get a long-term impersonal view. If all the time you take a personal view, then of course you end up saying, 'I don't want myself or anyone to lose his job.' But my point is that progress, evolution, change is inevitable, it's part of being human, and, if you accept that as a fact, you can't fail to see that the best policy is to help people to adapt.
ALAN	Up to a point I agree with you, but you're missing a vital point, because you seem to be suggesting that all change is good, as if all scientific progress has been for the best, and that if people protest it's just too bad – they're just trying to stop the clock. Whereas the real challenge is to adapt the scientific progress as best one can to the needs of humanity, not expect humanity to adapt to it.

An informal speech

Look at Mr Ellis's notes for the speech he is going to give on the occasion of Debbie Jackson's leaving the company she has worked for for five years. Listen to his speech, and Debbie's reply, before comparing the notes with his speech printed below. Find the points and note how they are linked together in speech.

1. My job to speak.
2. Debbie – 5 years' hard work/ putting up with us.
3. Very good work, charm, patience, tact.
4. Miss you – good wishes.
5. Gift presentation.

MR ELLIS   I'm sorry to interrupt the fun for a moment, but . . . I think we all know why we're here, and . . . the job of putting, the rather sad job of putting into words what I'm sure we're all feeling has fallen to me. As you know, Debbie Jackson has decided to leave us after five years of hard work and . . . putting up cheerfully with people like you and me. I know I'm talking for a lot of us, probably for all of us who have ever worked with her or for her, when I say that everything she's done in this company during her time here she's done conscientiously and well. And not only that, she's done it with a charm, patience and tact that are highly unusual in the working world these days . . . I hope somebody will be able to say that sincerely for me when I leave! That's why, Debbie, we're all sad to see you go, and we'll miss you a lot.

However, as we know we can't change your mind, we very sincerely wish you all the best for the future with your new job. As a small token of our appreciation we'd like you to accept this small gift, and we hope it will remind you now and again of all the colleagues and friends you're leaving behind here.

DEBBIE   Oh, it's lovely, really. It's really the nicest reminder of you all you could possibly have chosen. Thank you very much . . . I don't know what to say really. This party *did* come as a surprise, and the present even more so . . . All I'd like to say is that throughout my time here I've had the good luck to work with people who've always been tremendously helpful and nice as well as professional, and I shall miss you all a lot . . . Thanks again for everything.

Activity 3 – pair work

Each choose one of the people below and prepare and make a leaving/presentation speech to that person. The other partner should take the role of Virginia or Vincent and make a thank-you speech, similar to that of Debbie Jackson above.

Virginia, who is leaving her job as a reporter on a local newspaper, where she has worked for three years, to take a job on a big national daily newspaper.
Vincent, who is retiring after 25 years as the company's odd-job man. The gift is an inscribed gold clock. Vincent's great love is gardening, and his best-known routine odd job was making tea and coffee.

Formal speeches

Andreas Stephanides is a Greek scientist who has been attending an international conference in England. At the end of the conference, he has been asked to make a speech on behalf of all the visiting delegates.

Activity 4

The notes for his speech below are out of order. Decide on a logical order for presenting the points, then listen to the speech to see whether he followed the order you have chosen. Finally read through the speech below.

1 Atmosphere excellent. Planning helped delegates to concentrate on work in hand. Very noticeable to 'old hands' like self who have attended many such conferences.

2 Excellent planning – no language problems.

3 Next year conference in Athens. Trust that will be able to maintain high standard in handling complex task of organisation. On return will brief Greek organising committee. Important that conferences should continue as annual event for scientists everywhere.

4 Thanks on behalf of visiting delegates – conference valuable, informative. All made very welcome.

Ladies and Gentlemen! At the end of such a valuable and informative Conference, I would like to express my thanks to the Organising Committee on behalf of all the visiting delegates. You have made us welcome to your country in a way that we shall always remember. Everything has been perfectly planned, and whenever any of us got into a little difficulty because of our imperfect control over your delightful but – for a foreigner – puzzling language, there was always someone near at hand to sort the matter out.

Those of us who have attended a large number of such conferences in different parts of the world – the veterans of the circuit, like myself – cannot recall an occasion when things have gone so smoothly and when we have felt so relaxed and free to concentrate on the important work at hand.

In conclusion, I trust that when my own country is to have the honour of playing the host, a year from now, we shall be able to handle the complex task of organisation as efficiently. I can assure you that one of the first things I shall do when I return home is to brief our Committee on everything I have learned here, so that we can profit from your wonderful example and make sure that these conferences continue to be an indispensable annual event for scientists from all over the world.

Activity 5 – group work

Study the way in which the notes for a formal speech like this help the speaker to organise his thoughts. Make notes on speeches from the following list.

1 You are welcoming a group of visitors to your country for a conference. Without going into details about conference arrangements, make a speech to create a pleasant atmosphere.

2 You are the principal guest at a local event in your town, school or university. Reply to a speech of welcome, and comment on the success of the event.

3 The president of a professional association/club/ company you belong to is retiring. Make a formal speech thanking him for his work and commenting on his successful career.

Activity 6

Debates in the House of Commons are often reported in a mixture of direct and reported speech, as in the extract below. Read the extract, noting the changes in tenses and time expressions that are required from the verbs in italic.

If in doubt, look at the Reference Section, page 168. Then convert Mr Hunter's speeches into direct speech, what he actually said, and Mr Warne's into reported speech.

In proposing that the Government should continue to subsidise the shipbuilding industry for another year, Mr Richard Hunter, Secretary of State for Nationalised Industries, said that there *would have to be* a significant improvement in productivity. The industry's response to the targets set by the previous Government *had been* disappointing, since it *had produced* an increase of only 3% instead of the 20% that *had been* forecast. By the time the proposals *were reviewed* in a year's time, *he hoped* that the progress such a large investment *deserved would have been made*.

Mr Sydney Warne, Opposition Spokesman: 'The reason why the targets set by the Labour Government five years *ago have not been reached is* that the present Government's policy *has brought about* the collapse of manufacturing industry. As a result the demand for ships *has fallen*, as *it has* for everything else.

'The Labour Party *will fight* to defend all nationalised industries against such a policy, which *is* part of a strategy to cause massive unemployment. *We are* already *paying* the price for similar measures in the steel industry and *tomorrow we will be paying* it in the shipyards. I would like the Minister to give a categorical assurance that his policy *will not lead* to enforced redundancies.'

Mr Hunter replied that *he had frequently been asked* to assure members that there *would be* no redundancies among shipyard workers but *he could not give* such an assurance. It *would depend* on the success of the industry over the coming year, though it *had always been* his aim to achieve such security. Nevertheless, it *was* an objective that *could only be achieved* when it *was recognised* that it *was* not in the interests of young workers to keep unprofitable yards open.

The Houses of Parliament, London

Composition

1 You have been attending a successful summer course in Britain. Write a short speech to accompany a presentation made to your teacher.

2 Write out in full one of the speeches you have prepared notes for in Activity 3 or 5.

The past

My husband and I...

Before reading the texts below, listen to these extracts from the imaginary memoirs of the wives of famous men. Then decide, if necessary by studying the texts, who the famous men were.

1   I remember the night before it happened very well. It was one of those stormy nights in March when the sky seems to open, with thunder and lightning. My fortune-teller said it would be better if my husband stayed at home the next day because he might catch a cold in that draughty Forum, with nothing on but a toga. But when my husband came home, he told me he had endured far worse on his campaigns in miserable, foggy places like Britain, and took no notice of my warnings. I had a terrible nightmare that night, and, over breakfast, tried once again to persuade my husband not to go, but he just said, 'Think of Caesar's public image, woman.' He always talked about himself in the third person. So off he went. It was the last time I saw him alive.

2   I knew he had been a 'lady-killer' when he was younger – there had been five other wives before me and goodness knows how many other women – but I realised that what he needed in his old age was an intellectual companion. He prided himself on his knowledge of Latin and the Bible, but to be quite frank he wasn't very clear in his ideas of religion – he tended to behave as if he was God himself. I was a little taken aback when he proposed to me because I was already engaged to Tom Seymour, but of course I couldn't say no. No one who valued his neck ever did! Of course I married Tom, too, later on, but that's another story.

3   So there I was, with three young children, and the first thing I knew about his departure was a note on the kitchen table saying he had been called by his destiny; he was always fond of fine phrases like that. That's what comes of hanging around taverns talking to actors instead of mixing with decent people. We didn't see much of him for the next few years, and with his father getting into debt and his mother putting on fine airs, I had a terrible life, I can assure you. Then one day, he came back and built one of the biggest houses in town. He was quite famous, he told me, and even performed in front of the Queen. Of course I was glad he had made some money at last, but when he actually suggested I should go and see one of those things he had written and was acting in, I was shocked. What respectable woman would want to be seen at a theatre?

Write a similar imaginary extract from the memoirs of a famous man's wife or a famous woman's husband.

Two famous men

Miguel de Cervantes Saavedra was born at Alcála de Henares in Spain in 1547. His first known work appeared in 1569 in a collection of poems on the death of the queen. Early in the same year he travelled to Italy in the service of Cardinal Acquaviva, but shortly afterwards he joined the army, and, at the Battle of Lepanto (1570), he was badly wounded. After further service against the Turks in Tunis, he was returning to Spain in 1575 when the ship he was sailing in was captured by pirates. He was taken to Algiers, where he remained in captivity for five years and made four daring attempts to escape. In 1580 he was ransomed by the efforts of his devoted family.

As he could find no permanent occupation at home, he went to Madrid and tried a literary career. For some years he tried to earn a living by writing for the stage. By 1587 he had produced between 20 and 30 plays, of which only two have survived.

In 1587 Cervantes became commissary to the fleet at Seville and in 1594 he was appointed a collector of revenues for the Kingdom of Granada. Three years later, however, after failing to collect the sum due to the treasury, he was sent to prison at Seville. Although he was released on giving security, he was not reappointed. Local tradition maintains that he wrote the first part of *Don Quixote* in prison.

The first part of the book was published in 1605. It became popular at once, but, instead of giving his readers the sequel they asked for, Cervantes went on writing for the stage and composing short stories, or 'exemplary novels', as he called them. In 1614, another writer brought out a spurious second part of *Don Quixote*, which provoked Cervantes into completing the genuine second part (1615). He died in Madrid the following year.

Activity 1

If Cervantes **had not become** a soldier, he **would not have gone** to Lepanto. If his family **had not ransomed** him, he **might not have returned** to Spain and **might not have written** his great novel.

Consider what **would/might (not) have happened** in the following cases:
1   If he had not been captured by pirates.
2   If he had found a permanent job at home.
3   If his plays had been more successful.
4   If he had not failed to collect the sum due to the treasury.
5   If he had not gone to prison.
6   If another writer had not produced a spurious part of *Don Quixote*.

Activity 2 – pair work

It is interesting to speculate about Paul Gauguin's life. Read the text below and note down your own speculations, then compare yours with a partner's and discuss them. Think about: his relationship with his wife (and hers with him!), with his family, with Van Gogh; his personality; his wife's reaction to/opinion of his decision, art, etc.; life in the Pacific; his reasons for leaving. Your speculations should be in the form **He might have...**, your conclusions in the form **He must have...**

GAUGUIN, Eugène Henri Paul **(1848–1903)** French Post-Impressionist painter, was born in Paris, the son of a journalist and a half-Peruvian Creole mother, went to sea at seventeen, but settled down in Paris by 1871, married a Danish girl who bore him five children, and became a successful stockbroker who liked painting and collecting Impressionist paintings.

By 1883, however, he had already exhibited his own work with the help of Camille Pissaro and, determined to give up everything for art, he left his uncomprehending wife and family and travelled to Martinique (1887–88) and became the leader of a group of painters at Pont-Aven, Brittany (1888–90, 1894), where he met the theorist Emile Bernard.

He went south to Arles to work with Van Gogh (1888), but the two men quarrelled and Gauguin quickly left. In 1890–91 he moved in the Symbolists' circles in Paris. He gradually developed his own style, 'synthesism', in accordance with his hatred of civilisation and identification with the emotional directness of primitive peoples. Thus, from his Brittany seascapes and the stained-glass effects of the 'Vision after the Sermon' (1888), there is a conscious development to the tapestry-like canvasses of native subjects on Tahiti (1891–93, 1895–1901) and at Dominica on the Marquesas Islands from 1901. Gauguin also excelled in wood carvings of pagan idols, and he wrote an autobiographical novel, *Noa-Noa* (1894–1900). He never overcame his lack of basic early training, but he will be remembered not only because of the tragic choices he made, the subject of many popular novels (particularly Somerset Maugham's *The Moon and Sixpence*), but because he directed attention to primitive art as a valid field of aesthetic exploration and consequently influenced almost every school of twentieth-century art.

Britain between the wars

In describing a period in the past it is valuable to have access to accounts written by eyewitnesses. The two passages here describe life in Britain between the wars.

Many splendid parties were given during the summer of 1927, but I have never been to one that could hold a candle to Mrs James Corrigan's stunt party. It was fancy-dress, and everyone was invited to come prepared to do a turn on a
5 specially-built stage. Mrs Corrigan was a brilliant organiser and a shrewd business woman. She realised that even the most unlikely people were open to bribes, and, carefully assessing London society, dangled **Cartier** prizes under the highest-bridged noses.
10 When she first invaded London as an unknown American hostess few people went to her parties, but those who did came away with glowing accounts and glittering gifts. By the time she gave her stunt party everyone was elbowing each other for an invitation to her house in Grosvenor
15 Street.
Here entertaining took the form of huge dinner-parties of about 80 people seated at tables of sixteen, with a hostess for each group chosen by herself. The less favoured were asked in afterwards. A dismal-looking Pierrot with an
20 incongruous moustache acted as a sort of Master of Cere-monies, banging a gong and making speeches, which no one listened to, in an abortive struggle to dragoon the guests. All this became an affectionate joke among her friends, especial-ly the raffle, which she insisted on calling the tombola and
25 pronounced 'Tom Bowler', which was invariably won by the most exalted guest. I once had to make the lucky draw. I was blindfolded, and felt a very noble ticket being deliberately pushed into my fingers by the gloomy Pierrot. There was afterwards a second draw, which was genuinely
30 left to chance, and at the stunt party **Henry** won a pair of coronetted Cartier sock-suspenders with clips of solid gold.

From *Mercury Presides* by Daphne Fielding

Cartier: the Parisian jeweller
Henry: the writer's friend and escort at the party

Activity 3

1 From the context, decide on the meaning of: **hold a candle to** (line 2), **stunt party** (line 3), **do a turn** (line 4), **dragoon** (line 22).
2 How did Mrs Corrigan demonstrate that she was **a shrewd business woman** (line 6)?
3 What was the connection between **glowing accounts** and **glittering gifts** (line 12)? Why are these two adjectives used together?
4 Why were some of the guests **less favoured** (line 18)?
5 What was the point of the **lucky draw** (line 26), and why does the writer refer to **the most exalted guest** (line 26) and **a very noble ticket** (line 27)?

... In Wigan I stayed for a while with a miner who was suffering from nystagmus. He could see across the room but not much further. He had been drawing compensation of twenty-nine shillings a week for the past nine months, but the colliery company
5 were now talking of putting him on 'partial compensation' of fourteen shillings a week. It all depended on whether the doctor passed him as fit for light work **'on top'**. Even if the doctor did pass him there would, needless to say, be no light work available, but he could draw **the dole** and the company would have saved
10 itself fifteen shillings a week. Watching this man go to the colliery to draw his compensation, I was struck by the profound differences that are still made by *status*. Here was a man who had been half blinded in one of the most useful of all jobs and was drawing a pension to which he had a perfect right, if anybody has a
15 right to anything. Yet he could not, so to speak, *demand* this pension – he could not, for instance, draw it when and how he wanted it. He had to go to the colliery once a week at a time named by the company, and when he got there he was kept waiting about for hours in the cold wind. For all I know he was
20 also expected to touch his cap and show gratitude to whoever paid him; at any rate he had to waste an afternoon and spend sixpence in bus fares. It is very different for a member of the bourgeoisie, even such a down-at-heel member as I am. Even when I am on the verge of starvation I have certain rights attaching to my
25 bourgeois status. I do not earn much more than a miner earns, but I do at least get it paid into my bank in a gentlemanly manner and can draw it out when I choose. And even when my account is exhausted the bank people are still passably polite.

From *The Road to Wigan Pier* by George Orwell

'on top': on the surface of the mine
the dole: the equivalent of modern social security payments to the unemployed

Activity 4

1 Why was it in the company's interest that the miner should be passed fit for light work?
2 Why might he be expected to touch his cap?
3 What does the writer mean by 'status' (line 12)? Why does he use the word **demand** (line 15) and emphasise it, instead of 'ask for'?
4 In what ways is the writer different from the miner, and why is he treated differently in a bank, for example?
5 Explain what he means by 'even such a down at-heel member as I am' (line 23).
6 Why do you think he says his salary is paid in a 'gentlemanly' manner?
7 Compare this passage with the one on the opposite page. What does the comparison tell us about the organisation of society in Britain at that time?

Memories of India

In this passage an officer who served in the Indian army from 1914 to 1947 describes the climate in Upper India as he remembers it. Note the changes of tense from present to past and past to present and the use of *used to* and *would*.

In mid-April, something *happens*. The wind *drops*, the sun *gets* sharper, the shadows *go* black and you *know* you *are* in for five months of utter physical discomfort. *When* I *first went out* there *was* no electric light, there *were* no fridges and no electric fans – and to live in those conditions *is* pretty foul.

We *never slept* indoors in the hot weather. We *used to sleep* outside on the lawn under a mosquito net, with a little table by our side with a thermos flask or something with cold water in it – and with our shoes always on a chair because *if you left* them on the ground *they might be occupied* by a snake or a scorpion. One *used to lie* and look through the top of one's mosquito net at the stars. It *was* peaceful, but very hot. Then in the early morning it *would start* cooling down. At about four o'clock one *would drop off* to sleep. And then the sun *would come up* over the horizon and hit you a crack with its heat.

The glare *was* one of the things that I *found* most trying. It *used to strike* right through your eyes into the back of your head. The first rays of sun that *came* through the windows *struck* the floor almost like a searchlight. One *would wander* round outside when one *had to* with half-shut eyes. Heat, light, headaches – right up to September. You *think* it *is never going to finish*. Then one day you *hear*, miles up in the skies, the honk-honk of geese or wild cranes, and you *know* that they *are* the advance guard of the cool weather coming down from wherever it *may be* – Siberia or somewhere. And you *say* to yourself, 'Thank God *it's cooling down*. It*'ll be* all right in another fortnight or three weeks' time.'

From *Plain Tales from the Raj* edited by Charles Allen

Activity 5 – pair work

Describe a place you knew as a child where the climate is different, what you used to do there and what you would do at certain times of day or at repeated intervals. Alternatively, describe life at a school you no longer go to. Say where it is and how it is organised, if it still exists.

Composition

1 Write a short biographical account of a famous person.
2 Describe life as it must have been in your country 20, 50 or 100 years ago.
3 Describe someone you grew up with.
4 Describe the changes that have occurred in a place you knew well as a child.

The future

Film posters

Look at the four posters below. What sort of vision of the future is conjured up by each? Which vision says more to you? Discuss this in groups and then arrange them in order from the most realistic to the most fantastic.

Views of the future

These two pages contain passages about the possible near-future, the first real, the second imaginary. Compare the two and answer the questions.

According to **current forecasts**, the world's population, which is doubling every 35 years, will be at or near **7 billion** by the year 2000. This is unlikely to be an over-estimate for all previous forecasts have proved too low – demographers seem to find it hard to believe their own figures, and hope for a decline in the speed of advance. So far there is no sign of it. And of course it is not going to stop when it reaches 7 billion. It may double again by 2030 – if the world has found out how to feed 14 billion people.

This doubled population will, we must assume, be very much more industrialised than today. Advanced countries are expected to increase output by a factor of at least five times. Developing countries will at least have established **extractive industries**, backed by roads, airports and power-stations, and will be trying to export in order to be able to pay for imported food and skills. Technology itself will have become more sophisticated and various. Doubtless new materials, even harder to dispose of than glass and plastic, will have been invented. New drugs and pesticides with unsuspected side-effects will have been invented. New means of transport will abound: hovercraft will skim over lakes and commons to invade the silence of winter. A flurry of rocket-belted enthusiasts will leap about like grasshoppers, while overhead the skip-liners circumnavigating the globe in five or six hours, will emit their sonic booms.

More people with more technology spells more pollution, more environmental distortion and less privacy. Much of the damage will come from the attempts which will necessarily be made to feed the ever-increasing number of mouths, and to house their owners. The crash of falling timber, as forests are felled, will be echoed by the thunder of explosives, as canals and harbours are blasted into existence.

It is obvious that this process cannot continue for ever: when will the poison-point come? Some maintain the world could support 15 billion people; one or two have put the figure as high as 30 billion. The earlier figure could come in the lifetime of those now living, so the question is not an academic one. It is my belief that the collapse will come considerably before this level is reached, perhaps quite soon.

From *The Doomsday Book* by Gordon Rattray Taylor

current forecasts: current as of 1970 when this was published
7 billion: counting a billion as one thousand million
extractive industries: those that extract raw materials from the earth's surface, such as mining and the oil industry

Activity 1

1 On what experiences of the last twenty years does the author base his forecast of: 'new materials, even harder to dispose of' (line 12); 'pesticides with unsuspected side-effects' (line 13); 'New means of transport' (line 14); 'skip-liners … will emit their sonic booms' (line 17)?
2 What would appear to be the only peaceful way of averting the collapse he forecasts?

Behind Winston's back the voice from the telescreen was still babbling away about pig-iron and the over-fulfilment of the Ninth Three-Year Plan. The telescreen received and transmitted simultaneously. Any sound that Winston made, above the level of a very low whisper, would be picked up by it; moreover, so long as he remained within the field of vision which the metal plaque commanded, he could be seen as well as heard. There was of course no way of knowing whether you were being watched at any given moment. How often, or on what system, the Thought Police plugged in on any individual wire was guesswork. It was even conceivable that they watched everybody all the time. But at any rate they could plug in your wire whenever they wanted to. You had to live – did live, from habit that became instinct – in the assumption that every sound you made was overhead, and, except in darkness, every movement scrutinized.

Winston kept his back turned to the telescreen. It was safer; though, as he well knew, even a back can be revealing. A kilometre away the Ministry of Truth, his place of work, towered vast and white above the grimy landscape. This, he thought with a sort of vague distaste – this was London, chief city of Airstrip One, itself the third most populous of the provinces of Oceania. He tried to squeeze out some childhood memory that should tell him whether London had always been quite like this. Were there always these vistas of rotting nineteenth-century houses, their sides shored up with baulks of timber, their windows patched with cardboard and their roofs with corrugated iron, their crazy garden walls sagging in all directions? And the bombed sites where the plaster dust swirled in the air and the willow-herb straggled over the heaps of rubble; and the places where the bombs had cleared a larger patch and there had sprung up sordid colonies of wooden dwellings like chicken-houses? But it was no use, he could not remember: nothing remained of his childhood except a series of bright-lit tableaux, occurring against no background and mostly unintelligible.

The Ministry of Truth – Minitrue, in Newspeak – was startlingly different from any other object in sight. It was an enormous pyramidal structure of glittering white concrete, soaring up, terrace after terrace, 300 metres into the air. From where Winston stood it was just possible to read, picked out on its white face in elegant lettering, the three slogans of the Party:

WAR IS PEACE

FREEDOM IS SLAVERY

IGNORANCE IS STRENGTH

From *Nineteen Eighty-Four* by George Orwell

Newspeak: the official language of Oceania, a debasement of English

Activity 2

1 What form of government exists in Oceania? How do we know?
2 What technological 'advances' appear to have been made? How do they contrast with the condition of the city?
3 What is the political position of Great Britain? What has happened in the past to change London?
4 What has happened to the English language, judging from the Party's slogans?
5 Comparing the two passages, decide whether the first forecast could lead to the warning in the second, and how this would happen.

The distant future

Aldous Huxley's vision of the future, *Brave New World*, imagines Britain in 500 years' time. Lenina and Henry are privileged beings in a five-caste society, which is planned from birth and subsequently conditioned so that only Alphas, the highest caste, have some element of free will.

An incessant buzzing of helicopters filled the twilight. Every two and a half minutes a bell and the screech of whistles announced the departure of one of the light monorail trains which carried the lower-caste golfers back from their separate course to the metropolis.

Lenina and Henry climbed into their machine and started off. At 800 feet Henry slowed
5 down the helicopter screws, and they hung for a minute or two poised above the fading landscape. The forest of Burnham Beeches stretched like a great pool of darkness towards the bright shore of the western sky. Crimson at the horizon, the last of the sunset faded, through orange, upwards into yellow and a pale watery green. Northwards, beyond and above the trees, the Internal and External Secretions factory glared with a fierce electric
10 brilliance from every window of its twenty storeys. Beneath them lay the buildings of the Golf Club – the huge lower-caste barracks and, on the other side of a dividing wall, the smaller houses reserved for Alpha and Beta members. The approaches to the monorail station were black with the antlike pullulation of lower-caste activity. From under the glass vault a lighted train shot out into the open. Following its southeasterly course across
15 the dark plain their eyes were drawn to the majestic buildings of the Slough Crematorium. For the safety of night-flying planes, its four tall chimneys were floodlighted and tipped with crimson danger signals. It was a landmark.

'Why do the smokestacks have those things like balconies round them?' enquired Lenina.
20 'Phosphorus recovery,' exclaimed Henry telegraphically. 'On their way up the chimney the gases go through four separate treatments. P_2O_5 used to go right out of circulation every time they cremated someone. Now they recover over 98 per cent of it. More than a kilo and a half per adult corpse. Which makes the best part of 400 tons of phosphorus every year from England alone.' Henry spoke with a happy pride, rejoicing wholehearted-
25 ly in the achievement, as though it had been his own. 'Fine to think we can go on being socially useful even after we're dead. Making plants grow.'

Lenina, meanwhile, had turned her eyes away and was looking perpendicularly downwards at the monorail station. 'Fine,' she agreed. 'But queer that Alphas and Betas won't make any more plants grow than those nasty little Gammas and Deltas and Epsilons
30 down there.'

'All men are physico-chemically equal,' said Henry sententiously.

Activity 3 – pair work

1   Study the passage carefully. In the first paragraph, find evidence of   a) the society's efficiency;   b) its technological development;   c) its class distinctions.

2   Do you think Huxley is impressed by the society he has created, or disgusted? Compare his descriptions of a) the landscape and the factory (lines 6–10), paying special attention to the verbs and adjectives;   b) the houses of different castes (lines 10–12).

3   What are the moral implications of the treatment of the dead (last three paragraphs)?

4   What evidence is there that Henry, in particular, has been conditioned (or brainwashed) to form his attitudes?

5   How do these last three paragraphs relate to the first?

6   In what way does Lenina's comment point to a weakness in the society?

Activity 4 – group work

If Huxley's vision of the future proves to be true, what will have happened in the meantime? What sort of government will man have evolved? How will man have dealt with the problem of population? What sort of genetic development will have taken place? Take into account the description on the page opposite, and what it implies about the countryside, and people's houses and activities.

Activity 5 – group work

Do you think Huxley's vision of the future is likely to become reality? Or are the warnings presented on the previous two pages more likely to indicate the course the future will take? If you think none of the three is very attractive, make notes of the stages that would be necessary for them to be avoided. These should take the form of a series of conditional sentences, e.g. **If . . . happens, . . . will/will not happen . . . and then . . .**

Activity 6

Complete the following passage with appropriate verbs in the correct tense. Use modal forms (e.g. **can, should**) where necessary.

If the population of the earth . . . (1) to increase at its present rate, there will eventually not be enough resources to sustain life on the planet. By the middle of the 21st century, if present trends are maintained, we . . . (2) all the oil that drives our cars, for example. Even if scientists develop new ways of feeding the human race, the crowded conditions on earth . . . (3) it necessary for us to look for open space somewhere else. But none of the other planets in our solar system . . . (4) capable of supporting life at present. A few years ago, however, the American scientist, Carl Sagan, . . . (5) a typically ingenious solution.

Sagan believes that before we . . . (6) the earth's resources completely, we . . . (7) to change the atmosphere of Venus and so create a new world almost as large as earth itself. The difficulty is that Venus is much hotter than the earth, and there is only a tiny amount of water there.

Sagan proposes that algae . . . (8) in conditions similar to those on Venus, since they . . . (9) in extremely hot or cold atmospheres and at the same time produce oxygen. As soon as this . . . (10) the algae will be placed in small rockets. Spaceships . . . (11) to Venus and fire the rockets into the atmosphere. In a fairly short time, the algae . . . (12) the carbon dioxide into oxygen and carbon.

When the algae . . . (13) their work, the atmosphere . . . (14) cooler, but before man . . . (15) on Venus, it will be necessary for the oxygen to produce rain. The surface of the planet will be too hot at first but once the rain . . . (16), something like earth will be reproduced on Venus.

The first colonists . . . (17) get used to days and nights lasting 60 earth-days, but they . . . (18) longer because their hearts . . . (19) less strain. Apart from that, they . . . (20) in a new world while those on earth are still living in closed, uncomfortable conditions.

Composition

1 What do you think the world will be like in the year 2000?
2 The advantages and disadvantages of space travel.
3 Describe the world of the future envisaged in any of the films shown on page 77 and give your personal reaction to it. Would you like to live in such a world?

Education

Examination results

The tables below relate to the results obtained in the General Certificate of Education examinations at Ordinary and Advanced level in 1982. Study them, and then answer the questions that follow.

Ordinary (O) Level							
Subject	Entries (,000)	Boys (,000)	Girls (,000)	Proportion Boys	Girls	% Pass Boys	Girls
English Language	512	234	278	46	54	52	58
Mathematics	325	174	151	53	47	60	52
English Literature	250	104	146	42	58	58	66
Biology	235	84	151	36	64	59	51
Geography	194	107	87	55	45	57	53
Physics	184	135	49	73	27	60	61
French	158	63	95	40	60	60	62
Chemistry	146	87	59	60	40	63	60
History	132	64	68	49	51	59	58
Art	130	56	74	43	57	57	66

Advanced (A) Level							
Subject	Entries (,000)	Boys (,000)	Girls (,000)	Proportion Boys	Girls	% Pass Boys	Girls
Mathematics	66	47	19	72	28	65	69
English	63	19	44	30	70	58	73
Physics	56	45	11	80	20	69	70
Chemistry	47	31	16	65	35	74	73
Biology	43	18	25	41	59	68	68
Economics	43	27	16	64	36	63	58
General Studies	40	21	19	53	47	70	58
History	38	18	20	46	54	72	68
Geography	34	20	14	58	42	70	73
Art	26	10	16	38	62	71	72
French	25	7	18	27	73	73	73

1 Place the subjects in order of preference at O and
  A level for boys and girls. Are there any noticeable
  differences between the two lists? Which subjects
  are more popular with boys than with girls, and vice
  versa? Can you see any clear pattern of preference
  emerging for areas of study for each sex at:
  a) O level; b) A level, and does it seem to you
  logical?
2 Do any subjects become noticeably more or less
  popular at A level than at O level a) in general;
  b) with boys; c) with girls?

3 Are there any subjects at O level and/or A level
  where boys do noticeably better than girls, and vice
  versa? Are they the same subjects at each level? If
  so, it would suggest that boys or girls have greater
  aptitude for these subjects. If not, can you suggest
  any reason for the change? Do the results bear out
  what you would expect from your own experience of
  boys and girls being better at certain subjects?

Grading students

**Read the following text and then work in pairs on
the tasks that follow. It is the account of a teacher
who decides that as an experiment he will try for
a term to give back his students' homework
assignments with comments but no grades (marks),
although the grades would be entered in a book.**

Activity 1 – pair work

Work at your own pace. Note down your response to each
question below and then compare notes with a partner.

At first almost everyone was sort of nonplussed. The majority
probably figured they were stuck with some idealist who thought
removal of grades would make them happier and thus work
harder, when it was obvious that without grades everyone would
just loaf. Many of the students with A records in previous quarters
were contemptuous and angry at first, but because of their
acquired self-discipline went ahead and did the work anyway. The
B students and high-C students missed some of the early
assignments or turned in sloppy work. Many of the low-C and D
students didn't even show up for class.

His lack of harshness puzzled the students at first, then made
them suspicious. Some began to ask sarcastic questions. These
received soft answers and the lectures and speeches proceeded as
usual, except with no grades.

During the third or fourth week some of the A students began to
get nervous and started to turn in superb work and hang around
after class with questions that fished for some indication as to how
they were doing. The B and high-C students began to notice this
and work a little and bring up the quality of their papers to a more
usual level. The low-C, D and future F's began to show up for
class just to see what was going on.

After midquarter the A-rated students lost their nervousness
and became active participants in everything that went on with a
friendliness that was uncommon in a grade-getting class. At this
point the B and C students were in a panic, and turned in stuff
that looked as though they'd spent hours of painstaking work on
it. The D's and F's turned in satisfactory assignments.

In the final weeks of the quarter, a time when normally
everyone knows what his grade will be and just sits back half-
asleep, Phaedrus was getting a kind of class participation that
made other teachers take notice. The B's and C's had joined the
A's in friendly free-for-all discussion that made the class seem like
a successful party. Only the D's and F's sat frozen in their chairs,
in a complete internal panic.

The phenomenon of relaxation and friendliness was explained
later by a couple of students who told him, 'A lot of us got
together outside of class to try to figure out how to beat this
system. Everyone decided the best way was just to figure you
were going to fail and then go ahead and do what you could
anyway. Then you start to relax. Otherwise you go out of your
mind!'

From *Zen and the Art of Motorcycle Maintenance* by Robert Pirsig

1   What would *you* have thought of
    the teacher?

2   How would you explain the
    reaction of the A students?

3   And how would you explain the
    reactions of the others?

4   What do you suppose the students
    were suspicious of?

5   What sort of sarcastic questions do
    you suppose they asked?

6   How would *you* have reacted to
    the teacher's 'soft answers'?

7   How do you explain the reactions
    of the different groups in weeks 3
    and 4?

8   Why do you suppose friendliness
    was uncommon in a grade-getting
    class? Does that agree with your
    experience?

9   Bearing in mind factors such as
    student numbers, level and type,
    and the qualities of the teacher and
    school system in which he/she
    operates, under what conditions
    do you think this kind of
    experiment could be successful?

Activity 2 – pair work

Write down your own answers before comparing notes with a partner.

1   At the end of the term the students were asked to write an essay evaluating the system. None of them knew at the time what his or her grade would be. Given that the percentage of 'votes' in the essays fell into blocks of 9%, 37% and 54%, what proportion of the students do you think voted in favour/against/neutral? What would you have voted?

2   The majority of students wanted their grades as they went along, but when the teacher analysed the answers to his essay question according to the grades they eventually received, there were three basic blocks, formed by 1) A students; 2) B's and C's; 3) D's and F's. One group were evenly divided, one group unanimously opposed, one group in favour by 2 to 1. Which block do you think had which reaction, and why do you think so?
(The answers are at the back of the book.)

Discussion

Discuss the pros and cons of alternatives to the traditional marks system. Decide which one you prefer, giving reasons.

Discipline

Activity 3 – pair work

1 Whatever your own reactions to progressive views of education are, find an argument to *oppose* the following 'progressive' suggestions. *To improve education, the following things should be abolished: a) disciplinary systems; b) courses; c) obligations, e.g. fixed homework, exams; d) full-time administrators and administration; e) anything that in any way turns the school/classroom into a closed box.*

2 Before you go on to read the text below, discuss the following question with a partner.

Do you believe children learn best naturally or must they be taught?

In a beautiful large house nestling behind mature chestnut trees and forsythia in a leafy north London subsurb, a youth is shut in the bathroom for two days for bad behaviour.

At the lunch table a 15-year-old boy is ticked off for speaking with his mouth full and another has to put 2p in the swear box for foul language.

But if these children behave well they will go to the cinema on Thursday afternoon, or ice-skating, or riding. If they are rude, or don't do their work properly, they will not.

They accept this 'nursery discipline' and the punishments that go with it as they accept shopping, cooking and washing up after lunch. Yet these kids are among the toughest in London. Some are persistent truants, others have criminal records for robbery with violence, possession of offensive weapons or threatening behaviour. They are highly disruptive and teachers cannot cope with them in class.

But Sally Trench copes with them in one of the most unusual disruptive units in the country – her own home.

The author of *Bury me in my boots*, based on five years spent living with London's down-and-outs and drug addicts, has turned her attention to the dropouts from the classroom.

She has had 300 children through her doors since 1976 when she started the unit and her success rate is outstanding. Two of her school-leavers are in prison and two are on the dole. The rest are all in full-time employment. A handful of younger children have been referred to special schools – but all the others have gone back into mainstream education.

'Our magic is that this is a home first and school second.' said Sally Trench. 'We operate a tremendous discipline of formality and courtesy, with a flexibility which makes us caring.' In fact the unit is often the last hope for these youngsters before Borstal. 'I see us as a free spirit helping disadvantaged kids to come to terms with and contribute to the rest of the world. You cannot have free spirit unless you have discipline.'

From *At home* by Jane Last in *The Times Educational Supplement*

Activity 4 – pair work

Note down your reactions to the following questions and then compare them with a partner's.

1 How do you react to the disciplinary system described here? If you were Sally Trench what would you do to keep discipline?

2 How do you explain the success rate of the school? To what extent do you think it could be copied? (To what extent do you think it is the result of a particular individual with strong ideas *making* it work?)

3 How do you interpret, and do you agree with, the last sentence in the text?

4 Note down a series of questions you would like to ask: a) Sally Trench; b) Jane Last (the writer of the article); c) the youth who was shut in the bathroom. Then ask your partner the questions and discuss his/her answers.

5 Note down any possible explanation(s) why Sally Trench decided to dedicate her life to this activity. Then discuss it/them with your partner.

Activity 5 – pair work

Read the text and then note down your reactions to the questions below. Then compare your reactions with a partner.

'What would you like to be when you grow up?' I have asked the question hundreds of times. Only once did a child reply, 'A teacher'. I had to send her away from my school later when she turned out to be mentally defective.'

Over the years, Neill took a special delight in passing on this characteristically provocative anecdote to his lecture audiences. Yet, like many of his stories, it tells us as much about Neill himself as about the ambitions of his Summerhill pupils. From his self-appointed position 'on the side of the child', he never saw teachers as anything other than The Enemy. To him they represented authority, by far the dirtiest word in his vocabulary.

Like so much else in his life and work, the roots of this antagonism can be found in Neill's childhood, and in his bitter experience of the narrowly academic and thoroughly repressive Scottish school system around the turn of the century. Under the influence of the notorious 'payment by results' system, teachers demanded absolute obedience from their pupils, upon whose achievements their very livelihood depended. Severe punishment, in the shape of the **tawse**, was given not merely for misbehaviour, but also for inadequate work. The pupils learned history and geography by rote, and respect and obedience by intimidation.

This kind of experience marked Neill profoundly. It made him determined to create a school where children would be free to express their real nature, where learning would be less important than living, and where adults would hand out approval in place of punishment. These principles were, of course, central to the philosophy of Summerhill. But Neill's early years also played a part in shaping the way this philosophy was put into practice. This did not always make for an easy life for those who Neill took on as teachers.

In 1937, a reviewer of Neill's book *That Dreadful School* wrote in the *Observer*, 'Mr Neill has not yet outgrown the childish pleasure of trying to shock . . . he should really restrain himself from indulging in pleasantries such as the following: "I never visit lessons and have no interest in how children learn."' Far from being a pleasantry, this remark provides a very fair picture of Neill's attitude to lessons, which he considered the least important part of life at Summerhill.

tawse: a leather strap with one end cut into thongs

From *To hell with teachers* by Jonathan Croale in *The Times Educational Supplement*

1 What is your reaction to this?

2 To be 'on the side of the child' do you have to look on the teacher as an enemy?

3 To what extent is a bitter experience in youth a reliable basis for a belief in the necessity for radical change? If you had had Neill's experience, what sort of school would you have wanted to establish?

4 How do you interpret: a) the 'real nature' of children; b) 'learning would be less important than living'; c) 'approval in place of punishment'?

5 If you were a parent with a child you might send to A.S. Neill's school, how would you interpret this?

Finally, note down a list of questions that you would like to ask A.S. Neill. Then ask your partner the questions and discuss his/her answers.

Discussion

1 The extent to which people's ideas on education are reactions against (bad) personal experience.
2 The extent to which people learn in spite of the way they are taught.

State and private education

Study this information about the development of
secondary education in Britain since the war and then
read the article which follows.

Education in Britain is primarily the responsibility of local
educational authorities although the central government lays
down guidelines and provides or withholds money. From the
end of the Second World War until the 1960s education
under state control depended on the '11-plus' examination,
taken by all pupils between the ages of eleven and twelve.
The most successful went to grammar schools or direct-grant
schools (see below), while the rest went to secondary
modern schools. Since the 1960s almost all local authorities
have introduced comprehensive schools, where all pupils
attend the same school, even though there is usually an
attempt to separate them according to ability once they are
there. Local authorities where the Labour Party is usually in
control tend by now to be almost completely
'comprehensive'; those where the Conservatives hold power
have been more resistant to the change.

Throughout this period the public schools, which are
private in all but name, have continued to exist, independent
of the state system. Some became direct-grant schools,
accepting students who had passed the 11-plus examination
and were paid for by local authorities, but this system came
to an end in many cases when a Labour-controlled local
authority refused to go on paying the grants because of its
commitment to comprehensive education.

Comprehensive schools – for and against

The public debate in England and Wales between the supporters of comprehensive schools and those who want to retain or revive grammar schools continues unabated. Every year statistics are produced to demonstrate that comprehensive schools provide better education than grammar schools (and in some cases, better than the prestigious private sector). These statistics are immediately contradicted by others proving the opposite. The local authorities have on the whole been converted to the comprehensive system, in some cases with enthusiasm, in others with marked reluctance. Yet the real complication of the debate stems from the fact that although arguments are usually advanced in educational terms, almost all of them are rooted in political conviction.

It is clear that those local authorities that have abolished grammar schools completely were determined that their experiment should be seen to succeed because of their conviction that it is as wrong to separate children by intelligence as by social class. Such authorities tend to associate grammar schools with the private sector they would also like to abolish if they had the opportunity. In their view, any system that differentiates between children strengthens class barriers, and the fact that middle-class children tend to do better in the entrance tests to grammar schools and eventually claim a disproportionately high number of places at universities is not evidence that comprehensive schools are inferior; it is merely further evidence of the discrimination inherent in society.

The defenders of grammar schools use examination results to show that children reach their maximum potential when placed with others of similar intelligence and point out that even in comprehensive schools they are put in different classes according to ability. It is difficult to believe, however, that this defence is inspired purely by a desire for academic excellence. The belief in an educational elite, a meritocracy, is linked to a belief in a social elite; by preserving one it should be easier to preserve the other.

There is little doubt, on the one hand, that the meritocracy created by the '11-plus' examination favoured class divisions, if only because the average headmaster's obsession with distinctive school uniforms ensured that the neighbours could see at a glance which school a child went to. In one sense, the division was worse, since the uniform now seemed to proclaim the child's intelligence, rather than the parents' income or social position. On the other hand, the advantages of smaller classes, better-paid teachers and a home background more likely to contain books and room to study ought logically to have given the grammar-school child a better chance in competitive examinations.

In terms of the continuing debate, however, such common-sense considerations tend to be overlooked. The different circumstances in which comprehensive and grammar schools operate make accurate comparison difficult. But in any case no comparison would ever satisfy two opposing groups whose criteria have little to do with education as such. For one group the overriding consideration is equality and the need to eliminate privilege, even if it means ruling out any form of parental choice; for the other, the belief that its own children have the best chance of belonging to the educational elite is sufficient reason for perpetuating it.

Activity 6 – group work

Unlike the authors of the passages in Unit 11, the writer in this case does not seek to win an argument but to explain the reasons for opposing points of view. He is consequently putting arguments for *and* against comprehensive schools.

1 List the arguments advanced in favour of comprehensive schools, and then those against them. Does the writer devote a paragraph to each? If so, does the paragraph contain the point of view of the other side at the same time?

2 Examine the construction of paragraph 1. What is the connection between the topic sentence and the conclusion? Summarise the meaning of the paragraph in one sentence. How is the paragraph developed – by a series of examples, or by constant comparison and contrast? What is the overall effect of this?

3 In paragraphs 2 and 3, how does the writer suggest that he is not fully in agreement with either side? What technique does he use to emphasise his neutrality in paragraph 4?

4 How does the concluding paragraph relate to the topic paragraph? What important question is left unanswered? Give two reasons for this, in the writer's view.

5 Give each paragraph a heading. From these headings, you ought to be able to derive a suitable formula for organising paragraphs in writing this sort of essay, where your own point of view is neutral. Compare the five-paragraph plan or formula you have developed with that of other groups.

Arguing for *and* against

Activity 7 – pair work

The Government wants to reform the secondary school system, making it obligatory for all students to follow a course of eleven subjects from the age of eleven to the earliest permitted school-leaving age, sixteen. There would be examinations in all eleven subjects, which would be a mixture of arts and sciences. From sixteen to eighteen students would study eight subjects, again mixed. This system would replace the present one, in which students take eight subjects up to the age of fifteen or sixteen and then specialise, for the last two or three years, in three subjects, usually arts *or* sciences. Write an article, of about 400 words, giving a clear and balanced account of the arguments for and against each point of view, ending with a *neutral* conclusion.

1   First examine the lists of arguments for and against each side, and decide which are the strongest and which (if any) can be rejected.
2   Then, using the plan given, write the article.

Present system   vs   Suggested new system
Arguments for and against suggested new system

For
1   Children get more balanced education.
2   Less separation of subjects means less separation of children, therefore the new system will bring social benefits.
3   Easier to organise, assign staff to standard programme than one with so many specialist options.
4   Cuts out teaching of small groups in unpopular specialist options – better use of staff.

Against
1   More subjects must mean less learnt about each; superficial.
2   Classes will be full of unwilling, unmotivated students; e.g. arts students forced to study maths, which they may not be good at – therefore discipline problem.
3   Better students will suffer and be held back because general level of classes will drop.
4   System far too rigid – children need flexible system and many options so they can find out what they like and/or are good at – lack of choice.

Arguments for and against present system

For
1   The country needs more, not fewer, specialists.
2   Obviously in present system the subjects are covered in more depth.
3   Children get more individual attention because of smaller classes.
4   It is more satisfying to be able to choose subjects for specialisation.

Against
1   It breeds e.g. scientists who know nothing about the arts.
2   It is elitist, socially as well as academically.
3   Children forced to specialise too early – at fifteen you can't be expected to know what you really like.
4   Elitism has widespread negative social consequences – broader general education would reduce them.

Para 1:   Topic paragraph
(approx. 60 words)
Function: to catch the readers' interest, define the topic clearly, and contextualise it.

Para 2:   Arguments for present system
(approx. 100–120 words)
Remember that arguments against new system can be useful in this para.

Para 3:   Arguments for new system
(approx. 100–120 words)
Remember that arguments against the present system can be useful in this para.

Para 4:   Conclusion
(approx. 60–80 words)
Function: to make a clear general synthesis of the issue and leave the reader to decide.

Composition

1   Do you think boys have greater ability than girls in some subjects and vice versa? Can you account for the differences in achievement?
2   Do examinations serve a useful purpose?
3   What part should discipline play in the organisation of a school?
4   Is it better for children to concentrate on a few subjects at school, or be examined on a large number of compulsory subjects?

Advertisements

Choosing a flat

Abbreviations are often used in accommodation advertisements. Look at the list of abbreviations on the right and match each with its appropriate full form.

Abbreviation		Full form	
o/r	rms.	central heating	luxury flat
p.w.	sh.	telephone	minutes
lux. flt.	pref.	bedsitter	house
gge.	1st fl.	colour TV	own room
c.h.	furn.	per week	bedrooms
hse.	gdn.	sharing	preferred
tel.	min.	self-contained	first floor
bedsit.	s/c	rooms	furnished
col.TV	bed.	garage	garden

For the people in the FLATS WANTED column below, find a suitable flat or room from amongst those in the FLATS/ROOMS OFFERED list.

Flats Wanted

●**GERMAN FEMALE,** 19, seeks bedsit or o/r around Central London from Dec. until Feb, max £25p.w. Please contact Birgit Schmidt, Falltorweg 29, 6973 Braunschweig, West Germany.

●**AUSTRALIAN WOMAN SAXOPHONIST FEMINIST** needs o/r in friendly central flat (£30p.w.) 929 1188 evenings.

●**VISITING AUSTRIAN SCIENTIST,** wife & 2 children, 6 & 9, seek flat pref. 3–4 bedrooms for 18 months from end 84, up to £120p.w. NW London pref. Dr Kreisky 821 4499 ext 53/339 2205 evenings.

●**BRITISH-CANADIAN MALE,** 19, considerate, responsible, employed Cen. London seeks o/r, reasonable rent (£20–£25p.w.) anywhere considered, pref. approx. same age group. 793 0859, Terry, after 6.

●**TOP CLASS YOUNG PAINTER/ DECORATOR** seeks hse./flt. W/NW London. Anything reasonable considered but must be near tube station. Phone Tim, 275 8065.

●**VALERIE,** 26, quiet responsible non-smoker, vegetarian, into aerobics, yoga, animal-lover, wants o/r in flatshare West London pref. Ring 345 6392 ext.221.

●**THREE WOMEN** need flatshare central city. Ring Anne or Tamara, 772 8093.

●**RECENTLY WIDOWED DOCTOR,** 58, M. seeks flat, Cen. London, 2 beds. access gdn. gge. max. £100, Phone Dr Miller, 233 2467 evenings.

Flats/Rooms Offered

●**BEAUTIFUL** o/r in large c.h. furn. Bayswater flat, col. TV, 5 min. tube. Suit single professional person M or F, no animals allowed, access gdn. Ring Connie 358 3122.

●**MODERN PEACEFUL RIVERSIDE DREAMHOUSE** in West London (Chiswick), 5 min. walk Tube. 7rms, gdn, gge 2 cars & boat, furn. c.h. Phone 919 7217.

●**LARGE O/R** in spacious Cen. London flat (Queensway), 2nd fl., to sh. with 3 M into rock, motocross, etc. No bores wanted. 3 min. Tube. C.h. col. TV. Phone Eric 329 8571 evenings. Rent won't shock.

●**RESPONSIBLE SOLVENT M** (21–25) wanted for large o/r in c.h. riverside flat in SW London (Fulham). 2 min. bus stop. Would suit vegetarian football fan. Phone Dave or Graham, 219 2877.

●2 s/c. rooms in family house for students, single £22p.w. double £40p.w. cooking facilities available mornings only. Girls pref. 4 stops Oxford Circus. 209 2156.

●**RESPONSIBLE CAT-LOVING PERSON,** F preferred, for cheap, part-furn. o/r in c.h. W. London flat (Hammersmith). To sh. with group of 3 (F), into ecology, spiritual quests etc. £18p.w. Ring 393 6183 evenings.

●**O/R** in Central London (Victoria) flat for solvent F musician. Tel. in flat. Fully soundproofed. £33p.w. Phone 772 4736 evenings only.

●**NW LONDON** (Hampstead) 4 bed. flat, c.h, fully furn., access gdn. & gge, 3 min Hampstead Heath, 5 min. walk Tube, available Dec 15. £115p.w. Phone 441 5526.

●**EALING,** West London. Single rm. available now & double after Xmas in large lux. flat, c.h., col. TV, gge, gdn, near Tube. £160 per month. Ring 718 2054.

●**2 or 3 O/R** now available in spacious Cen. London (Camden Tn) part furn. flt. c.h. col TV. F preferred (sh. with 2 F already in) £35p.w. Ring 693 2813.

●**REGENT'S PARK** ground fl. flt. 2 beds. gdn. access gge. c.h. Quiet, suit professional person. £95p.w. 092 2461.

Activity I – group work

What is being advertised here? What would you do if you
wanted to reply to the advertisement? Why would it
interest you?

1 Countess of Beckenham. See
Domestic Situations.

2 Luxurious emperor-sized corner bath
(white), brand new, must go at £180
o.n.o. (£255 new). Tel. 0522 94680.

3 Our six-year-old Jack Russell needs a
good country home. Please phone
9392 31195.

4 Stop stuttering. New breakthrough.
Ring 627 1387.

5 Author seeks to edit Second World
War diaries and letters for
publications. Box 1735.

6 Squirrel. Sorry about last night. I
adore you. Oak tree as usual on
Friday, same time. Beaver.

Properties

**Mr and Mrs Clifford, who have lived for a long
time abroad, have decided to return to Britain for
their retirement, and see this advertisement in a
magazine. They write to their daughter Elizabeth
about it and ask her to investigate Burleigh House
for them. Opposite is her letter replying.**

*Flatlets especially designed for
Retirement.*

**BURLEIGH HOUSE
Nr BUMSTEAD,
Somerset.**

Burleigh House will give you peace of mind.
Each flat has its own 24-hour emergency call system
with qualified medical and nursing care available at
all times if needed. An excellent meal service is
available to your room or in The Great Hall. Guest
accommodation is also provided for relatives or
friends of residents.

Flatlets especially designed for a safe and secure retirement, offering:
Security in retirement.
24 hour qualified help on hand.
Complete audio contact.
Residents' Sitting Room.
Dining Room/Library.
Card Room.
Parking available.
Central heating.
Constant hot water.
Hairdressing service.
Personal shopping delivery service.

Laundry Room.
Laundry service if required.
Meal service if required.
Cleaning service.
Own minibus to town centre.
Lift to 1st and 2nd floors.
No fear of leaving home
because of ill health.
Nurses available 24 hours per day.
Doctor on call.

35 Park End Avenue,
Everglades,
BRISTOL,
22 Jan. 1985.

My dear Mum and Dad,

It's great to think that you will be coming back to Britain for your retirement. The day after I received your letter I went down to have a look at Burleigh House but I'm afraid it wasn't as good as it sounded in the advert.

To begin with the lift was out of order. It may just have been my bad luck, but I couldn't help thinking about Dad's bad leg and wondering how often he'd have to climb the stairs. (It's an old house and there are lots!)

Secondly, although all the services in the advertisement are available, the prices charged for them seemed to me to be really excessive. For example, there is a hairdressing service in the house, but I went to the village nearby to check, and it'd cost you, Mum, less to go there to have your hair done (by the same person, in fact!) than it would in the house. The meal service gave me the same impression; it was expensive and the menu on offer not very appetising.

However, in spite of that, the residents I met were happy and said they felt well looked after, which makes me think we must go on looking to see if other better places of the same type turn up. Leave it to me!

Take care of yourselves, lots of love

Liza.

Every home has its own garage – even though it's only just off the Queen's Road

We're building some particularly good Town Houses on the Chelsea/Fulham borders, around two half squares.

Each has a built-in garage, compact garden 2–3 living rooms, 1–2 bathrooms, fully equipped kitchen (Zanussi cooker, dishwasher & fridge freezer) and double glazing that makes it up to 30% cheaper to heat and run.

2 bedroom flats £65,000
2 bed Town Houses £89–92,000
3 bed Town houses £86–89,000

Showhomes now open (Clare St. off Turk Ave) from 11am 7 days a week.
EASY TERMS

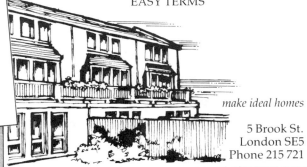

make ideal homes

5 Brook St.
London SE5
Phone 215 721

Activity 2 – group work

Imagine that some friends have written to you asking you to investigate the houses advertised here. Write your reply, drawing attention to the defects of the houses. In particular, think of what might be wrong with a compact garden, a built-in garage, and easy terms.

Jobs

Are you a salesman/woman residing in Devon, North Wales, Lincolnshire, Northumberland, Fife, and between 21 and 40 years of age? Have you the essential qualifications of a proven sales record, preferably with experience in the cash and carry/supermarket trade?

Could you increase area sales of bottled beer? Would you like the rewards this position would offer, a good basic salary, a sales commission, a company car, a non-contributory pension scheme, plus many other benefits?

YOU ARE? YOU COULD? YOU WOULD! Then write giving details of your sales career to: Mr Robert Martin, Sales Manager, Hodges & Co. Ltd., 5 Borough Lane, Milbury MG4 3DT.

CROSSLEY COLLEGE OF EDUCATION
Department of Social Studies
LECTURER IN SOCIAL POLICY AND ADMINISTRATION

Applications are invited for the above post from 1st September, 1985. The successful applicant will initially teach Social Studies as a main subject for the Teachers' Certificate and the B.Ed. degree. The course includes aspects of the Social Structure of Modern Britain with a particular emphasis on Urban Problems. Candidates with qualifications in social administration and/or sociology will be considered.

Salary on a scale currently £5,662 plus annual increments of £228 to £7,670 per annum.

Further particulars and application forms can be obtained from the Registrar, Crossley College of Education, Oak Road, Crossley CR11 4NT, to whom applications should be addressed by Friday, 13th June, 1985, together with the names of three referees.

Activity 3 – pair work

Study these advertisements and answer the following questions.

1 Are any restrictions placed on applicants regarding age, sex, residence, qualifications or previous experience? What are they?

2 How would you go about applying for the job in each case?

3 How many applicants will be successful in answering the first advertisement? What qualities will recommend them to the firm? What advantages does the job offer?

4 What is the possible disadvantage of the method of payment for the second advertisement, compared to the first? Which word indicates that the salary scale is subject to review?

Activity 4 – group work

Work together to apply for the two jobs, assuming you have all the qualifications necessary. Notice the differences in style in the advertisements. Why are these to be expected? Take this into account in writing a letter in each case that you think would impress the person to whom it is addressed.

Classified ads

Some classified advertisements are placed in the personal columns of newspapers by individuals, while others are really straightforward advertisements inserted by companies.

Activity 5 – pair work

Study the difference in style between the advertisements and the texts as they would appear in the form of a letter or an extract from a brochure. Then make notes for letters responding to the two.

Will anyone having knowledge of the whereabouts of D. K. Turner, formerly of 87 Berkeley Gardens, W1., please contact Simpson and Beardsley, Solicitors, Moorgate Chambers, London EC2.

Who were your ancestors? Are you of royal or noble blood? Send your family data to us and make use of our unique tracing service. From £150. Adam & Sons, Duke Street, Windsor BK3 1RH.

```
Mrs Angela Cavendish,
Flat 3,
Cavendish House,
Park Lane,
London W1 PX3.              19 November 1984

Dear Mrs Cavendish,
              We understand that until recently a
Mr D K Turner was a tenant of yours at
87 Berkeley Gardens but left the house without
leaving a forwarding address. We should be
most grateful if you could provide us with any
information that would enable us to discover
his present whereabouts, as we are anxious
to trace him in order to inform him of some
news that is to his advantage.

              Yours faithfully,
              Arthur Beardsley
              Arthur Beardsley
```

Half the people in England are siad to be descendants of King Edward III. The fascinating story of your own family's past can be revealed to you for as little as £150 if you take advantage of our unrivalled services and provide us with a copy of your birth certificate and any information you have about your parents and grandparents. Who knows what famous men and women will be found among your forebears? For prompt, efficient, discreet service, contact Adam & Sons for a complete genealogical tree.

Composition

1 Rewrite the house advertisement as if it were a card in the window of an estate agent.
2 Write a letter answering the advertisement for a student.
3 Develop your notes from Activity 5 into two letters.

DEVON-TORQUAY 12 mls. Det. brick-built hse., tiled rf., adj. vill., Sit. din. utility rms., study, kit., 3 dble beds. bath. Gge., gdn. lawn. fruit trees. Freehold £57,350. Brock & Badger, Estate Agents, Padstoke 053.

SWISS FAMILY – 4 children would welcome student (board and lodging) weekends at ski resort, possibility of attending courses in Geneva, in exchange one hour English conversation. Schindler, Rue Rousseau 69, Geneva 5.

Customs

Superstitions

Below you will find a list of common British superstitions and folklore traditions. Examine them and associate them wherever possible with any similar ones in your country. Tick (√) anywhere you find equivalents.

Animals
- Cats have nine lives; black cats are thought to be lucky.
- Horses were thought to be vulnerable to the evil eye (a look or glance supposed to have the power of inflicting harm or injury). Their owners protected them with brasses fashioned in traditional spirit-repelling shapes like the crescent moon or the sun.

Homes
- When a family moved to a new home it would take embers from the old fireplace and burn them in the new one, to signify that family ties will remain unbroken; the housewarming party is a development of this custom.
- Food will be spoilt if stirred anticlockwise.
- Breaking a mirror brings seven years' bad luck; associated with the idea that the image in the mirror is a person's soul. Possibly associated with some people's dislike of being photographed.
- Dropped cutlery is an omen of unexpected visitors. A knife for a man, a fork for a woman, and a spoon for a fool.

Hospitals
- Flowers should be removed from wards at night.
- Bunches of mixed red and white flowers are considered ominous because in Roman times flowers of those colours were placed on lovers' graves.

Sea and sailors
- Whistling at sea is taboo because it may call up a gale.
- If a sailor rescued a drowning man, he would probably be drowned himself, for he had cheated the sea of its due. It was this belief that gave earlier generations of seamen their fatalistic acceptance of drowning; they often withheld aid from drowning men, and very few ever learnt to swim.

Seasons and festivals
- In Celtic times great sacrificial bonfires were lit in honour of the sun on 23 June. Even in recent centuries, rural folk lit bonfires, and men and beasts passed through the embers to ward off disease and bad luck.

Cars
- The colour green is unlucky because it belongs to the fairies.
- Drivers carry medallions of St Christopher or lucky coins.

Theatre
- It is bad taste to wish actors or trapeze artists good luck before a performance.
- No real mirrors or flowers should be used on stage.
- *Macbeth* is notoriously unlucky; actors are reluctant to quote from it. The taboo on saying the last line of a play till the first performance is strictly kept to.

Farmers
- A farmer should live as though he were going to die tomorrow but farm as though he were going to live for ever.

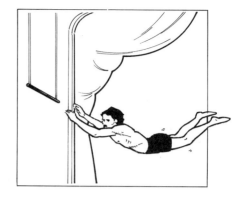

Marriage customs

Activity I – pair work

Read the following text about British wedding traditions and superstitions and compare them with those in your own country, answering the following questions.

1 What do most couples think is the best time of year to get married?

2 Who accompanies the bride and the groom in the wedding ceremony and what is their (ritual) function?
3 Are their any rituals or traditions about either the bride's or the groom's dress?
4 To what extent would a typical young couple take any notice of all these traditions? Are customs changing?

Wedding fantasia

For most people, weddings are a magical time when even the least superstitious will watch for portents of future happiness. As a result, the wedding preparations, ceremony and feast have all become loaded with ritual practices to ward off evil and bless the marriage with fortune and fertility.

The choice of date is important; May is traditionally unlucky for weddings because in ancient Rome, this was a month for remembering the dead and was an ill-omened time for lovers. Defying this augury, many modern couples marry between Easter and late May, a practice much encouraged by tax rebates. The tradition that the bride's parents should pay for the wedding dates from two or three centuries ago, when wealthy families would pay an eligible bachelor to take an unmarried daughter off their hands in exchange for a large dowry. Sometimes the groom would not wait to be asked, and would take the girl from her parents by force. His abettor in this act is represented at modern weddings by the best man, while the bridesmaids play symbolic roles as protectors of the bride.

Every bride regards her wedding dress as the most hallowed garment she will ever possess. At most formal weddings brides still get married in virginal white – many other colours are considered unlucky. Her veil is of great importance: it once had the double function of protecting the bride from the evil eye, and at the same time served to keep her in seclusion, in case her psychic powers at this time bewitched other people. A bride will also ensure that her wedding outfit includes something old and something new, something borrowed, something blue: 'old' maintains her link with the past; 'new' symbolises the future; 'borrowed' gives her a link with the present; and 'blue' symbolises her purity.

Even a modern bride will observe the taboos about wearing the dress before the ceremony. The groom must not see her in it until she enters the church. Nor must she wear the complete outfit before the wedding day. Some brides even believe that the sewing of the dress should not be finished till the day itself, and leave a few stitches to be completed on the wedding morning.

After the ceremony the couple are showered with confetti or rice as they leave the church, to bless the marriage with fertility.

From *The Readers Digest Guide to British Folklore*

Activity 2 – pair work

Read the following text and note down your reactions/ answers to the following questions before comparing them with a partner's.

I   In this account of a traditional wedding in an Indonesian island village, underline the occasions when the writer uses the present tense rather than the past, and explain why.
Bearing in mind the traditions in your country . . .
2   To what extent, and in which circumstances, do parents have any influence on their children's choice of marriage partners? (e.g. Does the groom have to make any formal approach to the bride's parents?)
3   What points could you make *in favour of* arranged marriages? To what extent do you think marriages 'of convenience' are arranged?
4   What are your reactions to the first paragraph?
5   Are there any traditions regarding: a) wedding feasts and food; b) presents; c) preparations for the wedding; d) invitations?
6   Which of the old traditions are tending to get lost and why?

An Indonesian island wedding

The people marry very young. While I was on Nus Tarian, a marriage was arranged between Daud, the youngest son of Pak Hashim, and a beautiful fourteen-year-old pupil of mine named Rahi. Her father, Saleh, discussed it with Pak Hashim, and a bride price of a paired team of buffalo, plus a bull for the wedding feast, was agreed on. The fathers made the arrangement entirely without consulting the young couple, but everyone knew they were lovers and expected it to be a good match.

The next important decision was the selection of an auspicious date. There must be a moon, since people have to walk all the way down from Desa Langit, and no party in either village was ever given on a moonless night. Pak Moudhi was consulted and agreed that two days after the next full moon would be ideal.

Saleh immediately started to enlarge his house in order to accommodate all the guests, and his wife, Petimo, began to make plans for the celebration. She invited guests by visiting each home with a present of *dodol*, a kind of sticky toffee made of glutinous rice and palm sugar. By this sign, the people knew that the feast was going to be on a grand scale and that appropriate gifts would be expected. Any guest invited to a meal always brings a *tjupak*, which is a large measure of raw husked rice. But for a feast of this kind *tembaga* were also necessary. These were old Chinese copper coins with a hole in the centre. Petimo was issuing invitations to all those who held outstanding obligations to her family, and on the day of the wedding these would be honoured in numbers of *tembaga*. In this way, money paid out over the year to other people's feasts is called back like a loan.

Three days before the wedding, Petimo summoned a number of women to help in *kerdja*, the work of preparing food. On the first day they gathered in the shade outside her home pounding spice in wooden mortars and shredding large quantities of coconut. The second day was given to the making of sweet rice cakes called *nasi kunjit* and of *djalor mas*, long golden strings of syrup and egg poured through a funnel of banana leaf. And on the third day, the bull was slaughtered and turned into a whole range of wonderful curries that sent beckons of fragrance out to every part of the village.

The wedding began at noon.

From *Gifts of Unknown Things* by Lyall Watson

98

Origins of soccer

Activity 3

The four paragraphs below are taken from a book by Desmond Morris, *The Soccer Tribe*, but they have been printed out of order. The topic sentences for each paragraph are printed in the correct position, first, but the other sentences have been moved round.

Decide on the order of the paragraphs by comparing the four topic sentences – which states the subject, which develop it and which reaches a conclusion? Then use the clues given by the words and phrases that provide the links between sentences to determine the correct order. These are printed in italic.

1   Our mental attitudes *also* had to change.
a) *Without active cooperation,* the human predator could not hope to complete with the larger and more highly specialised carnivores, such as lions and hunting dogs.   **b)** *The switch* from fruit-picking to prey-hunting *demanded* greater intelligence and cunning.   **c)** *Above all,* the tribesman had to improve *his ability to communicate and cooperate* with his fellow-hunters, as a way of increasing the efficiency of the hunt.   **d)** *It also required* the ability to concentrate on a long-term project, to avoid distractions and to keep doggedly after the main objective until a successful climax had been reached and the kill made.

2   Our bodies had to change from tree-climbing machines to *running machines.*   **a)** *If we were to catch our prey,* we not only had to be nimble and fast – good sprinters – we also had to be endurance athletes – good long-distance runners – which meant better breathing, with larger, deeper chests.   **b)** *Then,* at the kill, we required a superior aiming ability, calling for stronger arms, and hands better designed for gripping and throwing weapons.   **c)** We had to rear up on our hind limbs and stay there, our longer legs pounding the ground *as we sped after our quarry.*

3   *So* our early hunting ancestors became gradually *more athletic* and, at the same time, *more intelligent.*   **a)** And it is my contention that *this is no accident.*   **b)** Already, you will admit, *they are beginning to sound like* the perfect prototype for *a soccer team.*   **c)** Using *these advantages* and *working together as a team* – a hunting pack – they were able to plan strategies, devise tactics, take risks, set traps, and, finally, aim to kill.

4   *The roots of the Soccer Tribe lie deep in our primeval past,* when our early ancestors lived and died as hunters of wild beasts.   **a)** *And it* changed us dramatically from our nearest relatives, the monkeys and apes.   **b)** *It* moulded us and made us, genetically, what we are today.   **c)** To be good hunters we had to acquire *a whole new set of qualities,* both *physical* and *mental.*   **d)** Almost the whole of man's evolutionary history belongs to *that hunting period,* when the pursuit of prey was not a sport, but a matter of survival.

From *The Soccer Tribe* by Desmond Morris

If you have completed the exercise satisfactorily, you should be able   1) to give each paragraph a title;   2) to see a relationship between the topic sentence of the first paragraph, and the conclusion of the last. This relationship is grammatical, as well as logical.
Summarise the content of the four paragraphs in two or three sentences.

Composition

1   Discuss any superstitions common in your country, providing any evidence you have to justify them.
2   Describe a typical wedding or other official ceremony in your country.
3   Describe any folk custom or celebration you have taken part in, and, if possible, account for its origins.

Possibilities

'If I were Mayor . . .' is a half-hour regional TV programme of interviews and comment, based on letters sent in by viewers with serious problems or protests of general interest which might be solved if the 'Mayor' took action. Each week the five most interesting problems are selected and the five letter-writers are invited to be interviewed on the programme.

Activity 1 – group work

Work in groups of six. At first choose any five of the following list of problems. When that is done, allot roles for the programme; one person should act as the interviewer and the other five should take one of the roles each. The interviewer should prepare a brief list of questions and comments for each of the five; and the five should prepare to state their case and say what they would do if they were Mayor. The preparation stage is important. When everyone is ready, the programme can begin.

Letters received

1 A school in a working-class area has buildings that leak, very poor and often non-existent heating, very limited playing-field conditions and no access to TV or to laboratories.

2 The inhabitants of the suburb nearest the airport complain that with the increase of air traffic over the past five years, life has now become unbearable because of the noise.

3 People in one area of the city complain that because of inadequate street lighting it has become dangerous to go out at night, since the muggers take advantage of the darkness to attack.

4 One old district in the city has become fashionable as a site for ethnic restaurants, discos, late-night bars, etc. The residents are complaining about disturbances of the peace, 'lowering of the tone of the neighbourhood', etc.

5 In one district near the city centre there has been an uncontrolled growth in the number of sales stalls, street musicians, etc. The residents don't approve of this.

6 One district with a severe problem over dogs fouling the footpaths has found a successful solution by designating several places where dogs may be taken for that purpose. The inhabitants want to publicise the success of the experiment.

7 In one district the parking problem has become so severe that at night it is almost impossible to walk on the pavements because they are all occupied with cars.

8 In one district near the main railway station there is a need for some sort of reception service for people coming to the city for the first time (from other areas of the country) in search of work.

9 One TV programme glamourises the life of rock musicians to such an extent that a considerable number of young people have run away from home in search of fame. A parents' association is worried.

10 The river that passes through the city is being seriously polluted by factories in the new industrial zone, which prefer to pay high fines rather than invest money in anti-contamination measures. An ecological group has appealed to the City Council.

Activity 2 – pair work

Read the following model composition and then work on the questions that follow.

I once had a dream in which a wizard with a magic wand appeared to me and told me he was going to wave his wand and grant me a week in which my every wish would come true. I was a child then, and I remember most of my wishes revolved around toys and holidays, but if the wizard came back now, I wonder how much the wishes would have changed.

For one thing, the holidays, or at least, travel, would still be amongst them. In my seven days, assuming I could go anywhere, I would visit the Carnival in Rio, Holy Week in Seville, New York, Venice, the Sahara Desert and end the week, invisible, flying around the place where I was born, a small and beautiful old market town in the heart of England. I'd like to eat paella at a beachside restaurant in Valencia, pizza near the port in Naples, black bread and fresh cheese in Hamburg, tzatziki in La Plaka, Athens, and apple pie in London. And drink Vichy Menthe in Paris, Munich beer, Chianti, mango juice in Cairo . . . the list would never end.

I'm not so keen on toys now. Or am I? If the wizard allowed me unlimited money, there would be things I'd like to buy. For myself, I'd spend money on my hobby, music. I'd buy all sorts of different synthesizers and equip a room at home as a recording studio, where I could compose my own music. I'd gather all my family and best friends together and offer to buy them anything they dreamed of having but couldn't afford; the rest I'd give to charities or to movements like Greenpeace that I believe in, for them to buy what they need.

Finally, there are some experiences I'd like to have. I'd like to pilot a jet on a clear, starlit winter night, sit round a camp fire and tell creepy stories, drive a train, mingle with the crowd at a rock concert, smell freshly-made bread or coffee, throw sticks on a beach for my dog to run for, see the smile on an old woman's face, watch kids play age-old games . . . And one last thing, I'd like to know what it really feels like when a Proficiency student opens that envelope with the result inside and finds all the agony ended in a pass!

Suppose the wizard appeared to you and granted you seven days during which your wishes would come true. Answer the following questions individually at first and then compare your answers with a partner's.

1 Where would you want to go during those days and where would you want to be on the seventh day? Why?
2 What experiences would you like to have in those seven days, and why?
3 What would you like to buy or spend money on, and why?
4 What meals/food/drink would you like to have? Where? Why?
5 What films/TV programmes would you like to see? What books would you like to read? What music would you like to listen to?
6 What work of art would you like to have near you during the week? Why?
7 What things would you like to do or say during the week that you have always wanted to do but never dared?
8 Which routine occupations in your life that you *don't* like would you stop doing for those seven days?
9 How much of those seven days would you want to spend alone and how much in company? Why?
10 How would you plan to spend the seventh day?

Critical situations

Read the following passage about the difficulties of
being anything other than of average size in the army.

In the days when National Service still existed in
Britain, and I did it, the army was not the ideal
place for anyone out of the ordinary. The army had
difficulty, as all armies must have, not only in
5 dealing with soldiers who turned left when
everyone else was marching away to the right but
also with those whose height and shape were
unusual. If the army had had its way, every soldier
10 would have been 5 ft. 8 in. tall, his weight would
have been about 11 stone, and he would have
worn size 9 boots. Ignoring the evidence to the
contrary, the army chose to believe this was really
the case and consequently designed everything
15 from beds to bicycles with its ideal soldier in mind.

I happen to be 6 ft. 6 in. tall, weigh over 15 stone
and take size 12 boots (or took them when I wore
boots!). For the first few months, therefore, I had no
uniform and went around in denims, a khaki
20 version of prison clothing. This had some
advantages because I was always told to keep out
of the way when big parades took place, and that
was just as well because I would almost certainly
have been the one who turned left when the others
25 swung briskly to the right.

However, I did not escape drill altogether, and
my first problems arose in trying to lift a rifle to my
shoulder by the muzzle. Soldiers were supposed to
stand smartly to attention during this manoeuvre
30 and the sergeant was not impressed when I told
him I could not imitate the others unless he found
me a longer rifle. It was only just long enough for
me to balance it on the ground between my

35 fingertips, so there was no way of lifting it without
leaning over.

My most serious encounter with the army's
obsession with the average man occurred,
however, on the assault course. One of the
40 obstacles consisted of two wires slung about 25
feet off the ground between two telegraph poles.
The idea was to climb up one pole and walk across
the wires sideways, treading on the lower one and
grasping the upper one. It was not until I was
45 almost halfway across that I realised that the
tension was forcing the upper wire closer and
closer to my neck so that I would have been neatly
decapitated if I had gone much further. The
average man would simply have adapted his grip
slightly but I was obliged to duck under the wire
50 and in this position lost contact with the lower wire
and found myself hanging in mid air. I looked hard
at the upper windows of the gymnasium on a level
with my face and then down at the officer and men
on the concrete below. If I had fallen I would
55 probably not have been killed, but I would have
been lucky to escape with a broken leg. 'Don't
panic!' the officer shouted encouragingly, and I can
remember giving him a sour look as I struggled to
get my feet back on the wire. Eventually, I
60 managed it, but what was really hard was to move
my hand again on the upper wire and complete
the journey. Of course I must have done, or I would
not be writing this, but I cannot remember
anything about that part of the affair.

Activity 3

1 What was the army's 'ideal soldier' like and why?
2 Why does the writer say the army 'chose to believe'
   (line 13), not 'believed'?
3 Why does he change the tense from **take** to **took** (line
   17) when talking of the size of his boots?
4 Why did he have no uniform at first and why was this an
   advantage?

5 Explain his problem in being unable to lift his rifle
   correctly.
6 Draw diagrams to show what happened to him on the
   wire.
7 Why do you think he remembers everything about the
   incident except the last part of his journey across the
   wire?

Activity 4

Below you will find two situations in which certain key decisions, indicated in italic, were taken. Answer the questions with those decisions in mind.

Situation 1

Frank and Marge Gray had an only son, Keith, whom they loved very possessively, 'always wanting the best for him'. When Keith left school at sixteen, Frank made arrangements with a bank-manager friend for Keith to go and work in the bank, 'starting at the bottom and working his way up'. But *Keith refused the job* because he wanted to be a rock musician. Frank and Marge tried to dissuade him, but in vain, and one night, *Frank, tired of what he called Keith's 'ingratitude and sheer stubbornness', lost his temper* and told Keith that if he wanted to do that he would have to leave home and forget he had a father. Upon which *Keith left*, and Frank and Marge heard nothing more of him; until one day two years later, when Keith's band was beginning to be quite successful, and Frank heard one of Keith's songs on the radio. It was called 'I wish I had a father'.

Situation 2

Anne, a university librarian in Bristol, had applied for a job at an Australian university, but when she received the good news that the job was hers if she wanted it, *she decided to turn the offer down* because since making the application she had started going out with Mike, a quiet, shy but interesting student she often saw in the library. One day, Mike sent her a note telling her he loved her and proposing marriage; in the same note he told her he had been offered and had accepted a well-paid job in an African country. Anne, annoyed that he had taken it for granted that she would agree to go with him, *turned down the proposal*. Three years later she married another student, Vic, who turned out to be far less interesting and attractive than Mike, and *gave up her career* to look after their children. She often thinks, not to say daydreams, of what would have happened if she had decided differently.

1. What would you have done at each stage if you had been Keith's mother, Marge?
2. How would you have felt if you had been Keith? What would you have said at each stage?
3. How would you have felt at each stage if you had been Frank, and what would you have done?
4. What might have happened if Keith had gone into the bank?

1. What would you have done if you had been Anne?
2. What might have happened if she had gone to Australia?
3. What might have happened if she had gone to Africa with Mike?
4. What would you have done if you had been Mike?

Activity 5

Most people can recall certain crucial moments (turning points or close escapes) in their lives, about which they can say:

If I hadn't done that, or **if that hadn't happened, my life would have been different.**

Think of a similar incident and prepare to tell the class about it.

Embarrassing situations

Activity 6 – pair work

Some people get involved more often than others in embarrassing situations. The situations below all happened to a man called Tom and are fairly typical. First work through them individually, noting down what you **would have done**, then compare notes with a partner, and ask what Tom **should have done/said**, and what he **should have done/said** instead.

1 Tom went to a party with a friend who warned him that he might meet a very boring, talkative man there. At the party Tom was with his friend and a girl he had just been introduced to when a man entered the room. 'Is that the old bore who you warned me about?' Tom asked his friend. 'That,' said the girl, 'is my father'.

2 A friend of Tom's had just come off the stage after giving a very poor first performance in a play. Tom had agreed to take the friend out to supper, and went backstage to find out if he was ready. Still thinking of the performance, he said, 'We'll go as soon as you're better.'

3 Tom's little sister had the habit of innocently repeating to outsiders things that were meant to be kept in the family. One day when some family friends came on a rather unwelcome visit, she greeted them by saying, 'Oh yes, Mummy said when you phoned that you were fishing for an invitation.'

4 At a party, while people were queuing to serve themselves from a buffet, Tom introduced two people but then realised that one of them was a dogmatic vegetarian and the other a belligerent carnivore. As a conversation-opener the carnivore, looking at the array of bowls of salads, said 'look at all the rabbit food. Anyone would think we were cranky vegetarians or something.'

5 On behalf of the company he worked for Tom took a group of business visitors out to lunch in a restaurant near his office, making a point on the way there of saying how excellent it was. But that day, everything went wrong with the meal. Trying to pacify his guests, Tom said, 'It's normally good enough for the sort of visitors we get.'

6 Tom took an American friend to have tea with one of his aunts. As the aunt served the tea she said, 'Do you know, until quite recently our next-door neighbours were an American couple, and they were very nice, in spite of being American.'

Composition

Write a composition on one of the following:
1 If all my wishes were granted for a week, I . . .
2 A narrow escape.
3 A turning point in my life.

Sociology

Questionnaire

Complete the following questionnaire in the same way as the one on p. 59.

		++	+	o	−	=
1	Aggression is a natural human instinct and should never be suppressed in children.					
2	Ideas of crime and punishment in the world today should be completely revised.					
3	Telling the truth is often more of a vice than a virtue.					
4	Students should be able to choose what they are to be taught and how.					
5	Killing is never justified.					
6	The competitive spirit is essential for human progress.					
7	The countryside is always preferable to the city.					
8	Patriotism is out of date.					

All these topics have been set in past Cambridge examinations. It is hard to employ facts to deal with any of them. Answers may depend on moral belief (5), or personal prejudice (7), but usually the statement is either *vague*, depending on the definition of key words – e.g. 'progress' in (6); *extreme*, because it uses the words 'never' (1, 5), or 'always' (7); or demands *further definition* – e.g. which 'ideas'? (2).

Decide a) which of these three categories each statement belongs to, and why; b) whether any facts or personal experience affect your attitude – e.g. to (1) because you once saw a mother look on and say nothing as she watched her son hitting a smaller child. Having decided on the categories, approach them as follows:

1 *Vagueness.* Which words need a more precise definition? How would you define them and what alternative definitions exist? List them.

2 *Extreme statements.* How far do you agree? Would you change 'never' to 'sometimes' or 'occasionally'? In what circumstances would you accept or not accept the statement?

3 *Further definition.* Make clear, for example, which 'ideas' in (2) you are talking about.

In all cases, work together to produce a general statement you can accept – e.g. for (1) *Aggression is an instinct found in most human beings, so it is unwise to suppress it altogether in children, but there are obviously circumstances in which parents must intervene to prevent children being cruel to others and to show them this is wrong.*

Surveys and opinion polls

**The passages on these two pages deal with the role
of surveys in sociological studies and in taking
note of public opinion. The first explains their
value in sociology.**

The mere description of human behaviour, of its variation from group to group and of its changes in different situations, is a vast and difficult undertaking. It is this task of describing, sifting and ferreting out interrelationships which surveys perform for us. And yet this very function often leads to serious misunderstandings. For it is hard to find a form of human behaviour that has not already been observed somewhere. Consequently, if a study reports a prevailing regularity, many readers respond to it by thinking 'of course that is the way things are.' Thus, from time to time, the argument is advanced that surveys only put into complicated form observations which are already obvious to everyone.

Understanding the origin of this point of view is of importance far beyond the limits of the present discussion. The reader may be helped in recognising this attitude if he looks over a few statements made in connection with the behaviour of American soldiers during the Second World War, together with common-sense interpretations of them.

1   Better educated men showed more psycho-neurotic symptoms than those with less education. (The mental instability of the intellectual as compared to the more impassive psychology of the man-in-the-street has often been commented on.)

2   Men from rural backgrounds were usually in better spirits during their army life than soldiers from city backgrounds. (After all, they are more accustomed to hardships.)

3   Southern soldiers were better able to stand the climate in the hot South Sea Islands than Northern soldiers (of course, Southerners are more accustomed to hot weather).

4   White privates were more eager to become non-commissioned officers than Negroes. (The lack of ambition among Negroes is almost proverbial.)

5   As long as the fighting continued, men were more eager to be returned to the States than they were after the German surrender. (You cannot blame people for not wanting to be killed.)

We have in these examples a sample list of the simplest type of interrelationships which provide the 'bricks' from which our empirical social science is being built. But why, since they are so obvious, is so much money and energy given to establish such findings? Would it not be wiser to take them for granted and proceed directly to a more sophisticated type of analysis? This might be so except for one interesting point about the list. *Every one of these statements is the direct opposite of what actually was found.* Poorly educated soldiers were more neurotic than those with high education; Southerners showed no greater ability than Northerners to adjust to a tropical climate; Negroes were more eager for promotion than whites, and so on. . .

If we had mentioned the actual results of the investigation first, the reader would have labelled these 'obvious' also. Obviously something is wrong with the entire argument of 'obviousness'. It should really be turned on its head. Since every kind of human reaction is conceivable, it is of great importance to know which reactions actually occur most frequently and under what conditions; only then will a more advanced social science develop.

From *What is Obvious?* by Paul F. Lazarsfeld

In the passage below, the writer questions the value of public opinion polls.

I AM MORE than a little sceptical about those opinion polls which claim to show that support for the installation of cruise missiles has risen, or declined, or remained essentially stable, or whatever. One reason is that differently worded questions produce quite different results.

Writing in the current *Encounter*, Elizabeth Noelle-Neumann gives a revealing example. A July 1983 poll conducted for the West German television station, ZDF, asked people what should be done if the Geneva negotiations on medium-range missiles failed to produce agreement by the autumn (as has, in fact, happened).

From the three choices offered, an overwhelming 72 per cent selected *'Continue to negotiate about disarmament, and do not deploy any new missiles in the Federal Republic.'* There was even a majority support for this view among Christian Democrat and Free Democrat voters. Only 22 per cent of the total supported the official policy of negotiate and deploy.

In August, however, the Allensbach Institute got a very different result to what was essentially the same question. Forty per cent of those questioned said that American missiles 'should not be deployed' if the disarmament talks yielded no results, compared to 37 per cent who favoured deployment. Apparently a 50 per cent majority against deployment had fallen to 3 per cent in a single month. And minority Christian Democrat support for deployment had been transformed into a clear majority.

This discrepancy is, of course explained by the wording. The Allensbach question contained the clause *'. . . and (if) the Soviet Union keep its SS-20 missiles pointed at Europe . . .'*, whereas the ZDF question did not. Once reminded of this salient fact, about a quarter of the voters changed their opinions.

But this raises a more radical objection: if people alter their views in response to minor wording changes, in what sense can they be said to hold those views in the first place? Had many of those questioned thought seriously about missile deployment before a man with a clipboard suddenly appeared and read them a list of policy choices? Had they thought about it at all?

In fact, public opinion in general does not exist. It is no more than the insubstantial artefact of opinion polls.

On most political and international topics, 'public opinion' is created by the pollster's question. It has little or no relationship to irresistible waves of mass popular sentiment.

From an article by John O'Sullivan in the *Daily Telegraph*

Activity 1 – pair work

First passage

1. Study the first passage and then: a) briefly summarise the content of each paragraph – what is the writer saying?; b) consider whether the four paragraphs form a logical argument. If so, what is the purpose of each paragraph? How do they relate to each other – in particular, the second and the third?

2. Now study the construction of each paragraph in turn. a) In the first paragraph, note the way in which the writer prepares the reader for the content of the following sentence by the use of the connectors **And yet, For, Consequently, Thus.** What is the relationship between the topic sentence and the concluding sentence? b) In the second paragraph, what is the effect of the list of points, with the interpretation in brackets? Is it convincing? If so, why? c) What is the key sentence of the third paragraph? What is its effect on you, having read the second paragraph? d) How does the concluding paragraph resolve the question posed in the topic paragraph, and why do we find this conclusion convincing?

Second passage

3. To what extent does the second writer follow a similar technique in presenting his argument to the first? Compare the content of the four paragraphs, as in 1 a) above, and their purpose, as in 1 b) above.

4. In what ways do the subsequent paragraphs develop the point made in the topic paragraph and lead to the conclusion of the last paragraph?

Both passages

5. Although the second writer's technique is similar to that of the first article, there is a fundamental difference in the presentation of the examples. What is it?

6. The two writers appear to reach opposite conclusions about the value of surveys and opinion polls. Is it possible to reconcile their conclusions? If we accept that surveys are useful, what factors would be necessary to convince the second writer that an opinion poll was reliable?

Generalisations

General statements are seldom completely acceptable, either because they are inaccurate or because they are open to different interpretations. If you have sufficient information, you can question their accuracy.

Intelligence owes more to environment than to heredity

Some writers, such as J.B. Watson, have believed so strongly in this assertion that they have claimed that if they took charge of a child at an early age and could control his environment completely, they could turn him into a famous musician or scientist. In his book, *Uses and Abuses of Psychology*, H.J. Eysenck argues that, on the contrary, heredity is the more important factor in intelligence.

Eysenck uses three methods to prove his contention. First, he compares the intelligence of pairs of identical twins, where heredity is exactly the same, with that of fraternal twins, where heredity is only about 50% the same. Even when the fraternal twins were of the same sex, as identical twins always are, there was a correlation in intelligence of only 65% for them, while identical twins averaged 95%. So heredity, not environment, appears to be important.

A second test is to compare orphans, all of whom have been brought up in similar conditions with the same teachers and the same companions. Though the environment is the same, the spread of intelligence is almost as great as it is for children outside.

Finally, Eysenck points out that parents of the higher professional and administrative classes have an average Intelligence Quotient of 150, while their children average a little over 120. At the other end of the scale, adults who are

considered subnormal, with an I.Q. of 55, produce children who average 70, and at every stage in between, the children of parents of above average intelligence average less, while those whose parents' intelligence is below average, average more. Yet if environment were more important, we would expect the opposite to occur since the more intelligent the parents are the more likely they are to do everything to improve the child's cultural background, and vice versa.

Even so, Eysenck says it is meaningless to say human intelligence is 80% due to heredity because we cannot speak for human beings as a whole. A hereditary trait may be modified by the environment – for instance, if insufficient food is available. Height is almost entirely a matter of heredity, but if people are reduced to starvation level, the influence of heredity on the final height of a grown person can be reduced to as little as 60%. Eysenck therefore concludes that all we can say at this time is that in Britain, at present, differences in children's ability to do well in intelligence tests are determined to a much greater extent by heredity than by environment. Curiously (from the point of view of his critics) but logically, he adds that greater equality in society is likely to increase the importance of heredity in determining intelligence, not decrease it.

Activity 2 – pair work

The form of argument used here to criticise a general statement depends on two factors, logic and the use of statistics obtained by scientific research.

1 Trace the logic of Eysenck's three arguments. Can you see any way of contradicting it? What are the implications of the third argument for parents who spend a lot of money on education?
2 To what extent is the environment likely to modify the effects of heredity in: a) an advanced

democracy; b) a country where there are great differences in diet between rich and poor? How does this lead to Eysenck's eventual conclusion?
3 Despite this argument, the children of those of high intelligence in democratic countries tend to be more successful at school and in their careers than those whose parents have a low I.Q. What additional factor has Eysenck taken into account to explain this in the last paragraph, and what other factors has he not mentioned? Do these factors affect a) the validity of his argument; b) its practical application in real life?

Another way of dealing with general statements and questioning their validity is to insist on more precise definition. Very often, as in the argument that follows, the conclusion is that the real problem to be solved is something different.

In last week's *Tribune*, there was an interesting letter from Mr J. Stewart Cook, in which he suggested that the best way of avoiding the danger of a 'scientific hierarchy' would be to see to it that every member of
5 the general public was, as far as possible, scientifically educated. As a general statement, I think most of us would agree with this, but I notice that, as usual, Mr Cook does not define science, and merely implies in passing that it means certain exact sciences whose
10 experiments can be made under laboratory conditions. This point is of great importance. For the word 'science' is at present used in at least two meanings, and the whole question of scientific education is obscured by the current tendency to dodge from one meaning to the
15 other.

Science is generally taken as meaning either (a) the exact sciences, such as chemistry, physics, etc., or (b) a method of thought which obtains verifiable results by reasoning logically from observed fact. If you ask any
20 scientist, or indeed almost any educated person, 'What is science?' you are likely to get an answer approximating to (b). In everyday life, however, both in speaking and in writing, when people say 'science' they mean (a). Science means something that happens in a labora-
25 tory: the very word calls up a picture of graphs, test-tubes, balances, Bunsen burners, microscopes. A biologist, an astronomer, perhaps a psychologist or a mathematician, is described as a 'man of science': no one would think of applying this term to a statesman, a
30 poet, a journalist or even a philosopher. And those who tell us that the young must be scientifically educated mean, almost invariably, that they should be taught more about radioactivity, or the stars, or the physiology of their own bodies, rather than that they
35 should be taught to think more exactly.

This confusion of meaning, which is partly deliberate, has in it a great danger. Implied in the demand for more scientific education is the claim that if one has been scientifically trained, one's approach to *all* sub-
40 jects will be more intelligent than if one had had no such training. A scientist's political opinions, it is assumed, his opinions on sociological questions, on morals, on philosophy, perhaps even on the arts, will be more valuable than those of a layman. But a
45 'scientist', as we have just seen, means in practice a specialist in one of the exact sciences. Is it really true that a 'scientist', in this narrower sense, is any likelier than other people to approach non-scientific problems in an objective way?
50 Clearly, scientific education ought to mean the implanting of a rational, sceptical, experimental habit of mind. It ought to mean acquiring a *method* – a method that can be used on any problem that one meets – and not simply piling up a lot of facts. Put it in those words,
55 and the apologist of scientific education will usually agree. Press him further, ask him to particularize, and somehow it always turns out that scientific education means more attention to the exact sciences, in other words – more *facts*. The idea that science means a way
60 of looking at the world, and not simply a body of knowledge, is in practice strongly resisted. I think sheer professional jealousy is part of the reason for this. For if science is simply a method or an attitude, so that anyone whose thought-processes are sufficiently
65 rational can in some sense be described as a scientist – what then becomes of the enormous prestige now enjoyed by the chemist, the physicist, etc, and his claim to be somehow wiser than the rest of us?

From *What is Science?* by George Orwell

Activity 3 – pair work

1 Study the first paragraph and decide which proposition the writer is attacking. How does the concluding sentence indicate the form of this attack? In what way do the phrases 'as usual' and 'merely' in the second sentence show that the writer is preparing to contradict the statement? How does he draw our attention to his concluding statement?

2 In what way is the second paragraph a development of the first? Why do you think the article was called *What is Science?*

3 What is the connection between the second paragraph and the third? How does the writer exploit the confusion of definitions to reach an apparent conclusion that few people would accept? What is the effect of the phrase 'even on the arts' (line 43)?

4 What definition would the author accept of a valid 'scientific education'? Why does he think that his opponents would not accept it? What phrase, at the beginning of the third paragraph, has prepared us for this?

5 Devise a formula for a four-paragraph composition on any of the topics listed in the questionnaire at the beginning of this unit which can be attacked because of inadequate definition. What purpose should each paragraph have? Then compare your formula with those of other pairs.

Using the definite article

Activity 4

Before completing this exercise, consult the Reference Section, page 168. Complete the paragraphs by writing **the** in the spaces, *only where it is necessary.*

. . . . .(1) industrial psychology, in so far as it is concerned with . . . . .(2) improvement of . . . . .(3) working conditions, ...(4) increase of . . . . .(5) productivity, and . . . . .(6) problems of . . . . .(7) motivation and . . . . .(8) incentives has to live down a good deal of . . . . .(9) opposition. Under . . . . .(10) proud title of . . . . .(11) 'scientific management', it succeeded in antagonising workers to such an extent that . . . . .(12) 'efficiency expert' is now one of . . . . .(13) most-hated figures on . . . . .(14) contemporary scene. This hatred is understandable historically; is it an appropriate emotion in . . . . .(15) world today?

. . . . .(16) scientific management originated in . . . . .(17) brain of F. W. Taylor, an American in . . . . .(18) best tradition of . . . . .(19) English crank. He worshipped . . . . .(20) efficiency in all its forms, and carried this worship a little further than . . . . .(21) most of his contemporaries. He invented . . . . .(22) overhand pitch in . . . . .(23) baseball, which is now standard; he also constructed a spoon-shaped tennis racket because he was convinced that his shape was more efficient than . . . . .(24) more usual one. Unlike many other cranks, however, he put his theory to . . . . .(25) test, and went on to win . . . . .(26) American national championships with his racket.

When this apostle of . . . . .(27) efficiency looked at . . . . .(28) industry, he was appalled by . . . . .(29) waste and inefficiency he found there. He laid down a three-point plan for . . . . .(30) improvement, which in . . . . .(31) essence though not in . . . . .(32) detail may still be regarded as a kind of industrial psychologist's manifesto. His first point was: Employ only . . . . .(33) good men. By this he did not mean . . . . .(34) men who were morally good; although he was a Quaker, he did not try to mix . . . . .(35) morality and . . . . .(36) efficiency. He meant . . . . .(37) men who by . . . . .(38) inheritance and . . . . .(39) training possessed . . . . .(40) right combination of aptitudes for . . . . .(41) job in . . . . .(42) question.

From *Uses and Abuses of Psychology* by H.J. Eysenck

Composition

Write an essay on any of the eight topics listed in the questionnaire at the beginning of this unit. Disagree with the statement by using one of the following techniques: a) providing factual evidence to contradict it;   b) indicating that the statement depends on the definition of a word or words, which may vary;   c) suggesting that the real point at issue is something different.

Letters to the editor

Protest

The small village of Purblack, Burkeshire, is in ferment because of Transport Minister Mr Reginald Capstick's decision to give the go-ahead to a plan to build a motorway that will pass across farmland nearby. Below you will see the slogans on placards that were carried on the day the village took to the streets to demonstrate against Mr Capstick's decision. 'Translate' the slogans into statements and say what you think they refer to.

Opinion and reply

Activity I – pair work

Read the letter below. Note that the writer uses a number of techniques to persuade readers to accept his point of view, but also uses clichés, a sign of a weak argument that should not be imitated. Then answer the questions below.

Sir:

While I am no racist and believe that minorities within a country are entitled to receive their due from the powers that be, I would like to draw your readers' attention to a case where the natural order of things is being turned upside down
5 and the cart is unquestionably being put before the horse.

I refer to the fact that although I live in England there are frequent occasions during the day when I am only able to receive programmes in a foreign language, Welsh. I hasten to add that I have no axe to grind as far as Welsh people are concerned, nor would I wish to see programmes specially prepared for Welsh-
10 speaking audiences suppressed. But your readers will readily understand my frustration when I have settled down in an armchair, expecting to watch a programme I have been looking forward to, and find that it has been replaced by something I am not interested in and cannot begin to understand. What makes matters worse is that I do not even know when the programme is likely to be
15 changed, because the announcement itself is only given to viewers in Welsh.

The height of foolishness in this situation was reached last night when a Hungarian film was shown, with specially-made Welsh subtitles. Surely the expense and effort this must have involved can hardly be justified for an audience who all understand English, whichever side of the border they happen to live on?
20 As far as I was concerned, they might just as well have left out the sub-titles altogether, since I would have understood as much of the original Hungarian sound track.

R. MANNING-HOWARD, Offa's Dyke, Cheshire

1 Decide on the meaning of the following clichés: 'the powers that be' (line 3); 'the natural order of things' (line 4); 'the cart is . . . being put before the horse' (line 5); 'I have no axe to grind' (line 8).

2 Which phrase in the first paragraph and which sentence in the second show that the writer anticipates criticism of his views and is trying to defend himself against it?

3 How does he try to gain the readers' sympathy in the second paragraph, and why are readers likely to be sympathetic?

4 What possible question from readers is he preparing himself for in the last sentence of the second paragraph?

5 He uses an effective technique in argument, that of giving an extreme example of the results of one's opponents' actions or proposals. Find his use of this technique.

6 Why might the expressions 'the natural order of things' (line 4) and 'programmes in a foreign language' (line 7) be offensive to Welsh people?

7 Which phrase in the last paragraph really forms the basis for the whole argument?

Activity 2 – pair work

Read the reply to the letter opposite. Effective replies depend on techniques like those used here, so that this is a good model to imitate. Then answer the questions below.

Sir:

I must take exception to the tone of a letter published in the correspondence columns of your newspaper last Wednesday. Mr Manning-Howard, even if, as he says, he is not a racist, seems to consider his own comfort to the exclusion of
5   everything else. He is apparently unaware of the fact that it has been a long, hard struggle for Welsh people to gain public recognition of their native language in such important fields as education and broadcasting. Now that there has been a partial relaxation of the rigidly chauvinistic policy pursued until recent years, he complains about our hard-won rights (even though he is 'generous' enough not to
10   want to take those rights away altogether) just because he is disappointed at missing his favourite programme.
    I would have more sympathy for his point of view if, instead of wearying your readers with his complaints, he had addressed his letter to the Television Service. Surely it is their responsibility to ensure that people living in England can receive
15   programmes in English and those of us who live in Wales can enjoy programmes in our own language. I wonder what his reaction would have been if he had been forced to listen to the radio in a foreign language for most of his life, as I have been, and forced to write a foreign language to reach the understanding of 'little Englanders' like himself, as I am doing now.
20   MYFANWY HOPKINS, Mold, Clwyd

---

1 How does the writer immediately draw readers' attention to the previous letter and remind them of its content?
2 In the first paragraph, the writer attacks the first writer's attitude from two points of view. What are they?
3 Although the tone of this letter may appear reasonable, the writer seeks to influence readers by her use of emotionally charged adjectives. Find two phrases that aim to obtain sympathy for Welsh people and two that discredit their opponents.
4 Why is 'generous' (line 9) printed in inverted commas?
5 What should Mr Manning-Howard have done, according to this writer, instead of writing his letter to a newspaper? Why do you suppose he did not do so?
6 How does Ms Hopkins use phrases from the first letter in her conclusion to demonstrate the weakness of the argument, and why is this technique particularly effective here?

Activity 3 – group work

Make notes for a letter to the editor on one of the following topics. Use the techniques from Mr Manning-Howard's letter to make your argument convincing, and imagine the kind of person who would write the letter.

1 Protest about the number of immigrants coming into your country or city from other countries or parts of your own country.
2 Complain about films being shown in cinemas which in your opinion are in bad taste.
3 Draw people's attention to cruelty to animals in research laboratories.
4 Protest about increased taxes on petrol and cars.
5 Criticise the behaviour of students demonstrating in your city or country.

Comments on the news

The news item on the left, announcing a campaign
to suppress some traditional comics, provoked
letters from two readers of the newspaper, which
are printed alongside. Read the news item and
letters and answer the questions below.

ANTI-CANING GROUP BASH 'THE BEANO'

By MARGOT NORMAN
Education Staff

P ARENTS who are planning to put
'The Beano' annual in their child's
Christmas stocking were warned
yesterday that this apparently innocent
entertainment could badly affect the
child and encourage sado-masochism.

The anti-caning pressure group STOPP is
trying to persuade store chains such as W. H.
Smith and John Menzies to return all unsold
copies of 'The Beano', 'The Dandy' and 'The
Bash Street Kids' annuals to their publishers,
D. C. Thomson, because they are full of
stories about beating children.

Laughter and joy

SIR – I would like to say that the anti-
caning group are very silly to try and stop
an annual like *The Beano* which causes so
much laughter and joy to children. When my
sister and brothers were children they all had
the books that they are trying to stop. What
the anti-caning group are trying to do is the
horror story.

ROSEMARY JOY ALLDRED
Age 9
Blackwood, Gwent

No sense of humour

SIR – With reference to the 'anti-caning'
group STOPP's opposition to *The Beano*, as
an 11-year-old. I wish to express my
disapproval about their intended action.

My parents tell me that they read *The
Beano* and *The Dandy* as children and they
have never beaten me. I read and enjoy *The
Beano* and have done for five years and I do
not expect to grow up to be violent or beat
my children. I do not believe these people
can have a sense of humour. Therefore they
should not read children's comics.

THOMAS FORDHAM
Peterborough.

The Beano, The Dandy: traditional British children's
comics
annual: Christmas comic book, using the same
characters as in the comics.

Activity 4 – pair work

1   What is STOPP's case against these traditional comics,
    and why do the readers concerned disagree?
2   What evidence do the readers give in practical terms for
    their opposition?
3   Why are the views of these two readers particularly
    relevant?

Activity 5 – group work

Read the letters below, and decide from the content what the Government is proposing to do and what reasons have been given for its proposal. Which of the readers are in favour of the proposal, and which against, and what reasons do they put forward to support their point of view? Can you think of any reason why the two men may disagree with the two women?

£s of note

SIR – Congratulations on your editorial support (Dec. 23) of the new £1 coin. I know no one who dislikes this well-designed, attractive coin. As with so many things, it is the grumblers who make the news.

As for the argument that notes are light and fit into a wallet, who carries £1 notes in a wallet these days?

(Miss) M. Baldwin
Ludlow, Shropshire.

Too many coins

SIR – The pound has indeed declined in value, but it would make more sense to introduce a £2 note than to replace the £1 note with the coin. It is not simply a question of what is familiar, it is easier to carry a wad of notes, even tatty pounds, than a pocketful of jangling metal. There are too many coins already.

R. M. FRASER
London, N.1.

Enduring greenbacks

SIR – I am amazed that we apparently cannot afford to produce a £1 note 'because its life is only ten months.'

How on earth do other countries manage? In nearly 70 years I have seen no alterations in the currency of the United States, except the demise of the silver dollar, which like our crown was too big and heavy.

GEOFFREY LANCASHIRE
Berkhamsted, Herts.

Lone voice

SIR – May an apparently lone voice speak up in favour of the much-maligned £1 piece?

I find these preferable to dirty, germy £1 notes, and actually ask for them when cashing cheques at the bank.

PEGGY RAPHAEL
London, W. 13.

Composition

1 You live in the village of Purblack (see p. 111), write a letter to a newspaper protesting about the motorway plan.
2 Write the letter you planned for Activity 3, and then write a letter to the editor from the opposite point of view in answer to it.

Descriptive compositions

Planning your composition

In the examination you may be given topics such as the following, all to do with describing a house, but each from a different angle. You can use a similar plan for each, as shown in the table below, but the verb tenses you use will be different.

1   A house in the country
2   A house you knew as a child
3   Your ideal house

Basic plan of paragraphs	Questions to answer in each paragraph	Probable tense(s)		
		Topic 1	Topic 2	Topic 3
1 Establishment of time and place in topic paragraph.	Where is it/was it/ would it be? How did you find it?/Why would you go there? When or at what time of year did you go there?	Present or Past with some variants	Mainly Past, **used to** and **would. . .,** with some Present or Present Perfect at the beginning or the end	Conditional throughout (if answered literally) e.g. **My ideal house would have. . .**
2 Physical description	Built of what material? Number of rooms? Description of rooms. Garden? View?			
3 Colour . . . provided by people, location, incidents, special interest of neighbourhood, etc.	The inhabitants? Events or incidents related to it? Surroundings? There is room in this paragraph for imagination.			
4 Conclusion	How would you sum up in general terms the effect of your chosen house on you?			

Activity 1

Prepare notes for and then give a short talk on the flat or house where you live, or on one that has had an impact on you in your life.

Describing houses

Activity 2 – group work

Refer back to the plan on page 116. Choose *three* of the five houses illustrated; each should represent one of the following categories: 1) a house in the country;   2) a house you knew as a child;   3) your ideal house.

Then make a plan for a description, answering the questions suggested in the model plan; use the tenses appropriate to the topic you have chosen. When you have finished find out from other groups which of the houses you have both described and compare notes on your results.

Describing holidays

Activity 3 – pair work

Describe a typical seaside resort you have visited

Refer to the plan for Topic 1 on page 116, for guidance on the use of tenses. Then read the first paragraph below, and follow the instructions to write three more paragraphs of your own.

> _____ is at first sight a typical seaside resort on the coast of _____, but it has a personality of its own that makes it particularly attractive. Perhaps this is because, unlike many resorts that have been created for tourists in recent years, it was a village at one time and was originally built around a natural harbour. I have spent several holidays at _____ and although it has changed considerably since I first went there, I still find it delightful.

Discuss the instructions given with your partner, and write one paragraph each. Then compare notes in order to produce the last paragraph together.

Para 2: Describe the resort, using your own experience of such places. Consider the following questions: How big is it? What is the beach like? What sort of boats are there in the harbour? Where are the hotels, shops, etc.? What remains of the original village – narrow streets, a church? How has the resort developed in recent years? In which direction? What sort of view is there from the beach – islands, etc.?

Para 3: Describe what people do when they spend holidays there. Change to the past tense to describe an interesting incident that happened to you on your last visit. Consider the following questions: What sort of people go there? When is the tourist season? What is the weather like? How do people spend their time during the day, and after dark?

Para 4: Write a paragraph that completes the composition by explaining the content of the first, topic paragraph with relation to what you have said in the second and third.

Activity 4 – pair work

Write about a holiday you spent by the sea
Refer to the plan for Topic 2 on page 116 for guidance on the use of tenses. Then follow the instructions below to produce four paragraphs of your own. Discuss the content with your partner and write the first and last together, writing one intermediate paragraph each.

Para 1: Establish time and place. Where is the place? When did you go there? Had you been there before? How old were you? Who did you go with? Why did you choose the place? How long did you stay there? Where did you stay?

Para 2: Describe the place. Use the present tense if the holiday was recent, the past if you went many years ago and it has since changed (*When I went to _____, it was..... but....*). Say something about what you did in general terms and describe briefly any incident that was particularly memorable.

Para 3: Write about the people you met or saw there, how you met them or where you saw them. Were they local people or tourists? What did you do – excursions, fishing or sailing trips, dancing in the evenings, attending local festivities, etc.?

Para 4: Compare your paragraphs and write a brief conclusion. Would you like to spend another holiday there? Why? If not, why not? Has the place changed considerably?

Activity 5 – pair work

Imagine you could spend a holiday by the sea anywhere in the world. Where would you go?
Refer to the plan for Topic 3 on page 116, for guidance on the use of tenses. Then follow the instructions below to produce four paragraphs of your own on the same pattern as the previous exercise.

Note that before you answer the question truthfully, you should be sure that if you choose an exotic place you have never visited, like Hawaii or the Bahamas, you will have to describe it accurately and know very well what you would do there. It is wiser to choose a place you already know and transfer your past experiences to a hypothetical future. Use the composition you have already written above for the facts but modify it as indicated below.

Para 1: Why have you always wanted to go to this place? Have you read about it? Have friends of yours been there? How would you go there? Where would you stay?

Para 2: Describe the place in the present tense but begin: *From what I have heard/read...* You can describe an incident in the past by attributing it to a friend.

Para 3: Although you will have to concentrate on what you *would* do you can vary the tense by describing the typical activities of the place in the present – what people usually do there, what customs or festivities it is famous for – or by describing a further incident you have heard about from friends in the past.

Para 4: Work together on the conclusion, as before. Repeat your main reasons for wanting to go to the place, and decide whether you will ever have the opportunity to do so.

Composition

Use your own experience to write a composition on any one of the topics listed on pages 116, 118 and on this page.

Narrative compositions

A party

1   The bar's car park was empty apart from a new Ford which seemed to belong to the only other customers, two young men. As we were ordering the wine, I noticed one of the young men looking across at us. For a moment he looked puzzled, as if he couldn't believe his eyes. Then he limped slowly across, his eyes fixed on Gerry, who had his back to him. When Gerry finally turned round, the young man was standing by him, smiling. 'I might have known we'd meet in a bar!' he said.

2   One party I remember took place on July 14, Bastille Day, in 1968, when I was working in Sousse, a coastal town in central Tunisia. I was sharing a flat with two other teachers, an American called Gerry, and Henri, a Frenchman, and it was Henri who invited us along to the party, which had been organised by the local community of French teachers. They had chosen a site on a beautiful rocky beach north of Sousse, and the party began in the early evening, just as the sun was going down over the hills to the west, behind us.

3   The moment in the party I will never forget, however, came around midnight. By that time the stocks of wine were running low, and Gerry and I drove with Henri across the rough, sandy track that led back to the main road where there was a bar. For some days Gerry hadn't wanted to talk much, and we knew what was on his mind. He had a younger brother, Gary, who had been drafted to Vietnam the previous spring. Six weeks before, Gary had written to say his company was probably going into action, and Gerry had heard nothing more. Gerry had taken the silence to mean that Gary might have been either killed or captured.

4   The young man, as you have probably guessed, was Gary. He had been wounded in the leg at the battle of Da-Nang, had been demobbed as a result and had decided to spend his pay on a visit to Gerry. I remember very clearly how, several hours later, when the sun rose over the sea, the 30 or so of us who remained were drinking coffee, eating what was left of the roast sheep, and listening while Gary told tales of Vietnam in his halting French.

5   There must have been about 70 people there. Everyone had contributed something to the food and drink, but the centrepiece was a whole sheep that was roasted over an open fire, around which we all gathered. We ate, we drank, we sang French songs, we swam, we danced on the beach to music from someone's record-player, and above all we talked, because there had been dramatic events in France only a month or so before, and many of the teachers were planning to return to France shortly for their summer holidays.

Activity 1 – pair work

1 The paragraphs opposite are in jumbled order. Read the paragraphs and put them in the correct order.
2 Study the passage opposite and briefly note down what actually happened *at* the party. Notice which tense(s) are used to describe the party events, and explain why the Past Continuous appears so frequently.
3 Find examples where the writer explains or describes things which, though not events at the party, give the reader the background to what happened. In these cases which tense is used and why?
4 There is one example of direct speech. Why is it used at this particular moment?
5 Now study the function of each paragraph, and decide why you ordered them the way you did. Summarise the content of each paragraph in a sentence. What elements do the introduction and conclusion have in common?

Activity 2 – pair work

Write an account of an eventful party you attended

The following two paragraphs form the beginning of another story about a party. Write a third paragraph describing the consequences of the incident at the end of paragraph 2, and a suitable conclusion describing how the party finished.

I'll never forget that hot August evening when Vernon, my flatmate at the time, gave a fancy-dress party to celebrate his engagement to Sylvia. We were living in a ground-floor flat in a house in London, and as the only party we had had there before had ended in trouble with the neighbours and a visit from a nice but firm policeman (one guest had insisted on playing his saxophone loudly), I suppose I should have had the common sense to dissuade Vernon from risking it again.

Probably nothing unusual would have happened if Vernon and Sylvia had not chosen to go to the party as Antony and Cleopatra. Or possibly events would have been different if they had not both been short-sighted and vain and decided not to wear their glasses. Or it may have been just fate. Anyway, the cause of what later happened was the unfortunate coincidence that at the party there were two Antonys, or rather two Romans, since the other one thought he was Nero. To most people at the party the difference between the two was obvious, and no doubt it would have been to Sylvia if only she had had her glasses on. To complicate matters still further, Nero was Vernon's boss. So imagine my feelings when I went into the kitchen midway through the party, and was confronted with the scene of Sylvia advancing towards Nero with her arms outstretched, saying, 'Now we're alone, Antony darling, why don't you give me a Roman Kiss?'

First meeting

Activity 3 – pair work

Describe your first meeting with a person who influenced your life

Plan:
1. Topic paragraph. Establishment of time and place and reason for meeting, if any.
2. First impressions of the person and conversation. Use direct speech here for the important points affecting the subject.
3. How the meeting ended. Direct speech can again be used.
4. Subsequent meetings. Reasons for them.
5. How the person has influenced your life.

Read the three paragraphs of the narrative below, and then write two more to complete the story, using the guidance given. Discuss the content with your partner and write one paragraph each. (The story is told by Brian Reeve, aged twenty-six.)

It is strange that so many of the important meetings in people's lives take place quite by chance. I could have sat anywhere in the train I caught to London on the day I left university because it was almost empty. For some reason, however, I did not want to be alone and sat opposite a man with greying hair who was so engrossed in his newspaper at first that I could not see his face.

After a few minutes he put the paper down with an impatient gesture. He had not realised I was there, and, probably because of his surprise, made a remark about the weather. He had penetrating, but kindly, blue eyes, a firm mouth and an air of authority, as if he was used to giving orders and expecting them to be carried out. He looked older than he really was, because at that time he could have been only 41. He glanced at my jeans and shirt, the scarf round my neck, and my battered suitcase, and said, 'End of term?'

'The end of university for me,' I said. I had not really got used to the idea that from then on I was no longer a student.

'Well, now you've got your degree, I expect you're looking forward to a long summer break.'

'Not exactly,' I said. 'The first thing I must do is look for a job. I've got my name down for three or four interviews, but to tell the truth, they don't excite me much.'

For the rest of the journey, we talked about my studies – I had done Economics – and all the time I felt he was not just making polite conversation. Now that I know Stephen Merrick well, I know that he never asks questions to pass the time. By the time we reached London, he knew almost all there was to know about me. As I was saying goodbye, he handed me a business card with his name on it and the address of Merrick Enterprises Ltd. in the City. 'If you run out of ideas during the summer,' he said, 'give me a ring.'

Para 4: How do you think Brian met Mr Merrick again? What happened when they met? Remember that at the time of writing Brian knows Merrick well. What do you suppose Merrick does? Why was he interested in Brian? What do you imagine Merrick's office (or house) is like? Describe their second meeting.

Para 5: What do you think their relationship is now (five years later)? What do you imagine has happened in the intervening five years? The narration suggests they are still on good terms. How would you end the story?

A quarrel

Activity 4 – pair work

Describe a quarrel you witnessed

Plan:
1. Topic paragraph. Set the scene for the quarrel. Who was involved? What was their relationship to you?
2. How did the quarrel start? Consider the events that led up to it. Where did it take place?
3. The beginning of the quarrel. Use direct speech at the important points.
4. The development of the quarrel. What happened? Use direct speech again.
5. The result of the quarrel and the present situation. The three paragraphs given below are the last three. Read them and then use the guidance given to write the first two. Discuss the content with your partner and write one paragraph each. (The story is told by Catherine's younger brother, Tim, aged fourteen.)

It was clear from the expression on Ronald's face that there was going to be trouble. He walked onto the dance floor and said loudly to Catherine, 'Hey, Catherine, I want to talk to you.' Trevor and Catherine took no notice, but when the music stopped, he barred their path as they were going back to their table. Ronald was working himself up into one of his rages and I wondered what Trevor would do.

'What are you doing here with this creep?' Ronald said, ignoring Trevor and speaking only to Catherine.

'That's my business,' Catherine said defiantly. 'I can go to a dance without asking you, can't I?'

'No, you can't,' Ronald said. 'You're my girl, remember.'

Catherine looked up at Trevor, expecting him to react but he still stood beside her, saying nothing. Ronald probably under-estimated him for that reason. He took a step forward to grab Catherine's arm and found Trevor had stepped between them. 'Why don't you shut your big, ugly mouth and leave us alone?' Trevor said very clearly, so that everyone could hear.

He told me afterwards that Ronald reacted exactly as he had planned. He threw a wild punch at Trevor. Trevor moved to his right and hit him hard in his fat stomach. Ronald gasped and sat down on the floor, surprised. He did not get up, and no one helped him. 'Let's dance,' Trevor said to Catherine. 'He won't bother you again.' He was quite right. In fact, we haven't seen Ronald in the neighbourhood for the last six months. As for Trevor and Catherine, they're planning to get married next year.

Para 1: What do you think the relationship between Ronald and Catherine was before this? What do you imagine Tim thought about it? How do you imagine Trevor got to know Catherine? How old do you think the three characters are? What do you think they look like?

Para 2: How and why did the quarrel take place? Consider the events leading up to the dance. Why did Catherine go with Trevor? How did Ronald find out she was there? Link the paragraph to the third one. Did Tim see Ronald come in? Did Ronald speak to him? What did he say?

Composition

Use your own experience to write on the three topics in this unit, but organise your composition along the lines suggested.

Discussion essays

Approaches

The units devoted to discussion in this book (3, 6, 11, 15 and 19) have indicated various ways of responding to general composition questions, and the appropriate techniques to use. The approaches 1–4 in this Unit summarise the alternatives, indicating useful phrases that may be helpful to you in building up your argument. They can be used for reference in writing your own compositions. Note that the present tense can be used in almost all cases, except for references to personal experience (past) and hypothesis (conditional sentences).

The first step in choosing an approach is to decide where you stand, as you have done in the questionnaires in Units 11 and 19. Note that the neutral position should only be adopted in an examination if you can genuinely see both sides of the case, or you feel that the statement is unacceptable without redefinition. Do not answer such questions if you have no opinion on the subject.

Approach 1: Arguing for the proposition
Examples on pages 62, 112 and 113.

1   Topic paragraph. Define the question and indicate your favourable reaction to it in the concluding sentence. Imply reasonableness of own views. – *Most people would agree that. . .; While I am not (biassed, unreasonable), I . . ., nevertheless, that. . .*

2   List your main reasons for agreeing with the statement, supporting them by facts or by examples, whenever possible based on personal experience. – *In the first place, Secondly, Apart from that, Finally, Above all,. . .*

3   Recognise the opposing point of view. Choose two or three arguments used against the proposition and attempt to destroy them by   a) facts; or
b) examples from personal experience; or
c) suggesting their absurdity by a hypothetical demonstration of what would happen if they were

put into practice. – *Of course, However, Although. . ., In fact, In my experience. We could easily imagine. . .*

4   Repeat main arguments as the logical point of view for anyone to take in the light of the evidence. Suggest the beneficial results of this approach. – *In conclusion, therefore. . ., Summarising the position, . . . As a result, In that case. . .*

Approach 2: Arguing against the proposition
Examples on pages 108 and 113. (Note that this approach is only possible on page 108 if you have enough facts at your disposal.)

1   Topic paragraph. Define the question and indicate why you are opposed to the statement in the concluding sentence. – *Many people seem to think that. . .; In fact, However, All the same. . .*

2   Define the kind of people who hold such views, and list two or three of their arguments. Use the techniques suggested in Approach 1, Paragraph 3 to suggest they are limited or ridiculous. The same phrases are useful.

3   Indicate in contrast your main reasons for disagreeing (as in Approach 1 Paragraph 2). The same phrases are relevant, together with *In contrast, On the other hand.*

4   Link to third paragraph to summarise your point of view. Compare statement to facts, personal experience, and suggest advantages if your view were widely held. – *In consequence, The logical result of this is that. . ., In theory, In practice, In fact, My experience suggests that. . ., In that case. . .*

For *or* against

Look back to the paragraph plan for Approach 1 on page 124 before reading the composition below. Note the connectors and modifiers used.

Rock Worship or Are we all going mad?

While I am not by nature an unreasonable or biased person, two vivid and striking personal experiences of rock music over the past two weeks have persuaded me that it has become a duty for those of us with enough common sense to see its potential dangers to point them out. My first experience, – perhaps a minor one, but highly symptomatic – was the realisation that if I speak to my teenage son when he is listening to rock music through headphones, he replies in an unnaturally loud voice, as if there was something wrong with his hearing. The second occurred when I went with him to a 'concert' and witnessed for myself what these affairs are like.

Till I went to that concert, my first and assuredly my last, I had always adopted the 'live-and-let-live' attitude that rock music was simply not my taste but that other people had every right to enjoy it if it was theirs. But what I saw and heard convinced me that we are allowing something very powerful to take possession of the younger generation. *In the first place*, I noticed a collective madness, a mass hysteria, brought about by the noise level. But *secondly*, and far more dangerously *in my opinion*, I observed that after a time everyone was carried along by the noise, and gave up his/her individuality. *By the end* I was in the middle of a faceless crowd who clapped and stamped and jumped around like demented monkeys. It was the most degrading human spectacle I have ever had the misfortune to witness, and I seriously believe that *in time to come* our present young generation would thank us if we managed to put a stop to it now.

Of course, the rock business has its defenders. There are, *to start with,* the so-called serious music critics who write glibly and hypocritically about the musical 'quality' of rock in their columns, *although* they know full well that most of these rock 'musicians' can't even play their instruments properly. *Then* there are people who defend the right of the young to enjoy themselves, ignoring the fact that your hearing system has to last you all your life and there are few things more frustrating than deafness. *Last but not least,* there is a powerful group that defends the vulgar, brash commercialism of the rock world by claiming that it gives the young the freedom to choose what they like. To which I reply, '*in fact* they choose what they like from amongst the few options you choose to offer them.'

In conclusion, however, what haunts me *above all* about my rock experience is the sheep-like attitude of the fans. It is as if the mere fact of standing up on a stage, striking absurd provocative poses and shouting stupid, unintelligible words into a microphone creates a world of fantasy, and the fans begin to live in it at the expense of their own lives. *In short,* those jerking marionettes on the stage turn the audience into mindless zombies, but anyone present with any common sense left after witnessing the process is bound to ask, 'And those marionettes. . . . . who pulls their strings?'

BY STEPHEN MURGATROYD

Activity 1

Study the article on rock music above.

1 In paragraph 1, how does the writer indicate his attitude to rock music? According to what he says in paragraph 1, on what is he going to base his main arguments against it? In what way are the two experiences with his son connected? Isolate specific words or phrases that reveal his attitude.

2 In paragraph 2, list his main reasons for disliking rock music. Isolate words and phrases that indicate his strong disapproval of it. List any words or phrases you consider to be undue exaggeration. Does the writer add any arguments to those set out in paragraph 1?

3 In paragraph 3, list the opposition arguments the writer mentions. Does he give a fair or logical answer to them all? Isolate words or phrases where you feel he is being unfair to the opposition, or exaggerating; find those where you feel he is fair. Find words or phrases you would consider to appeal more to emotion than to reason.

4   In the conclusion, which argument(s) from paragraphs 1, 2 or 3 does the writer refer to? Find any words or phrases you feel to be appealing more to emotion than reason.

5   In all four paragraphs isolate the topic sentence.

Activity 2

Briefly note down your personal reactions to each paragraph, and write down against each one a list of questions you would like to ask the writer.

Activity 3

Refer back to the notes on Approach 2 on page 124. Suppose you disagree with Stephen Murgatroyd's viewpoint as expressed in his article, and decide to write a reply. A possible introductory paragraph is given. Following the model given write three more paragraphs to express your *disagreement*.

Stephen Murgatroyd's article about rock concerts, which he wants to ban 'for the good of the younger generation', deserves a reasonable reply. Many parents, like him, seem to think that young people need a leader, who will tell them, in their own interests, of course, what to think and do. In fact, however, if one reads his article more carefully, one sees that he isn't writing only because he wants to help the young. He has other reasons, which he may be not be aware of. Possibly the main one is that he is afraid. Rock music frightens him; he doesn't understand it, and therefore he wants to ban it. And not only that. It seems rock music for him is one sign of how the world is changing, whereas what he wants is to stop that change and bring back the things he understands.

The balanced approach

Approach 3: Neutrality (balanced argument)
Examples on pages 88 and 127.

1 Topic paragraph. Examine the question and suggest reasons for the different points of view held. – *Yet, However, although. . ., even though. . ., even if. . ., On the other hand.*

2 Indicate the point of view of those in favour, and say what sort of people they are. Say how far you sympathise, and whether you can see weaknesses in their argument (because it is illogical, selfish or overlooks important points). – *for example, for instance, in their opinion (view), from their point of view,*

However, Nevertheless, All the same, although. . .

3 Present the point of view of those against in the same way.

4 Give a personal assessment, indicating how far you agree with each side, and if possible suggesting a third solution that would either satisfy both sides or provide the opportunity for more intelligent discussion between them. – *Personally, In my opinion (view), My own conclusion is that. . ., On the one hand. . . On the other hand, While. . .*

The punishment should fit the crime
Read the paragraph plan for Approach 3 above before reading the following composition. Note the connectors and modifiers used.

This expression appears to represent a natural human demand for justice but it raises the question of how literally we should interpret it. In some Muslim countries, *for example*, thieves are punished by having their hands cut off. *Even if* everyone accepted this sort of appropriate punishment for crime, it would not be easy to find a suitable way of dealing with every sort of offence.

People likely to favour this statement are *probably* those who have been brought up with a strict sense of right and wrong, and believe everyone else should share it. *Essentially*, they consider that everyone is responsible for his own actions and must pay for the consequences. They base their attitudes on the Old Testament motto: 'An eye for an eye, and a tooth for a tooth.' This motto can represent an idea of natural justice, *of course, but* it can *also* be an excuse for revenge.

People such as social workers, *on the other hand*, tend to put the blame for crime not on the individual but on society. They emphasise that most crimes are committed by those in a disadvantageous social position, *such as* young people who are out of work, and *therefore* they see the solution in terms of reforming society as a whole and rehabilitating the criminal. They argue that the abolition of the death penalty has not resulted in a noticeable increase in the number of murders, *but in any case* they would oppose its reintroduction because for them execution is *also* a criminal act, and 'two wrongs don't make a right'.

Personally, I suspect that the insistence on strict punishments hides a desire for revenge and may be a way of giving people's own violent tendencies some sort of moral justification. It was not so long ago in so-called civilised countries that public executions were a popular spectacle. *Nevertheless*, those who concentrate entirely on the rehabilitation of criminals can easily give the impression that they care more about them than about their victims. *My own view is that* the average man simply wants crime to be prevented. *On the one hand*, he finds the idea of physical punishment barbaric but *on the other* he is annoyed when he reads about violent criminals being given short terms of imprisonment and committing further crimes soon after they are released.

The analytical approach

Approach 4: Redefinition or analysis of the preposition

Examples on pages 109 and 128.

This approach questions the terms of the statement and/or implies that the statement misses the real point at issue.

1 Investigate the statement made, paying close attention to the words employed. Use the techniques suggested on page 105, and ask which interpretation is to be adopted. In the concluding sentence, raise the question that seems to you more relevant. – *As a general statement, . . . A literal interpretation of this statement means/implies that. . .*

2 Consider how the majority of people interpret the statement. Give reasons for this interpretation.

Suggest that they are really more concerned with an answer to the question you have raised. – *If you ask the man in the street. . ., For the majority of people,. . .*

3 Consider the inadequacy of such interpretations by means of practical examples. Attempt a more satisfactory redefinition or indicate any possible solution to the question you have raised. – *However, All the same, In fact, The fact of the matter is. . ., If, on the other hand, . . .*

4 Either indicate why you consider the redefinition to be satisfactory or suggest that no general statement along these lines can be completely acceptable. Phrases as, in (3) above, also *in theory, in practice.*

The punishment should fit the crime

Read the paragraph plan for Approach 4 above before reading the following composition. Note the connectors and modifiers used.

If this statement is meant to be interpreted literally, it must imply that the suffering inflicted on the victim should be imposed in the same proportion on the criminal. *Clearly, while* it may be possible in some cases, *for example,* to fine a businessman who has been found guilty of fraud the exact sum he has taken, human ingenuity could not always devise an appropriate punishment. *In any case,* the statement raises the question: 'Is the object of punishment to satisfy a feeling of justice, or is it an attempt to deter further crime?'

There is *little* doubt that *most* people have a conception of natural justice which can *only* be satisfied by what is felt to be adequate punishment. In the past, no one doubted that murderers should be executed but people were outraged when the punishment seemed out of proportion to the crime; *for example,* when the same punishment was imposed on a man who had stolen a sheep. In modern society, the same sense of injustice exists in reverse. The widespread demand for the reintroduction of the death penalty is *only partly* due to a desire to see those who kill in cold blood similarly treated. What influences people *most* is the knowledge that *most* murderers are released within ten years, *even though* their sentence was life imprisonment, and *consequently* their punishment is proportionately not much more severe than that of many whose crimes do not involve violence.

Even if we accept the statement as meaning that punishment for crime should satisfy people's conception of natural justice, *however,* it does not help us to resolve the more important question of whether such punishments really prevent crime. The evidence with regard to the abolition of the death penalty in Britain in the 1960s, *for example,* is contradictory. *While* it did not lead to a spectacular increase in the number of murders committed, it certainly encouraged professional gangs to carry guns, *even if* they did not always make use of them.

This points to a conclusion that would be as difficult to reach *in practice* as it would be to find a suitable punishment for every crime. Should there be one law for professional criminals who calculate their actions against the punishment they are likely to receive if they are caught, and another for the majority of people, who commit crimes without taking the consequences into account?

Composition

Plan and write a composition on one of the following, using one of the four approaches presented.

1 People should be allowed free choice of schools and medical services.

2 Colonialism is responsible for all the problems of the third world countries.

3 We should find alternative sources of energy, instead of relying so much on oil.

Official language

Formal/informal letters

Activity I

This activity is in three parts.

Part I   Read the letter below.
1   Identify elements which show it is an informal, friendly letter.

2   Note down your impressions of Mum's attitude to Dad's idea of building a garage.
3   How would *you* try to persuade the Council to give you planning permission? How would you present your case in the letter?

Burre Croft,
44 London Rd,
Gormley-on-Ouse,
Burkeshire,
ENGLAND.
27th May 1984.

Dear Lesley,

I hope things are going all right with you in Florence. I can't help envying you when I think of you in that lovely city with that beautiful food!

Here, there was a tremendous thunderstorm last night. I was safe inside the house when it started – Dad had just dropped me off at the door – but Dad got caught in it because he'd taken the car round to put it in the garage and there's no shelter between there and home. He was so furious about it that he's finally going to write to the Council to ask for planning permission to build a proper garage in the garden. I'm not so keen because it will mean cutting down the old cherry tree to make way for the gate out into the avenue, and, after all, the rented garage is pretty cheap and quite near, but your Dad's set on it so.

That's really all for now. Dad's busy with his letter to the Council now so I won't ask him to add any lines to this.

Love from us both,

Mum
x

Part 2

Now read Dad's letter to the Council.

1 Look at points 1–4 in the letter. Dad is anticipating four possible arguments the Council might use against the garage. What are they?

2 Why do you think he adds point 5 about the neighbours?

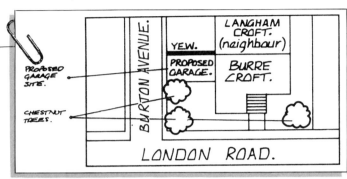

Burre Croft,
44 London Road,
Gormley-on-Ouse,
Burkeshire.
28 May 1984

The Planning Committee,
Gormley Urban District Council,
Gormley Town Hall,
Market Square,
Gormley-on-Ouse,
Burkeshire.

Dear Sir,

I am writing to make a formal application to the Urban District Planning Committee for planning permission to build a garage in the garden of my house, which stands on the corner of London Road and Burton Avenue.

The proposed garage, as you will see from the sketch map attached, would measure 15 feet by 11 feet, and would have direct access to Burton Avenue. It would be built in rustic brown brick to tone in with the bricks of the surrounding houses, and would in fact be largely hidden from public view by the large spreading chestnut tree in our garden. Since our neighbours have a thick yew hedge dividing their garden from ours, they would not be aware of its existence, and so would not be at all inconvenienced.

My reason for applying for this permission is that the only alternative garage accommodation available in this area is a five-minute walk away from my house, at the Haddon Park Garage Rentals, and the inconvenience of this is increased by the fact that I have no satisfactory parking place near the house, since as you know parking is prohibited on this stretch of the London Road and Burton Avenue is too narrow for any car to be parked there. I should add here that Burre Croft is the only house without a garage in the whole of Burton Avenue.

I should be most grateful if the Committee could give due consideration to the circumstances causing my application, as I believe they constitute a genuine case of hardship and need.

Yours faithfully,

J. Martin Sutcliffe

J. Martin Sutcliffe

Part 3

1 Before you read the reply from the Town Council Planning Committee, note down any possible objections you think the Council might have to the building of the garage.

2 Identify in the letter any language you would consider to be 'typically bureaucratic', giving reasons why you think so.

3 Why is this an unsatisfactory reply for Dad?
  a) Briefly express it in ordinary language, as if you were Dad telling the news to a friend.
  b) Sum up in one sentence the content/meaning of each paragraph of the Council's letter.

4 Finally, write a letter to (your daughter) Lesley in Italy, telling her about your two letters, the Council's reply, and your plans for future action.

Planning Committee,
Gormley Urban District Council,
Town Hall,
The Square,
Gormley-on-Ouse,
Burkeshire.

17 August 1984

J. Sutcliffe,
Burre Croft,
44 London Road,
Gormley-on-Ouse,
Burkeshire.

Dear Mr Sutcliffe,

Thank you for your letter of 28 May. Your application for planning permission to build a garage in the garden of your house, Burre Croft, on the corner of London Road and Burton Avenue, has been given due attention by the Council Planning Committee, after consultation with the Ouse National Park Planning Office, and it is with much regret that I have to pass on to you the news that in the circumstances the Committee is unable to grant you that permission.

Their decision is based on the customary interpretation of Sub-Section 2A of Clause 4 in Bye-Law No. 357, according to which a building of the type of your house, which was originally constructed as one dwelling but later converted into two, though it may, and in fact in your case undoubtedly still does, contain two entirely independent dwellings (that is, is to all intents and purposes a semi-detached house), is invariably considered, for planning purposes, as one building, with the consequent implication that it has rights to only one garage access, and since that single garage access already exists, albeit for the sole benefit of your neighbour, you therefore have no right to build another.

In addition, it was also felt by the Committee that your particular hardship case, that of having to garage your car in rented accommodation in Haddon Park, was not of sufficient gravity to merit the Committee making any fresh interpretation of Sub-Section 2A.

May I once again express my regret that this permission cannot under the circumstances be granted.

Yours sincerely,

Herbert Magehot

Herbert Magehot
Secretary
Gormley UDC Planning Committee

Formal protest

Activity 2

Listen to and then read the following telephone dialogue and list Steve's reasons for complaint to the airline concerned, to be used in a letter.

Steve	Hello. . . .hello. . . .hellooo. . .
Val	Hello, Valerie Sutton here.
Steve	Val, it's Steve, Steve Kemble here.
Val	Steve! We were worried about you. Where are you?
Steve	That's just it. I'm here at the railway station. Just arrived.
Val	At the station? I thought you were coming by plane!
Steve	I was, but I. . .it's a long story. They simply cancelled the flight, last night, with no warning at all.
Val	Honestly, that's the limit. Just left you there standing?
Steve	Well, I got to Frankfurt all right, and then I should have changed to another flight, which goes Stockholm–Frankfurt–Rome, and at the check-in desk there was this infuriating man who just looked at my ticket and smiled and said, 'Sorry sir, but that flight won't be running till Thursday.' And I said, 'What?' and he said, 'Sorry, but the Rome flight has been cancelled', and I said, 'But I've got an important meeting in Rome tomorrow morning.' And he simply shrugged his shoulders!
Val	So what did you do then?
Steve	Well, I played the tough guy – actually, I really lost my temper – and thumped the desk and said, 'Well, what's your precious airline going to do about it, now you've landed me in this mess?' And he just said, 'There's nothing we can do about it. These are circumstances beyond our control.'
Val	Really, how can they? What a cheek!
Steve	So I said, 'Look here, my man, your airline sold me a ticket and that ticket guaranteed I would get to Rome this evening, and I am going to Rome tonight and your airline is going to arrange it.' And he had the nerve to say there were no more flights to Rome and even if there had been he wouldn't have been able to fix anything.
Val	I would have asked to see his boss or somebody above him.
Steve	Well, I did then, but of course it was late and he wasn't there.
Val	They're never around when you want them, are they?
Steve	So, to cut a long story short, I said, 'Night train then. There must be a through night train from Germany to Italy. First class on that, that's what I've got a right to, paid by your airline.' Then he paled a bit, and took out his little book of regulations, and at first he said, 'There's no reference to that here', so I got so furious that I grabbed it from him and there it was as clear as day. . .
Val	Fancy that!
Steve	So in the end he wrote me a voucher for the train –I practically had to write it for him, he was so obstructive, just downright stubborn about it, you know. I didn't get a sleeper, but you are entitled to a first-class seat. And here I am. But the first thing I'm going to do when I get home is to write to the airline about it.

Composition   Write Steve's letter of protest to the airline, Air Hawk.

132

Prescribed books: Plot and theme

Points to note

Tenses

In telling the story of a book, play or film or in making. critical comments on it, we use the Present Simple, not the Past Simple, as the main narrative tense. This is because a work of art, unlike a normal narrative, is considered permanent.

Consequently, the following combinations are likely to occur:

The novel **takes place** in 1814.

The narrator **explains** that before the story **begins**, the heroine's mother **died**.

At the beginning of the story, the heroine **does not realise** that at the end, she **will marry** her brother-in-law.

During this speech, which **appears** incoherent, Miss Bates **is** in fact **giving** us useful information about other characters; we learn that Frank **has been helping** her, and Mr Knightley **has given** her some apples.

Useful terms

	Book	Novel	Play	Film and TV
Author	author writer	novelist writer	playwright dramatist	scriptwriter author of screenplay
Divisions of the work	chapter page line	chapter scene dialogue	act scene speech line	episode (TV) scene shot (one picture)
Performance	read by readers	read by readers	acted on the stage by actors for audiences	shown on the screen to audiences; TV programmes watched by viewers

Definition

People in books, plays and films are called **characters** (*not* 'personages' which means 'important or distinguished people'). The main characters are the **hero** (e.g. Othello), the **heroine** (e.g. Desdemona), the **villain** (e.g. Iago). The others are **minor characters**.

The **plot** is what happens, the sequence of events; the **theme** is what the book or play is about – e.g. marriage, jealousy, etc.

Characters who lack individual personality are **types** (e.g. the tyrannical father, the clever servant, etc.); sometimes they are **personifications** of abstract qualities or vices (e.g. Molière's miser is the personification of avarice).

Symbols are the objects with a meaning in the book or play – the macaroons (sweets) Nora eats at the beginning of Ibsen's *The Doll's House* **symbolise** her situation as a child-wife.

Allegory is the use of characters in a story that has another significance – Orwell's *Animal Farm* is an allegory of the Russian Revolution.

Drama

In writing compositions on prescribed books it is necessary to distinguish between these two terms. **The plot** refers to the events in a novel or play, while **the theme** indicates what the book is about. All stories have a plot but it is not always easy to discover what the theme of a novel or play is unless the author states it in the title – *War and Peace*, *Crime and Punishment*, *Pride and Prejudice* – and some stories, especially those of adventure, may have no real theme at all.

At Proficiency level, you are more likely to be asked questions about the theme than simply required to tell the story. But it is impossible to discuss the themes convincingly without showing a knowledge of what happens. It is therefore useful to make a synopsis of the book as you read it for the first time so that when you answer questions during the year or reread the book in preparation for the examination, you can easily remember the order of events.

In dealing with a play, it is helpful to note the characters taking part in a scene and when they come on and go off the stage, as well as the events that take place. A synopsis for a scene from a play could well be like this one for the first scene of *Othello*.

Synopsis of *Othello*, Act 1, Scene 1.
Scene: Venice, a street. Time: night.
Characters: Iago, Roderigo; enter Brabantio, exit; exit Iago, re-enter Brabantio.

Iago, an ensign (junior officer) in the Venetian army, tells Roderigo, a foolish young gentleman, that he hates the commander, Othello, a moor (black man), because Othello has chosen Cassio as his lieutenant although Iago is more experienced. Roderigo, in love with Desdemona, Brabantio's daughter, is angry because he has given Iago money to try to win Desdemona's favour but now discovers that she has run away to marry Othello. Iago reassures him and tells him to wake Brabantio and tell him the news. Brabantio, shocked, calls his servants. Iago leaves Roderigo because he says he must not break openly with Othello yet. Brabantio discovers Desdemona has gone. He and Roderigo go in search of her and of Othello.

Activity I – pair work

The themes of most books can be expressed in abstract terms. From your knowledge of Shakespeare's most famous plays, *Hamlet, Othello, King Lear* and *Macbeth*, decide which of the groups of themes listed correspond to which play: a) ambition, the corruption of power, the force of evil;   b) envy, the destruction of love, jealousy;
c) revenge, betrayal, appearance and reality;
d) relationships between parents and children, ingratitude, man's place in the universe.

> KEY QUESTION
> Do you remember what happens in the opening scenes or chapters of the book you are reading? Briefly compare notes with your partner.

Sir Laurence Olivier as Othello

The relationship between plot and theme in
Othello

It is well known that Shakespeare borrowed his plots from other writers but it is important to add that the painstaking scholarship that has identified the sources of his plays serves mainly to demonstrate how great his dramatic genius was. What is incredible, once we compare the plays with the originals, is not what he borrowed but what he made out of the borrowings. At the same time, a study of the sources is of great value because it enables us to find out what his intentions were by concentrating on the changes he made; for the most part, they have to do with heightening the dramatic tension, but in some cases they indicate the true theme of the play.

Othello is based on a story by the Italian writer, Cinthio. The story covers the second half of Shakespeare's play, roughly equivalent to the last three acts. It mentions that Othello married Desdemona in spite of the opposition of her relations but does not introduce the characters of Iago, Emilia, his wife, and Cassio, his rival, until they reach Cyprus, where the action takes place. In Cinthio, Iago is in love with Desdemona. Incapable of understanding how she can go on preferring a black man to him, he imagines that she must be in love with Cassio; as in Shakespeare's version, he gets Cassio discredited and uses a handkerchief as the means of confirming the suspicions of his wife that he has already aroused in Othello's mind. Iago and Othello kill Desdemona together. Cassio, persuaded by Iago, who is afraid that Othello will give him away, accuses Othello of murder. He is arrested, but not convicted. Eventually, he is killed by Desdemona's relatives and Iago confesses his part in the affair when he is in prison for another crime.

The difference between Cinthio's story and Shakespeare's play are clear. In Cinthio, Iago's motive is lust for Desdemona, not envy and hatred of Othello; Emilia, in the original story, knows the whole plot, while in Shakespeare she is faithful to Desdemona and condemns her husband; the murder in Cinthio is quite different, with Iago acting as an accomplice. Above all, there is no sub-plot, involving Roderigo, and the first two acts of the play scarcely exist in Cinthio.

The theme of Cinthio's story is jealousy and the black general's gullibility, and some critics have assumed that these are the principal themes of the play. If that is the case, why did Shakespeare invent a complicated sub-plot between Iago and Roderigo? Why did he include the scenes of Othello and Desdemona justifying their marriage in front of the Venetian Senate, and the story of their courtship? Surely it was because on the one hand he wanted to demonstrate the implacable self-interested cleverness of Iago, who deceives everyone in the play, not just Othello; on the other, he meant us to feel Othello's essential dignity and nobility and Desdemona's love for him as a fact, so that later on in the play we know what is being destroyed, instead of simply assuming it. Cinthio's Othello is a man without dignity, not a tragic hero. Shakespeare's has magnificent qualities as a man and as a leader, though Shakespeare, even in the early scenes where Othello is most impressive, points to the roots of his later insecurity; he is a middle-aged soldier who knows little about women and cannot really understand himself why this beautiful, sophisticated young white girl has fallen in love with him.

If Shakespeare had simply dramatised Cinthio's story, the play would have been a melodrama, not a tragedy; indeed, the theme of jealousy, especially of jealous husbands, has traditionally been thought comic. But the main themes of Shakespeare's play are different -- the destruction of love by envy and implacable malice – and that is why it is so unbearable in its tension because we echo Othello's words: 'The pity of it, the pity of it', and, when he says this to Iago, cannot rise out of our seats to tell him what we know about Iago and he does not.

Activity 2 – pair work

Having read this article, point to the differences a) in plot and b) in theme between Cinthio's *Othello* and Shakespeare's. Why did Shakespeare make these changes, in the writer's opinion?

KEY QUESTION
What do you consider to be the main themes of the book you are reading? What events in the plot make them clear?

The novel

It is more difficult to summarise the content of a chapter of a novel in the form of a synopsis than it is a scene of a play, and the themes of a novel are not always immediately apparent on first reading. Nevertheless, a synopsis is even more important because of the number of events that take place. Apart from the events, you should also note the introduction of new characters and pay attention to comments the author makes about characters, comments the

characters themselves make that indicate their personality, and comments they make that illustrate the relationships between them.

Before attempting the activities on the next page, which should help you to recognise the relevant points to note in any novel you are reading, study the synopsis below in order to become familiar with the book used as an example here and in the following units, *Emma*, by Jane Austen.

Emma: An outline of the plot

Emma Woodhouse, a wealthy young lady of 20, lives with her father, a widower, in an English village, Highbury. The date is 1814. Emma has been brought up largely by her governess, Miss Taylor, who has just married a neighbour, also a widower, Mr Weston. Mr Weston has a son by his first marriage, Frank, who has been adopted by his rich uncle in Yorkshire and has taken the family name of Churchill. Emma's elder sister, Isabella, is married to a London lawyer, John Knightley, and his elder brother, Mr Knightley, a man of 37, and a bachelor, is the neighbouring landowner. Emma's social position and pride in her ability to understand people lead her to attempt to arrange marriages between her acquaintances against Mr Knightley's advice. First, she befriends an orphan, Harriet Smith, and discourages her friendship with a farmer, Robert Martin, one of Mr Knightley's tenants, because she hopes to marry her to the clergyman, Mr Elton. Elton believes Emma is interested in him herself. When Frank Churchill arrives, Emma imagines a romance between them, and also supposes that Jane Fairfax, an orphan and the niece of a neighbour, Miss Bates, has a liaison with a married man in Ireland. In fact, Frank and Jane are secretly engaged, but he dares not announce it for fear of offending his all-powerful aunt and losing his inheritance. Eventually, Mrs Churchill dies, and the mystery is resolved. Emma, already sorry for her behaviour on an outing, when she was rude to Miss Bates and Mr Knightley was angry with her, understands that in flirting with Frank and believing the worst of Jane she has caused pain and could have destroyed their relationship. When Harriet tells her that she loves Mr Knightley, Emma understands how dangerous it is to interfere in people's lives; her comprehension of what she has done leads to her discovering her own feelings for Mr Knightley, who is in love with her but hesitated to tell her because of the difference in age between them.

The following brief synopsis of the first chapter is an example of the kind of synopsis you should make yourself.

Emma's strengths and weaknesses are described. Her governess, Miss Taylor, has just married a widower, Mr Weston, and Emma must now get used to living alone with her father, a timorous old man who exaggerates all difficulties. Mr Knightley calls on them and they talk about the Westons' wedding. Emma claims credit for bringing the couple together, and plans to find a bride for the clergyman, Mr Elton. Mr Knightley tells her she really had little to do with the Westons' marriage and warns her against meddling in other people's affairs – 'leave him (Mr Elton) to choose his own wife.'

The extract below is taken from the first chapter of
Emma.

1 Mr Knightley, a sensible man about seven or eight-and-thirty, was not only a very old and intimate friend of the family, but particularly connected with it as the elder brother of Isabella's husband. He lived about a mile from Highbury, was a frequent visitor and always welcome, and at this time more welcome than usual, as coming directly from their mutual connections in London. He had returned to a late dinner after some days absence, and now walked up to Hartfield to say that all were well in Brunswick square. 2 It was a happy circumstance and animated Mr Woodhouse for some time. Mr Knightley had a cheerful manner which always did him good; and his many inquiries after 'poor Isabella' and her children were answered most satisfactorily. When this was over, Mr Woodhouse gratefully observed,

'It is very kind of you, Mr Knightley, to come out 3 at this late hour to call upon us. I am afraid you must have had a shocking walk.'

'Not at all, sir. It is a beautiful, moonlight night; and so mild that I must draw back from your great fire.'

'But you must have found it very damp and dirty. I wish you may not catch cold.'

'Dirty, sir! Look at my shoes. Not a speck on them.'

'Well! that is quite surprising for we have had a 4 vast deal of rain here. It rained dreadfully hard for half an hour, while we were at breakfast. I wanted them to put off the wedding.'

'By the bye – I have not wished you joy. Being pretty well aware of what sort of joy you must both be feeling, I have been in no hurry with my congratulations. But I hope it all went off tolerably well. 5 How did you all behave? Who cried most?'

'Ah! poor Miss Taylor! 'tis a sad business.'

'Poor Mr and Miss Woodhouse, if you please; but I cannot possibly say 'poor Miss Taylor.' I have a great regard for you and Emma; but when it comes to the question of dependence or independence! At 6 any rate, it must be better to have only one to please, than two.'

'Especially when *one* of those two is such a fanciful, troublesome creature!' said Emma playfully. That, is what you have in your head, I know – and what you would certainly say if my father were not by.'

'I believe it is very true, my dear, indeed,' said Mr Woodhouse with a sigh. 'I am afraid I am sometimes very fanciful and troublesome.'

'My dearest papa! You do not think I could mean 7 *you*, or suppose Mr Knightley to mean *you*. What a horrible idea! Oh, no! I meant only myself. Mr 8 Knightley loves to find fault with me you know – in a joke – it is all a joke. We always say what we like to one another.'

Mr Knightley, in fact, was one of the few people 9 who could see faults in Emma Woodhouse, and the only one who ever told her of them: and though this was not particularly agreeable to Emma herself, she knew it would be so much less so to her father, that she would not have him really suspect such a circumstance as her not being thought perfect by everybody.

J. Austen

Activity 3 – pair work

Which of the ringed comments show us the authoress's opinion of her characters? In which of them do characters show their own personality? Which illustrate the relationships between them? What do we learn about the three characters as a result?

KEY QUESTION
In the book you are reading, does the author inform the reader about the characters by direct comment, by means of dialogue or by means of characters' personal confessions?

Composition: Theme

'*Emma*, like the rest of Jane Austen's novels, is concerned with the proper preparation of a young woman for marriage.' Do you agree?

In planning an essay of this kind on the theme of a book, it is assumed that you would have made a synopsis and so be able to base your answer on your knowledge of the plot and characters. In *Emma*, Mr and Mrs John Knightley are already married when the novel begins, Mr and Mrs Weston marry in the first chapter, and four subsequent marriages take place: Mr and Mrs Elton (Ch. 22), Emma and Mr Knightley, Frank Churchill and Jane Fairfax, Harriet Smith and Robert Martin (at the end). The main point of an answer here depends on the suitability of the eventual marriages made and the alternative combinations for the characters suggested in the course of the novel. It is assumed that you would have notes from a synopsis with a few relevant quotations to work on, as below. Note that it is useless to try to remember long quotations, but short phrases that you can remember easily may be of value in your essay. The numbers refer to chapters of the book.

Mr Elton Emma discourages Harriet's relationship with Robert Martin, and tries to interest Elton in her (4). Elton assumes she is interested in him herself. Both feel insulted when they discover the truth (15). Elton marries a rich, vulgar woman from the city for her money (22). Mr Knightley: 'Elton may talk sentimentally, but he will act rationally' (8).

Jane Fairfax Emma supposes Jane fell in love with Mr Dixon at Weymouth (19); Mrs Weston believes Knightley cares for her (26). Frank Churchill pretends to find her dull (24), but is really keeping his engagement to her secret. He buys her a piano, causing everyone to think that it is a present from Mr Dixon or Mr Knightley (26), and flirts with Emma at Box Hill (43). The engagement revealed (46).
Frank: 'One cannot love a reserved person' (24).
Mrs Weston: 'She has always been a first favourite with him' (Mr Knightley) (26).
Mr Knightley: 'She has not the open temper that a man would wish for in a wife' (33).

Harriet Smith Mr Knightley dances with her when Mr Elton will not ask her (38) and Frank rescues her from the gypsies (39). Harriet is very grateful to 'him' (40). Emma thinks she means Frank but discovers she means Mr Knightley (47), and then realises she is in love with Mr Knightley herself. 'It darted through her with the speed of an arrow that Mr Knightley must marry no one but herself.' (47)

Emma Attracted to Frank before meeting him (14). The Westons favour the match (29). Frank about to confess to her, but she thinks his confession is his love for her (30). Believes she is in love (31) and he loves her (37) but unwilling that relationship should go further. Admires Mr Knightley at dance (38). Flirts with Frank at Box Hill and is reprimanded by Mr Knightley (43). Realises she loves Mr Knightley herself (47).

Mr and Mrs John Knightley
'The extreme sweetness of her temper must hurt his' (11).

'*Emma*' like the rest of Jane Austen's novels, is concerned with the proper preparation of a young woman for marriage.' Do you agree?

Plan: 1 Preparation for marriage for a woman in Emma's situation in effect preparation for life. Few alternatives available. (Jane Fairfax destined to be governess, if unmarried.)
   2 Examples of potential marriages – Harriet Smith and Mr Elton. Mr Elton's motives for marriage, Harriet's eventual marriage.
   3 'Good marriages' – comparison of Mr and Mrs John Knightley, Frank and Jane, Emma and Mr Knightley.
   4 Importance of maturity for happy marriage – preparation for life.

It is not surprising that marriage should be the principal theme in a novel about a young woman in a small village in the early nineteenth century. Beneath the brilliant surface of social comedy in *Emma* lies the assumption that marriage was almost the only career an educated woman could follow, and choice of the wrong partner would be fatal to her future happiness. For those with no money and little freedom of choice, like Jane Fairfax, the alternative might be the life of a governess, where she would be treated like a servant.

The novel offers several examples of marriages that take place and more of potential marriages Emma and other characters imagine. Emma herself is clearly unprepared for marriage at the beginning because her standards are false and her judgement of others immature. She discourages Harriet's attachment to Robert Martin for snobbish reasons but fails to see that Mr Elton is ambitious enough to aim at her, not Harriet. Mr Knightley is justified in his belief that Elton 'will act rationally', when Elton marries a vulgar woman for the worst of motives, money. Harriet is happier with a kind man of her own social class than she would have been with someone far more intelligent and better educated.

On the other hand, love is not in itself a sufficient motive, either, if the man behaves irresponsibly, like Frank Churchill. His secret engagement to Jane embarrasses her by raising Emma's suspicions of a relationship with a married man, and his anonymous gift of a piano seems to confirm them. His motive for secrecy is selfish, and he could have hurt Emma, too, by flirting with her if she had returned his apparent affection. It is evident, too, from Jane Austen's comments on John Knightley and Isabella that she thinks a wife should not be too dependent on her husband. She implies that Emma and Mr Knightley will be happier because there is mutual respect between them, as well as affection, and her youth and vivacity will complement his maturity and common sense.

It is clear that the importance of preparation for marriage is not a matter of upbringing – Emma has been spoilt but she can overcome that with the right partner – but of choosing the right moment as well as the right person. For this satisfactory ending to be reached, Emma must 'grow up'. It is not until she has realised that the series of errors she has made could have interfered with others' happiness and until the thought of Harriet marrying Mr Knightley makes her aware of her own feelings that she is ready for marriage. In this sense, the novel is certainly about 'the proper preparation of a young woman for marriage', but only if we understand this as growing up sufficiently to deal with life itself and become a sensitive, responsible human being, not merely to run a household.

Activity 4 – pair work

Trace the source for what is said in the essay in the synopsis and notes on the opposite page.

Prescribed books: Character

Character and plot

The relationship between characters and the plot in a novel or play can be looked at in two ways, depending on which affects the other. Characters affect the plot by their actions (what they do) but the plot is only convincing if the characters' actions seem appropriate to what we know of them (why they do it). On the other hand, the plot can affect characters by causing them to change or develop according to what happens. In such contexts, unlikely events, such as the sudden discovery of long-lost parents, popular in melodrama, are an unconvincing explanation of changes in character, and characters who change abruptly from good to evil or vice versa without sufficient explanation in the plot also fail to make us believe in them.

In considering these relationships, it is also important to take the minor characters into account, since their actions may influence the protagonists, or they may exist primarily to demonstrate the effect of the protagonists' behaviour. The examples given here are given to help you to look for similar features in the book you are reading.

The effect of character on plot (motivation)

Othello

Iago is almost entirely responsible for what happens in *Othello*. Yet the motives he himself offers the audience in soliloquy are not entirely convincing, and it is not clear he believes in them. He says he hates Othello because Cassio has been promoted above him; he shows his prejudice against Othello's race and colour; he pretends to believe Othello has slept with his wife, Emilia. But none of these is sufficient to justify his course of action. The most convincing explanation of Iago's behaviour is that he hates everything most human beings respect – love, honesty, loyalty – and is driven by his obsessive envy of others' happiness to destroy it, perhaps to prove to himself that virtue, as he says, does not exist.

Emma

The plot of *Emma* depends mainly on Emma's attempts to bring together people whom she thinks would be suited to one another, ignoring or misinterpreting any evidence she finds to the contrary. Whereas in a play, unless the author explains the characters' motives in stage directions (which are in any case not available to the audience in the theatre) we must deduce them entirely from what is said, in a novel the writer is free to explain them directly. Jane Austen makes it clear in the first chapter of *Emma* that Emma takes up matchmaking because she is spoilt and a little bored: 'The real evils of Emma's situation were the power of having rather too much her own way, and a disposition to think a little too well of herself.' . . . 'She was now in great danger of intellectual solitude. She dearly loved her father, but he was no companion for her.' Given the advantages of her social position and influence in such a small community, it is the sort of game we would expect a rich young girl of twenty to play.

> KEY QUESTION
> Do you consider the motivation of the characters in the book you are reading sufficiently convincing to justify their actions?

The effect of plot on character (transformation)

Othello

Critics who concentrate entirely on the written text of plays find it unbelievable that Iago can transform Othello from a loving husband into a man driven mad by jealousy in the course of one scene, even though it is one of the longest in Shakespeare. In the theatre, however, the scene is immensely effective. Iago begins his attack slowly, drawing Othello's attention to the interview between Desdemona and Cassio, who leaves her in a suspicious manner. His technique is to excite Othello's curiosity by incomplete statements as if he were reluctant to tell the whole truth. When he hints that Desdemona has secret motives in pleading for Cassio's reinstatement as Othello's lieutenant, he still avoids direct accusation.

Critics have remarked that Iago is a master of improvisation, rather than a careful planner, but it is also true to suggest that a man who despises human values senses that all men have weaknesses and it is enough to sow doubt in their minds for their basic insecurity to show itself. When it does, in Othello's case, Shakespeare indicates in a few lines why Othello is convinced. In a soliloquy that is vital to an understanding of Othello's character, he refers first to Iago's reliability and wide experience of the world, a view of him shared by the other characters; then to himself, as a black man and a rough soldier not used to flattering women; finally, to his age – he is no longer young, though not yet very old. It is at this point that he suddenly exclaims: 'She's gone. I am abused.' The transformation carries conviction not so much because of Iago's cunning, but because Shakespeare suggests that he could only succeed by exposing the insecurity already latent in Othello, and the reasons for this insecurity are plausible.

The effect of minor characters on the plot and on the main characters

Emma

In Dickens' novels minor characters often appear whose main purpose is simply to entertain, and a reader not familiar with Jane Austen's technique might imagine that the talkative spinster, Miss Bates, is of this type, too. Yet in the course of her apparently confused, delightfully amusing monologues she is the means of telling us a great deal of useful information about other characters, and this is natural, since she is the village gossip. She also unwittingly causes Emma to commit the social indiscretion that brings down Mr Knightley's anger on her head and makes her realise how she has been behaving.

The bored young people on a day out in the country have proposed a party game in which everyone must say either one very clever thing, two reasonably clever things or three dull things, and poor Miss Bates says that the last task will be easy enough for her. 'Emma could not resist. "Ah! ma'am, but there may be a difficulty. Pardon me – but you will be limited as to number – only three at once."' When Mr Knightley points out that this remark was unforgivable because Miss Bates is a harmless, middle-aged woman who cannot defend herself against the mockery of someone of Emma's age and social position, Emma is forced for the first time to examine her own conduct. Miss Bates is the means by which Emma ceases to be a spoilt child and grows up into a woman sensitive and responsible enough to become Knightley's wife.

KEY QUESTION
In the book you are reading, does any character change noticeably and is the change convincing in terms of the plot?

KEY QUESTION
What part do the minor characters play in influencing the course of action and affecting the development of the main characters?

Character and theme

Characters or types?

If the relationship between character and plot in a novel or play is largely a matter of what characters do and why, and how far the action affects them, that of character and theme is mainly determined by the degree to which they are representative or typical – what do they stand for?

At one extreme, characters may be no more than types. Melodrama expresses this idea in its simplest form – the heroes are heroic, the heroines innocent and the villains devils. The minor characters are also stereotypes: fathers tend to be tyrants or weak failures, mothers long-suffering housekeepers or dominant women. At the other extreme, characters may be so unusually presented that they can stand for nothing but themselves, in which case they are likely to appear grotesque. Dickens, whose work is closely allied to melodrama, offers both extremes in his novels; on the whole, his grotesques are preferred to his types because his enormous imaginative vitality makes them so entertaining.

It is sometimes said that Shakespearean heroes represent certain values and even that they personify abstract characteristics, such as jealousy (Othello), ambition (Macbeth) or lack of resolution (Hamlet). Nevertheless, while satirical dramatists since Aristophanes have frequently given characters type names, in comedy they indicate the vices the dramatist is satirising, and novelists in the eighteenth century did much the same thing, characters demanding our emotional involvement in their fate, such as tragic heroes, require a personality of their own. The same is true of the main characters in novels that aim at realism.

Consequently, what makes Othello a great character on the stage is not that he is jealous, or black, or middle-aged, or a general, or that he is meant to personify any of these things, but that he is a combination of all these characteristics. It is this combination in the situation in which he finds himself that makes him believable, since his actions are appropriate to it. If Shakespeare had created him as the personification of jealousy, there would have been no need to make him a general, for example, since generals are not necessarily jealous, any more than they are necessarily black.

Emma is a similarly complex creation. She is typical of young ladies of her time in being interested in marriage and fond of having her own way, but Jane Austen herself was aware of the individuality of the character she had created when she said she was a heroine 'whom no one will like but myself'. She gave Emma untypical wit and liveliness in a situation where neither can be displayed to the full. It is this combination of untypical qualities and weaknesses in a typical situation of the time that makes her an interesting character, not a type.

Frank Finlay as Iago

The interrelation of characters

Parallels

Othello

Many plays and novels possess a sub-plot involving secondary characters whose actions parallel or contrast with those of the hero or heroine. In *Othello*, Shakespeare invented a sub-plot of his own, using a new character, Roderigo, as Iago's victim. Roderigo takes some part in the action; he stirs up Brabantio against Othello in the first scene and later provokes Cassio into the duel that brings about his dismissal. But these incidents were suggested in the original story and do not justify his inclusion. Clearly, his situation is parallel to Othello's; both are tricked by Iago and deceived about Desdemona's character against their better judgement. Yet Roderigo and Othello are not in the least alike, and in focussing on Roderigo in the first scene of the play, always an important guide to his

intentions, Shakespeare is doing more than giving us a foretaste of what will happen to Othello later. Elsewhere, in *Richard III*, he allows the villain to speak to the audience alone and build up a kind of ironic sympathy; here, he uses Roderigo to prevent us from sympathising with Iago, and to show us his mean-minded love of money and cynicism about human values as well as his cleverness. With only Iago's conversation with Roderigo to guide us, we would expect Othello to be very different from the magnificent, self-confident figure who first appears on the stage. So Roderigo is not only a parallel to Othello, but also a contrast, and while Iago's deception of Roderigo, a foolish young man, is comic, his destruction of the noble Moor is a tragedy.

Contrasts

Emma

Emma is full of neatly contrasted couples and potential candidates for marriage. Emma herself, vivacious and witty, contrasts directly with the heroine of the sub-plot, Jane Fairfax, who is quiet and serious. Mr Knightley's maturity and common sense contrast with Frank Churchill's youth and irresponsibility. When Knightley marries Emma and Frank marries Jane, it is suggested that the good qualities of one partner will compensate for the other's limitations. But even in subtler details, Jane Austen provides contrasts that explain why Knightley and Emma will eventually make a good match. Isabella, Emma's elder sister, and John Knightley, Knightley's younger brother, are already

married when the novel beings. They live in London, away from Mr Woodhouse, Emma's timorous father. In one delightful scene, when John Knightley begins to show his impatience with the old man, and Isabella, who is like her father, can do nothing, Mr Knightley skilfully changes the conversation to avoid a family quarrel. At the end of the novel, when Emma feels she cannot abandon her father and Knightley agrees to share the house with him so that they can get married, we realise that he will be capable of managing the old man without upsetting his wife while his brother would have been driven mad by the situation.

Jane Austen

KEY QUESTION
In the book you are reading in what ways are minor characters used as parallels or contrasts to the main characters? Do these parallels or contrasts help you to understand the theme?

143

Composition: Character

'Othello stands out as the archetypal figure of jealousy in literature.' Do you think this is a just assessment of Othello's character and his part in the play?

In planning an essay of this kind, it is assumed that you would have made a synopsis and so be able to base your answer on your knowledge of the plot and characters, using notes and a few relevant quotations, as below.

Othello's actions

I ii First appears, contradicting impression given by Iago and Roderigo in opening scene. Brave, self-confident.

I iii Defends his marriage to Desdemona in the Senate. An outsider, open and direct, admired by everyone.

II iii In Cyprus, with firm authority dismisses Cassio for drunkenness.

III iii (Temptation scene) Refuses Desdemona's pleas for Cassio at first, so as not to show favouritism. Iago sows suspicions in his mind. Emilia finds Desdemona's handkerchief and Iago takes it. Iago claims proof of Desdemona's infidelity. Othello thinks of Iago's honest reputation, his own ignorance of women, his colour and age. He is convinced and resolves on revenge.

III iv Othello asks Desdemona for the handkerchief, saying it has magic powers. She says that she has lost it and that he is making excuses to prevent her pleading for Cassio. Othello is enraged.

IV i He has an epileptic fit. Iago has dropped the handkerchief in Cassio's lodgings, and he has given it to his mistress, Bianca, to copy. Othello sees Iago talking to Cassio, but cannot hear them; believes they are joking about Desdemona, not Bianca. Sees Bianca give back the handkerchief to Cassio. Hits Desdemona in front of the Venetian ambassadors. Tells Iago he will kill her, and Iago promises to arrange Cassio's death.

IV ii Questions Emilia and accuses Desdemona, who denies guilt.

V i Sees Cassio wounded, and thinks he is dead.

V ii Kills Desdemona, intending it as just execution. Emilia accuses him and later discovers truth and reveals it. Iago kills her. Othello tries to kill Iago, fails, and after explaining his actions, kills himself.

References to jealousy and to Othello's character

I iii	BRABANTIO:	She has deceived her father, and may thee (you).
I iii	OTHELLO:	She loved me for the dangers I had passed,
		And I loved her that she did pity them.
II i	IAGO:	The Moor . . . is of a constant, loving, noble nature.
III iv	EMILIA:	Is not this man jealous?
	DESDEMONA:	I never gave him cause.
IV i	EMILIA:	But jealous souls will not be answered so;
		They are not ever jealous for the cause,
		But jealous for they're jealous.

V ii   LODOVICO: Is this the noble Moor whom our full Senate
                             Call all in all sufficient? Is this the nature
                             Whom passion could not shake?
         OTHELLO: That's he that was Othello. Here I am.
V ii   OTHELLO: Then must you speak
                             Of one that loved not wisely, but too well;
                             Of one not easily jealous, but being wrought,[1]
                             Perplexed in the extreme.[2]

1   being worked up into a passion
2   totally bewildered

'Othello stands out as the archetypal figure of jealousy in literature.' Do you think this is a just assessment of Othello's character and his part in the play?

Plan: 1   The meaning of jealousy. Emilia's definition.
        2   How far is it reasonable for Othello to accept Iago's proofs?
        3   Othello before the temptation scene. Transformation worked by Iago.
        4   Othello's self-justification. Is it acceptable?

It is clear that Othello shows all the signs of a jealous man in the play once Iago has sown the seeds of doubt in his mind, but if he were to be considered an 'archetypal figure of jealousy' he would need to fit Emilia's definition when Desdemona says she never gave him cause for jealousy – 'jealous souls will not be answered so: They are . . . jealous because they're jealous.' Othello's own defence of his actions in his final soliloquy hangs on whether we can accept that he had sufficient cause. Even then, this does not necessarily mean that jealousy is the theme of the play and that he exists to personify it.

Shakespeare uses a number of circumstances that favour Iago in order to make Othello's behaviour more convincing – Cassio leaves the stage hurriedly at the beginning of the temptation scene; Emilia finds the handkerchief and Iago deceives Othello into thinking that Desdemona has given it to Cassio; at the crucial moment when Othello asks for it, she makes a fatally ambiguous reference to Cassio's reinstatement, and a similar ambiguous remark in front of the Venetian ambassadors causes him to strike her. But Shakespeare also concentrates our attention on Othello's insecurity. It is at the moment when he ruminates on Iago's 'honesty', on his own roughness and inexperience with women, his colour, and above all, his age, that he first convinces himself that Desdemona is unfaithful.

The first half of the play, which Shakespeare invented, does not stress Othello's potential jealousy but his qualities, which carry in them his fatal weakness. He is 'of a constant, loving, noble nature'. He is superbly self-confident in the face of danger, as befitting a soldier, and loving in his simplicity and directness when he defends his marriage in front of the Senate. But this defence, while it explains his love for Desdemona, is so simple that it suggests he does not understand her love for him:
       She loved me for the dangers I had passed,
       And I loved her that she did pity them.

Othello is an outsider in the sophisticated world of Venice, and is unaccustomed to women. It is significant that when he believes she is unfaithful, he considers that Desdemona's making him a cuckold will end his military career. Iago has not only filled him with jealousy but has destroyed his self-confidence. When he eventually realises he has committed a murder, instead of the execution he had intended, he answers Lodovico by saying:

> That's he that *was* Othello. Here I am.

He understands the transformation that has taken place.

Shakespeare gave Othello a final speech of self-justification in which he argues that he was

> One that loved not wisely, but too well.

He means that his love for Desdemona was so great that he could not bear to see it made dirty and meaningless. He claims that he was 'not easily jealous', that he was unsuspicious until Iago began to work on him. Othello's tragedy is not that of the naturally jealous man but of the outsider, magnificent in his familiar soldier's world, but insecure in a society where his straightforwardness and lack of experience with women make him vulnerable to Iago's malice.

Activity – pair work

Study the construction of this essay to see: a) the use of the synopsis;   b) the use of quotation;   c) references to the plot;   d) the writer's personal opinion.

Frank Finlay and Sir Laurence Olivier in *Othello*

Prescribed books: Narrative technique

Structure of the novel

A novel can be long or short; it can contain anything from a handful of characters to a hundred. The action can last a few hours and be confined to a single house, or cover a period of years and be extended to many countries. Despite these variations, novels have a structure depending on the narrative technique, and you can understand this structure more easily if you imagine it visually.

Linear structure

The simplest narrative structure is linear. A story based on a journey and concentrating on a single character or group, one of whom may be the narrator, begins and ends with the journey itself. All the events take place in relation to the travellers, and other characters meet them briefly and disappear, or accompany them for a time, so that the structure looks like this:

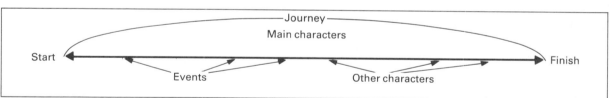

Examples: Homer, *The Odyssey*; Defoe, *Robinson Crusoe*; many folk tales, and modern stories of escapes from prison, etc.

A similar construction is applicable to novels in autobiographical form or those that tell the story of one person's life. As we follow the main character's experiences, the incidents that occur and characters introduced are important only in so far as they relate to him or her.

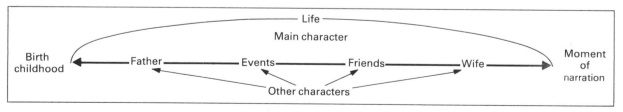

Examples: Dickens, *David Copperfield*, and similar autobiographical or biographical books.

Family structure

Many novels are constructed around a family tree or family rivalries and the relationships between them over a number of generations. An interesting example is Emily Brontë's *Wuthering Heights*.

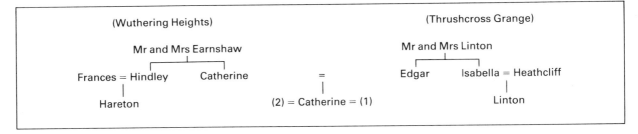

The story concerns the love between Heathcliff, adopted by Mr Earnshaw, and his love for Catherine before and after her marriage with Edgar. After her death he gains control of both houses by gambling with Hindley and marrying his son, Linton, to Catherine's daughter. Eventually, after his death and Linton's, Catherine marries Hareton. The neatness of the plot is emphasised by this equation:

Catherine Earnshaw wanted to be Catherine Heathcliff but became Catherine Linton. Catherine Linton was forced to become Catherine Heathcliff but eventually became Catherine Earnshaw.

Activity I – pair work

Work out how the equation happened from the family tree.

> KEY QUESTION:
> What advantages and disadvantages can you see in the forms of narration indicated above in terms of ease of storytelling, and development of characters?

Community structure

Novels concerned with presenting society depend normally on the interrelationships between characters in a community. In such novels the social position of the characters is often important in determining the degree of influence they have on others and this position is usually defined according to the norms of the period. Jane Austen liked to work with 'three or four families in a country village'; other novelists have attempted a much more ambitious panorama, e.g. the life of a town (George Eliot, *Middlemarch*) or of a country (Tolstoy, *War and Peace*).

At the beginning of *Emma*, the relationships between the families in the village of Highbury look like this:

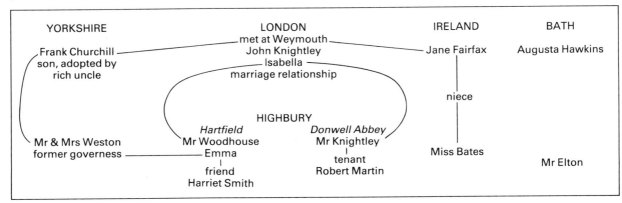

148

In the course of the novel, a number of possible marriages are discussed and at the end of the novel a number take place. The first are marked . . . . the second ────────.

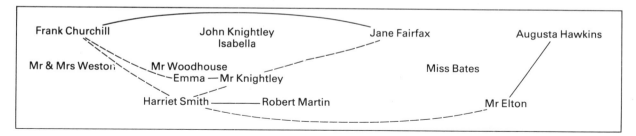

Jane Austen's skill in construction is shown in the way in which she prevents us from drawing the shortest, most logical lines between Emma and Mr Knightley and Harriet and Robert Martin until the end of the book by interesting us in a wide variety of alternative links.

> KEY QUESTION
> What advantages and disadvantages can you see in this form of narrative structure in terms of ease of organisation, and the degree to which such a picture may be representative of society as a whole? Why is a more representative structure, in a town or city, likely to be more difficult to construct? Why is it more likely to be difficult to construct now than 150 years ago?

Point of view in narrative

First-person narrative

We may not recognise the structure of a novel until we have finished reading it but we are influenced by the narrator's point of view from the start. In some novels the story is told in the first person, either as pseudo-autobiography by the hero (*Robinson Crusoe*), or by a witness who is in a privileged position to interpret the main characters' actions (*The Great Gatsby*). Joseph Conrad, in *Heart of Darkness*, tells most of the story in the first person as Marlow, but the real narrator is an anonymous 'I' listening to it.

1 I was born in the year 1632, in the city of York, of a good family, though not of that country, my father being a foreigner of Bremen, who settled first at Hull. (Daniel Defoe, *Robinson Crusoe*)

2 Only Gatsby, the man who gives his name to this book, was exempt from my reaction – Gatsby, who represented everything for which I have an unaffected scorn. (F. Scott Fitzgerald, *The Great Gatsby*)

3 . . . it was only after a long silence, when he said, in a hesitating voice, 'I suppose you fellows remember I did once turn fresh-water sailor for a bit,' that we knew we were fated . . . to hear about one of Marlow's inconclusive experiences. (Joseph Conrad, *Heart of Darkness*)

Even when the story is told in the third person, the novelist may intervene in his own voice. In Victorian novels, which were often first published in serial form in magazines, novelists often address the reader personally.

1 Dead, Your Majesty. Dead, my lords and gentlemen. Dead, Right Reverends and Wrong Reverends of every order. Dead, men and women, born with heavenly compassion in your hearts. And dying thus around us every day. (Charles Dickens, *Bleak House*)

2 Picture to yourself, O fair young reader, a worldly, selfish, graceless, thankless, religionless old woman, writhing in pain and fear, and without her wig. Picture her to yourself, and ere you be old, learn to love and pray. (William Makepeace Thackeray, *Vanity Fair*)

3 We must now take leave of Mr Slope, and of the bishop also, and of Mrs Proudie. These leavetakings in novels are as disagreeable as they are in real life . . . What novelist can impart an interest to the last chapter of his fictitious history? (Anthony Trollope, *Barchester Towers*)

4 It may be possible to do without dancing entirely. Instances have been known of young people passing many, many months successively, without being at any ball of any description, and no material injury accrue either to body or mind . . . (Jane Austen, *Emma*)

Activity 2 – pair work

What tone of voice does the novelist adopt towards the reader in these examples? Do you find it irritating to be addressed in this way? If so, do you find some examples more objectionable than others?

Third-person narrative

In a first-person narrative, the storyteller has the advantage of appearing to be genuine (the reason why this technique was adopted by Defoe in *Robinson Crusoe* at a time when many readers still distrusted 'fiction') and of describing events with a precise knowledge of what happened and how he felt. This gives immediacy and credibility to the narrative. The disadvantage is that the novelist-narrator can only guess or record the feelings of others and must continually find ways of explaining how he heard of events when he was not present.

In a third-person narrative, the novelist can claim to understand the thought processes of any or all of his characters, but this also carries risks. In the first place, if he attempts to focus our attention on too many characters we may lose interest in the main protagonists and in the thread of the story as a whole. Secondly, novelists' own experience of life may not be sufficient for them to deal convincingly *from the inside* with the minds of people of the opposite sex or from a different social class.

Jane Austen provides an excellent example in *Emma* of how these problems can be satisfactorily resolved. Emma is a character with defects that are overcome in the course of the novel. If the story were told in the first person by Emma herself, she would do so from the mature perspective of the end of the novel and would be forced to condemn and apologise for all her errors, losing the vivacity and wit that attract the reader to her. If Mr Knightley, for example, told the story as an observer, he would bore us by saying how right he was all the time when Emma was mistaken. Jane Austen allows us to follow the story through Emma's eyes but with Mr Knightley's more mature standards constantly intervening to guide us. By focussing on Emma, she is also able to conceal from us the secret engagement between Frank Churchill and Jane Fairfax, which she herself, as all-seeing novelist, is obviously aware of from the start, so that we share Emma's sense of mystery and surprise.

Jane Austen was unmarried and knew her limitations in terms of personal experience, though she did not live such a retired life as some critics have supposed. Unlike many novelists, however, she never got out of her depth. She never attempted a detailed examination of a man's mind from the inside. In fact, although we are not conscious of it, there is no conversation in *Emma* where a woman is not present! People from social classes other than her own are mentioned but she confined her study of the manners of society to the class she belonged to. This helps to explain why, although *Emma* may be limited in scope and theme, it could be said to the most perfect novel in the English language.

KEY QUESTIONS

Is the narrative you are reading written in the first or third person? If first person, is the narrator one of the main characters? Does the novelist account for events convincingly? How does the narrator hear about them if he/she is not present? If third person, does the novelist intervene? Does he/she attempt to focus on the thoughts of more than one character? Is this successful in all cases?

Arousing interest

There are many ways of arousing our interest in a novel, as the examples of opening sentences from a number of well-known novels printed on this page indicate. The most straightforward are references to time, to place or to a character.

1   On the 1st of September, in the memorable year 1832, someone was expected at Transome Court.   (George Eliot, *Felix Holt*)
2   At the little town of Vevey, in Switzerland, there is a particularly comfortable hotel.   (Henry James, *Daisy Miller*)
3   No one who had ever seen Catherine Morland in her infancy would have supposed her born to be a heroine.   (Jane Austen, *Northanger Abbey*)

In order to excite our curiosity the author may vary these conventional beginnings by creating atmosphere through physical description or through suggesting from the first moment the idea of mystery.

Parlour in Chawton Cottage showing Jane Austen's desk

4   Fog everywhere. Fog up the river, where it flows among green aits and meadows; fog down the river, where it rolls defiled among the tiers of shipping, and the waterside pollutions of a great (and dirty) city. (Charles Dickens, *Bleak House*)
5   When a day that you happen to know is Wednesday starts off by sounding like Sunday, there is something seriously wrong somewhere.   (John Wyndham, *The Day of the Triffids*)

In all these cases we expect to learn something of the subject of the book or at least to get an idea from the tone of the opening sentence, paragraph or chapter what it is like and how the theme is to be treated. Jane Austen's openings are apparently straightforward, though often ironic, like the one quoted above. She begins *Emma* like this.

Emma Woodhouse, handsome, clever, and rich, with a comfortable home and happy disposition, seemed to unite some of the best blessings of existence; and had lived nearly 21 years in the world with very little to disturb or vex her.

Apart from giving us a lot of information about Emma in an economical way, what is intriguing about this opening sentence is the use of 'seemed', suggesting that Emma should have been contented but probably is not, and the impression given to us by the final phrase that Emma may have been spoilt from having had such an easy existence; in order to grow up and mature (the theme of the novel) she will have to be disturbed. For all these reasons, we are encouraged to read on to find out more about her.

Activity 3 – pair work

What would you imagine the theme of the novels quoted above to be? What do you imagine comes next? How does the beginning encourage us to read on? What do we expect to find out? (Suggested answers are given at the back of the book, but discuss your reactions with your partner first.)

> KEY QUESTIONS
> How does the author of the book you are reading arouse your interest?   Does he/she use any special techniques, like those indicated above?

Maintaining interest

Just as there are many ways of arousing our interest in a story, there are many ways of maintaining it. The most obvious possibilities are to introduce a number of exciting events, strategically placed in the novel to create a series leading up to a climax, and to introduce interesting minor characters or make them reappear from time to time; in many novels such characters may hold our interest by their conversation or behaviour alone, though they should really advance the plot in some way at the same time.

Chapter endings are often a sign of the author's technique. Just as we feel satisfaction if the end of a novel seems appropriate and therefore convincing, a good chapter ending concludes one part of the story but leaves us anxious to find out what happened as a result. In Victorian novels like Thackeray's *Vanity Fair*, published in monthly instalments, it was vital for the novelist to end each episode in this way so that readers would buy the next.

(Sir Pitt Crawley, a rich landowner, has just proposed to Rebecca Sharp, an adventuress interested in marrying for money.)

Rebecca started back, a picture of consternation. In the course of this history we have never seen her lose her presence of mind; but she did now, and wept some of the most genuine tears that ever fell from her eyes.

'O Sir Pitt!' she said. 'O Sir – I – I'm *married already.*'

The point of this is that Thackeray has not told us about it, so we share Sir Pitt's surprise, and would have bought the next episode to find out who she had married.

This is an example of 'withholding information', similar to Jane Austen's technique in *Emma* of concealing Frank Churchill's engagement to Jane Fairfax from Emma and so from the reader. We share Emma's interest in what seems to be curious behaviour and are as eager to solve the mystery as she is.

Novels concentrating on a single character and covering a considerable period of time tend to bore us unless the character has many difficulties to overcome or shows some sign of development. Completely virtuous heroes and heroines tend to be dull, and supermen whose appearance in an adventure story guarantees easy victory are far less interesting than

heroes struggling against the elements, even though we are sure they will be successful in the end. Emma holds our interest largely because she is capable of development. Compare her reaction to her first serious error (that Mr Elton is in love with Harriet Smith) to her recognition that she has been unpardonably rude to Miss Bates at Box Hill.

1   . . . she went to bed at last with nothing settled but the conviction of her having blundered most dreadfully.

To youth and natural cheerfulness like Emma's, though under temporary gloom at night, the return of day will hardly fail to bring return of spirits . . . Emma got up on the morrow more disposed for comfort than she had gone to bed.

2   Time did not compose her. As she reflected more, she seemed but to feel it more. She never had been so depressed . . . Emma felt the tears running down her cheeks almost all the way home, without being at any trouble to check them, extraordinary as they were.

Activity 4 – pair work

In what way do these passages indicate a development in Emma's character, showing her transformation in the course of the novel?

> KEY QUESTION
> Which of the devices mentioned above does the author of the book you are reading employ in order to maintain the reader's interest?

Composition: Narrative technique

How does Jane Austen arouse our interest in Emma and maintain it throughout the novel?

As we have seen on the previous two pages, Jane Austen uses many of the techniques outlined there. From a synopsis of the novel and a few relevant quotations marked, it is possible to build up a table noting the introduction of the main characters, the first references to them, and the principal events, particularly those that affect Emma's character and behaviour and bring about her gradual transformation.

Chapter	Characters		Events
	Introduced	First referred to	
1	Emma, Mr Woodhouse, Mr Knightley	John Knightley, Isabella, the Westons, Mr Elton	Novelist describes Emma.
2	The Westons	Frank, Miss Bates	
3	Harriet Smith		
4		Robert Martin	Emma discourages Harriet.
5			Mr Knightley's view of Emma.
6	Mr Elton		
7			Harriet refuses Robert Martin.
8			Mr Knightley's reaction.
10		Jane Fairfax	
11	John Knightley, Isabella		
15			Emma discovers Mr Elton's aims.
17			Mr Knightley's view of Frank.
19	Miss Bates		Emma imagines Jane's romance.
20			Novelist describes Jane.
22		Mrs Elton	
23	Frank Churchill		
26	Jane Fairfax		
29			Emma imagines romance with Frank.
32	Mrs Elton		
38			Mr Knightley dances with Harriet.
39			Frank saves Harriet from gypsies.
40			Harriet's gratitude.
43			Emma rude to Miss Bates.
44			Emma's remorse.
46			Frank and Jane's engagement revealed.
47			Harriet and Mr Knightley. Emma realises real feelings.
49			Mr Knightley proposes.
54			Harriet accepts Robert Martin.
55			Emma marries Mr Knightley.

Useful quotations

1 The real evils of Emma's situations were the power of having rather too much her own way and a disposition to think a little too well of herself.

8 She did not repent what she had done.

16 She was quite concerned and ashamed, and resolved to do such things no more.

26 (to Mrs Weston) 'Mr Knightley and Jane Fairfax . . . Mr Knightley must not marry!'

31 (of Frank) . . . the conclusion of every imaginary declaration on his side was that she *refused him*.

38 She was more disturbed by Mr Knightley's not dancing than by anything else.

43 Not that Emma was gay and thoughtless from any real felicity; it was rather because she felt less happy than she had expected.

47 A few minutes were sufficient for making her acquainted with her own heart.
She was . . . ashamed of every sensation but the one revealed to her – her affection for Mr Knightley. . . . She was proved to have been universally mistaken; and she had not quite done nothing – for she had done mischief.

53 (of John Knightley's letter of congratulation to his brother) 'I honour his sincerity. It is very plain that he considers the good fortune of the engagement as all on my side, but that he is not without hope of my growing, in time, . . . worthy of your affection.'

EMMA:

A NOVEL

IN THREE VOLUMES.

BY THE

AUTHOR OF "PRIDE AND PREJUDICE,"
&c. &c.

VOL. I.

LONDON:
PRINTED FOR JOHN MURRAY.
1816.

Facsimile of the title page of the first edition of *Emma* (1816)

How does Jane Austen arouse our interest in Emma and maintain it throughout the novel?

Plan: 1 Presentation of Emma's character at the beginning. Introduction of characters and events. Emma's viewpoint varied by Mr Knightley's opinions and novelist's.

2 Emma's development through successive errors.

3 Development of character through: a) overcoming faults; b) recognition of true feelings, understanding herself.

4 Interest in heroine who is not ideal, but develops.

Emma is a novel in which the heroine's character is explained quite clearly at the beginning. She is spoilt and has 'a disposition to think a little too well of herself', which encourages her to attempt to arrange other people's lives. The events of the novel are apparently not very exciting, consisting of a series of meetings, parties and excursions, and the characters introduced, while very realistic and often highly amusing, would not justify a novel in themselves. But Jane Austen's timing in introducing them at intervals and in varying the viewpoint so that we see them through Emma's prejudiced eyes but hear Mr Knightley's sensible comments and sometimes the novelist's own, maintain our interest, even though the novel must stand or fall according to our interest in Emma herself.

Emma makes a series of errors, but she does not make the same mistake twice; consequently, as we follow her development we never doubt her real intelligence and capacity for learning from them. After the initial error of discouraging Harriet's attachment to Robert Martin and misreading Mr Elton's intentions, her subsequent mistakes are the products of her situation and of her ignorance of the true state of affairs between Frank Churchill and Jane Fairfax, which Jane Austen has also carefully concealed from us. These mistakes reflect the imagination and energy of an intelligent, rather mischievous, young woman, who is bored in a limited society.

Emma must learn to correct her defects, and Jane Austen maintains our interest by showing how easily she gets over her initial setback, when Mr Knightley is angry with her for interfering over Robert Martin; then, her first doubts about herself when she is proved wrong over Mr Elton; finally, her real remorse when she understands the effect her behaviour has had on Miss Bates, Jane and Harriet. In the same way, she must learn to understand her own feelings, and this process is also more carefully planned than her sudden realisation that she loves Mr Knightley might suggest. We see her first shocked at the idea of his marrying Jane Fairfax; then imagining herself in love with Frank, but knowing it is not serious; then admiring Mr Knightley physically for the first time at the ball, and happy to dance with him; finally, when she has suffered herself from shame at her own actions, recognising her feelings for him.

A novel about a long-suffering, consistent, quiet girl like Jane Fairfax would not interest us as much as one about a vivacious girl whose experiences enable her to develop her best qualities and reject her defects. We would neverthelss find it unrealistic if Emma were transformed into a penitent and made excessively serious. Her maturity, and also her attraction for us, is demonstrated at the end when she keeps her sense of humour, laughing a little at John Knightley's letter of congratulation, without doubting that Mr Knightley is more worthy of her affection than she is of his.

Activity 5 – pair work

Trace the source for what is said in the essay in the table and quotations on the opposite page.

Prescribed books: Dramatic technique

Setting the scene

Plays are normally written to be acted, not read. Drama depends on the ability of the dramatist to establish a context economically and to develop it through words and action in a limited space of time. The events in drama, whether they take place on or off the stage, must be sufficiently clear for an audience to grasp them by eye and ear alone, without the detailed explanation available to the novelist. The essence of drama is an atmosphere of tension and potential surprise in which we are constantly interested in what is going to happen next and how the situation is to be resolved.

Like the novelist, the dramatist must establish from the beginning who the characters are, where they are and when the action is supposed to take place, but he can hardly do so by means of straightforward statements unless he appears on the stage himself. In a theatre such as Shakespeare's, where there were no programme notes or reviews of plays in newspapers for the audience to read beforehand, where scenery was rudimentary and the plays were usually acted in open-air theatres without curtains or lighting, every piece of information to be conveyed to the audience in order to establish time and place, to introduce characters and indicate the relationships between them, had to be contained in the speech and action on the stage.

The opening scene of *Hamlet* is a superb example of Shakespeare's technique, not only in suggesting time and place (night in the castle of Elsinore in Denmark) but also in producing from the first moment an atmosphere of tension appropriate to the play, in suggesting the theme and in creating a feeling of expectation in the audience for the entrance of the principal character, Hamlet, in the second scene.

Two sentries are changing guard at midnight as the scene begins. What is curious about the staccato dialogue between them that opens the play is that Bernardo, the sentry coming on guard, says 'Who's there?' before he is challenged. Something is wrong in an army where a man is so nervous that he is not sure

Marcellus (Michael Godfrey) and Bernardo (Esmond Knight) see the Ghost in the opening scene of *Hamlet*

who he will find on guard. We discover the cause of this nervousness soon afterwards when Horatio and Marcellus, both introduced by name, discuss with Bernardo a strange figure he and Marcellus have seen on previous nights. Horatio is sceptical until the Ghost, dressed like the recently dead king of Denmark, Hamlet, appears. Even then Horatio believes it may be the Devil, who is 'usurping' the form of the dead king. This is highly relevant to the theme, not only because Hamlet's initial quarrel with Claudius, his uncle, is that he has usurped a throne that should have come to him, but also because his delay in revenging his father's murder until Claudius has given proof of his guilt is much more the result of his own doubts about the reliability of the Ghost than of any natural lack of resolution in his character.

The Ghost disappears, and Horatio and Marcellus talk about the dead king, who killed the King of Norway, Fortinbras, in single combat, and about young Fortinbras, an active, hot-blooded prince. They are convinced that the Ghost, whatever it may be, is an ominous sign for the country. Shakespeare is building up tension by this reference, but when the Ghost reappears, and they try unsuccessfully to stop it leaving, he tilts the balance in its favour from the audience's point of view by making Marcellus say:

> 'Tis gone!
> We do it wrong, being so majestical, (since it
> looks so majestic)
> To offer it the show of violence.'

The scene ends with Horatio suggesting that they should relate what they have seen to 'young Hamlet', who is mentioned here for the first time. The audience await the second scene with expectation, knowing from the title – *Hamlet, Prince of Denmark* – that he is the main character. What will he do in this situation? Will he be hot-blooded like Fortinbras? The modern audience knows he will not, because Hamlet thinks before he acts. But the audience the play was written for did not know that.

KEY QUESTION
In the play you are reading, how does the dramatist indicate place, time, the names of characters and the relationships between them? Does he create an atmosphere from the beginning that makes you anxious to know what will happen next?

Stage directions and symbolism

Modern dramatists frequently tell the reader a great deal about the characters in the stage directions. This custom, which enables them to explain the behaviour of characters in a similar way to the novelist, is used to a considerable extent, for example, by Shaw, who also provides long introductions discussing the themes of his plays. It must be remembered, however, that almost all of Shaw's early plays were published and read before they were performed, and that the audience in the theatre are unaware of these aids to understanding and must still depend entirely on what they see and hear. In reading a play, while you should take advantage of such help as the stage directions give, you should also try to imagine how the play would be performed in the theatre.

Ibsen is the greatest master of naturalistic stagecraft in modern drama. Like Shakespeare, he aimed at presenting the themes of his plays as well as setting the scene and introducing the characters at the beginning, but he did so against the background of scenery that faithfully represented the middle-class homes of his time in terms of furniture and decoration. This advantage was to some extent counteracted, however, by his need for suitably naturalistic language, which did not allow him the same opportunities as Shakespeare had had for creating atmosphere through language. Ibsen's stage directions are particularly important because his use of symbols extends beyond words to the settings, the objects seen on the stage, and the characters' actions; his ideas on the staging, which bring out the symbolism, are found in these stage directions.

Two examples of this use of symbolism will suffice. At the beginning of *Hedda Gabler*, Hedda is already married to Tesman and living in his house. The setting for the play is a living-room, with a small room at the back, Hedda's sanctuary, the interior of which is sometimes visible to the audience, sometimes curtained off. In the centre of the stage, within this room, the audience can see a portrait of General Gabler, Hedda's father. The portrait and the title of the play both indicate that Hedda, despite her marriage, is still her father's daughter, not her husband's wife.

A Doll's House is a play about the relationship between a married couple. Their marriage is one in which the husband treats the wife as a child (a doll), so that their home is like a doll's house. Their relationship is suggested at the beginning of the play, not only by the way Nora behaves and by Helmer addressing her by pet names like 'skylark' or 'squirrel', but also by Nora eating sweets in secret. The stage directions are of vital importance to an understanding of the play, but whereas in Shaw, they are only of use to the actor or reader, in Ibsen their effect is clearly felt by the audience in the theatre, who have not read them.

It is just before Christmas, and Nora has just come in with a Christmas tree and a lot of parcels.

(Nora shuts the door. She is laughing to herself as she takes off her hat and coat. She takes a bag of macaroons out of her pocket and eats one or two; then she goes cautiously to her husband's door, and listens.)

NORA   Yes, he's in. *(She begins humming again as she goes to the table on the right.)*

HELMER   *(from his room)* Is that my little skylark twittering out there?

NORA   *(busy opening the parcels)* Yes, it is.

HELMER   Is that my little squirrel bustling about?

NORA   Yes.

HELMER   When did my little squirrel get home?

NORA   Just now. *(She stuffs the bag of macaroons in her pocket and wipes her mouth.)*

Activity 1 – pair work

Study the stage directions in the play you are reading. Do they simply give instructions to the actors and director, or do they comment on the characters?

> KEY QUESTION
> In what ways, other than speech, does the dramatist in the play you are reading make you aware of the theme and the relationships between characters?

Claire Bloom as Nora in *A Doll's House*

Maintaining interest

Conflict and tension

If we ask ourselves (in real life, as well as in the theatre) 'What is dramatic?', we are likely to answer in terms of conflict or tension. Either a situation develops into a struggle between two people, or political ideas, or philosophies of life, or we are on edge because we do not know how a situation will be resolved. Conflict on the stage can be presented in terms of a battle between two personalities, such as that between the married couple in Edward Albee's *Who's Afraid of Virginia Woolf?*, where husband and wife pour out their hatred of one another throughout the play. Alternatively, as in Sophocles' *Antigone*, or Jean Anouilh's version of the same myth, Creon and Antigone represent two fundamentally different views of life in opposition, and we are interested not only in who will win, but who is right in moral terms and in whether a moral victory can be won in spite of physical defeat, or death.

Tension is felt in such situations partly as a result of the emotions expressed, which we may recognise because we have felt them in real life ourselves, or because we are drawn to sympathise with the attitudes of one or other of the characters, but also because we are uncertain of the outcome. We are involved to the extent that we take sides, and want our side to win, or we can see both points of view and want the situation to be resolved fairly, or happily. The tension we feel is most noticeable and lends itself best to dramatic exploitation when we understand the situation better than some of the characters on stage.

Elizabeth Taylor and Richard Burton as George and Martha in *Who's Afraid of Virginia Woolf?*

KEY QUESTION
Can you find instances of conflict in the play you are reading? Are they conflicts between characters, of ideas, or both?

Suspense and surprise

The dramatist can control the audience's reaction to events on the stage by the amount of information he provides, and above all by choosing the moment when he imparts it. One way of producing a dramatic effect is to surprise the audience by a twist in the plot that they have not been prepared for and do not expect: a character they thought was dead reappears, or turns out to be the heroine's long-lost father, or the suspected murderer is really a policeman in disguise. In such situations, the audience are expected to react like the other characters on stage, and their knowledge of the situation is the same.

The greatest tension (and also the most entertaining comedy), however, tends to be produced when all or most of the characters on stage are unaware of the truth, but the audience have already been informed. In a serious play, the tension arises from suspense; we wonder whether the hero will discover the truth in time to avert disaster, for example. In comedy, we are amused by the confusion of characters who are ignorant of the real state of affairs, which we already know.

Activity 2 – pair work

Study the play you are reading to discover whether there are: a) events that come as a surprise; b) moments when the audience knows more about the situation than some of the characters. Is this used to create tension or for comic effect?

Tension and surprise

Act 3 of Shakespeare's *Macbeth* demonstrates his skilful handling of a variety of dramatic techniques to control the audience's reactions. The act deals with the murder of Banquo, and begins with Banquo, alone, voicing his suspicions that Macbeth was responsible for the murder of King Duncan. Macbeth, now king, enters with his wife, asks Banquo about his plans for the afternoon and evening, and invites him to a dinner with the other nobles at seven. Banquo explains that he must go on a journey with his son, Fleance, whom Macbeth also plans to murder, and will return in the darkness by seven o'clock. 'Fail not our feast', Macbeth says (although he has every intention of making sure that Banquo will not return) and Banquo replies, 'My lord, I will not.'

Afterwards, Macbeth interviews the murderers and gives them instructions to ambush Banquo and his son on their way back. He talks to Lady Macbeth, revealing his state of mind but not his plan. He says that that night 'there shall be done a deed of dreadful note.' Throughout the scenes leading up to the murder of Banquo, the tension is maintained by constant reference to him. At all times, the audience is aware of him, offstage, riding to meet his fate, and as that fate draws closer, Shakespeare gives us memorable lines of poetry that remind us of the approaching night and associate the oncoming darkness with the murder:

> 'Light thickens
> And the crow makes wing to the rooky wood;
> Good things of day begin to droop and drowse,
> Whiles night's black agents to their preys do
> rouse.'

This technique of word pictures, apart from indicating the passing of time, also emphasises that in the greatest drama, action takes place off the stage as well as on. Our minds are in two places at once, listening to Macbeth and his wife and thinking of Banquo. At this point, the scene changes to the murderers preparing for Banquo's arrival and to the murder itself, from which Fleance escapes.

Throughout this act, the audience have been in the position of Macbeth, knowing what is going to happen while Banquo does not. Shakespeare creates tension by making us constantly aware of time and place while the event we are expecting draws closer. At the scene of the banquet, however, he at first places us in a superior position, as we watch Macbeth anxiously awaiting news from the murderers, knowing, as he does not, that his plan has only been partially successful. The arrival of the murderers is a prepared surprise, since we have seen the murder, but what follows, the appearance of Banquo's ghost sitting in the chair set aside for Macbeth, is a surprise to us as well as to him. As we see him recoil in horror from a sight only he (and the audience) can see, the irony of his earlier insistence on Banquo's presence at the feast is brought home to us. Banquo has not broken his word. He has not 'failed the feast', even though he is dead.

Banquo (Edgar Barrier) and Macbeth (Orson Welles)

KEY QUESTIONS
In the play you are reading, what use does the dramatist make of tension and surprise? How does he maintain tension, once he has created it? Are the surprises prepared, or is the audience as surprised as the characters on the stage?

Composition: Dramatic technique

How does Shakespeare create and maintain tension in *Othello*?

	Audience's information (from Iago)	Action	Sources of tension
I iii	Plot to have Cassio dismissed and make Othello jealous.	Iago encourages Roderigo to annoy Cassio.	
II iii		Cassio dismissed. Iago advises him to seek Desdemona's help.	
III iii	Explains plot in detail. (Temptation scene)	Iago sows doubt in Othello's mind. Desdemona drops handkerchief. Emilia finds it. Iago takes it.	Othello shows insecurity. (Will Iago succeed?)
	Tells us he will leave handkerchief in Cassio's lodgings.	Tells Othello he saw Cassio with handkerchief.	
III iv		Emilia lies to Desdemona.	First chance of truth.
		Desdemona lies to Othello. Cassio has found handkerchief, gives it to Bianca.	Second chance. (Disaster averted?)
IV i		Othello thinks Cassio's conversation is about his wife. Bianca throws the handkerchief at Cassio.	
IV ii		Emilia says Othello is being tricked. Iago persuades Roderigo to kill Cassio.	Will Iago give himself away?
V i	Explains need to kill Cassio and Roderigo.		
		Cassio wounded, Roderigo killed.	One (but not both) witness dead.
V ii		Othello kills Desdemona. Emilia accuses him, Iago is called as a witness and she confronts him.	Will truth be discovered?

Quotations

II iii	IAGO:	So I will turn her virtue into pitch (black, tar-like substance) And out of her own goodness make the net That shall enmesh them all.
III iii	IAGO:	Ha! I like not that!
	OTHELLO:	What dost thou say?
	IAGO:	Nothing, my lord: or if – I know not what.
	IAGO:	Did Michael Cassio, when you wooed my lady, Know of your love?
	IAGO:	For Michael Cassio, I dare be sworn I *think* he is honest.
	IAGO:	O beware, my lord, of jealousy!
III iv	DESDEMONA:	This is a trick to put me from my suit: Pray you let Cassio be received again.
IV ii	EMILIA:	The Moor's abused by some most villainous knave, Some base notorious knave, some scurvy fellow.
	IAGO:	. . . There is no such man! It is impossible.
V ii	OTHELLO:	O, I were damned beneath all depth in hell, But that I did proceed upon just grounds To this extremity. Thy husband knew it all.
	EMILIA:	My husband?
	OTHELLO:	Thy husband.
	EMILIA:	That she was false. . . ?

Sir Laurence Olivier as Othello strikes Desdemona (Maggie Smith)

How does Shakespeare create and maintain tension in *Othello*?

Plan: 1 At all times, Iago directs action, and audience know plot beforehand from his soliloquys.
     2 Tension depends on sympathy for Othello and Desdemona, fear of Iago's success. Will Othello be convinced?
     3 Once convinced, tension depends on opportunities for truth to be revealed in time, or Iago giving himself away.
     4 After murder of Desdemona, will Iago's guilt be discovered?
     5 Conclusion – why tension is continuous and unbearable.

Tension is almost always present in *Othello* from the moment when Iago first tells the audience of his plot to have Cassio dismissed and to make Othello jealous. This is because Iago directs the action throughout and there are no surprises. Everything turns out as he plans until he is finally discovered, even though the plan is not complete at the beginning and he improvises when he has the good luck to be presented with the crucial piece of evidence to support his case, Desdemona's handkerchief. At all times, his soliloquys make the audience aware of what is going to happen, while the other characters are unsuspecting:

     'So I will turn her virtue into pitch
     And out of her own goodness make the net
     That shall enmesh them all.'

For us to be involved in this tension, Shakespeare must first make us sympathetic towards Othello and Desdemona, which he achieves in the scene before the Senate, and at the same time cause us to fear Iago's cleverness. The ease with which Iago deals with Roderigo and retains Cassio's confidence in spite of his dismissal prepares us for the much subtler approach he employs in the Temptation Scene. The muttered comment, as Cassio leaves Desdemona, 'Ha! I like not that!' arouses Othello's curiosity. Throughout the scene, Iago skilfully leads Othello into asking the questions and inferring the worst from the non-committal answers, first about Cassio's acquaintance with Desdemona before the marriage, then as regards Cassio's trustworthiness. It is Iago who first mentions jealousy, but only to tell Othello to beware of it. When Othello is left alone, and his soliloquy reveals his own insecurity, we sense that Iago is likely to succeed, but the handkerchief must serve as the proof Othello demands before acting.

In the next scene, Shakespeare exploits tension in a different way. Now that Othello is convinced, can the truth be revealed in time to show him he is wrong? The audience watches, fascinated, but with growing pity and horror, as the opportunities for the truth to come out are thrown away; first Emilia lies to Desdemona about finding the handkerchief, and then Desdemona lies to Othello, pretending she has not lost it, and in her fear of his rage, makes the fatal reference to Cassio:

     'This is a trick to put me from my suit:
     Pray you let Cassio be received again.'

From this point on, as we watch Othello's degradation in the fourth act, our only hope must be that Iago will give himself away. At one moment, he seems as if he might, when Emilia says Othello is deceived by 'some most villainous knave', words that apply to himself, and he is angry.

Even after Othello has killed Desdemona, Shakespeare prolongs the tension. He delays the discovery of Iago's part in the crime, when Othello, accused by Emilia, claims Iago's evidence as his justification, and she refuses to believe him:

OTHELLO: Thy husband knew it all.
EMILIA: My husband?

She responds like this three times until she is driven to confront Iago with the evidence, and the plot is at last revealed with her confession of having found the handkerchief.

Othello is the Shakespearean tragedy where the tension is sustained for the longest period of time because it is the only one where the audience is always one step ahead of the principal character and must watch his destruction helplessly while every possibility of his being undeceived in time to avoid it disappears.

Appendix: Connectors and modifiers

The presentation of information in English is greatly helped by the correct use of connectors and modifiers. Whenever you are in doubt about the most appropriate form to use – for instance, when writing a composition – use the examples below as a guide. Whenever you come across any of the phrases listed below in the course of your reading, note how they are used to develop and link paragraphs. For exercises on their use, see *Book 3*.

1 Appearance and Reality

The establishment of facts usually appears in contrast to appearance, what appears to be true, or what is commonly but incorrectly believed to be true. Look at this sentence:

At first sight (**on the face of it**) connectors may seem unnecessary, but **in fact** they are essential to the development of an argument in good modern English.

The same sentence can be written with the use of adverbs as modifiers:

Connectors are **apparently** unnecessary to the development of an argument in good modern English but they are **really** (**actually**) essential.

Stronger forms of **in fact** for establishing contrast are **the fact is that** . . . and **the fact of the matter is that** . . .

The aeroplane may appear to be a modern conception but **the fact of the matter is that** Leonardo da Vinci designed a flying machine five hundred years ago.

As a matter of fact has the same meaning, but carries the idea that the listener or reader may be surprised to hear it:

It is not the first time I have met the Duke. **As a matter of fact**, he was in the same class as I was at school.

In practice is almost always used in contrast to **in theory** or **in principle**, and means 'when carried out in a real situation':

These ideas are all very well **in theory**, but will they work **in practice**?
In principle I have nothing against the proposal, but I am still not convinced that it will work **in practice**.

In effect is close to **in fact** in meaning and usage; it implies 'for practical purposes'; an alternative form is **to all intents and purposes**:

Officially we are still an independent company but **in effect** we belong to Exports Ltd, because they own most of the shares.

Indeed is used with the meaning of **in fact** or 'as you may imagine' but as a continuation of a previous statement, not as a contrast:

We expected an improvement in the situation, and **indeed**, things have turned out as we expected.

2 Developing an Argument (Sequence)

Most people develop a complex argument by making a series of points. This can be done numerically – **first, second, third** – but the following phrases are most commonly used:
Point 1: **In the first place, To begin with, To start with, First of all. For one thing** is more conversational, and may suggest that the speaker is still thinking of his reasons and has not listed them in his mind.
Point 2: **Secondly, In the second place.** These lead the reader to expect further reasons.
In addition to that tends to be used for the second and final reason.
Apart from that, Moreover (more formal) and **What is more** (conversational) indicate second reasons of a rather different kind, but tending towards the same conclusion:

I am not sure whether we really need a second garage. **Apart from that**, we must take the cost into consideration.

Besides raises a second, conclusive point which often makes the first reason seem irrelevant:

I am not sure whether we really need a second garage. **Besides**, we can't afford it.

Final Point: **Finally, Lastly.**
Above all, indicating that the last point is the most important.
In the last resort suggests 'if everything else has failed' or 'if all other arguments fail to convince':

Of course, they may not accept any of these reasons for negotiation. **In the last resort**, we would have to use force.

Conclusion (not the last point, but a summary of all of them):

In conclusion, To sum up. These indicate to the reader that you have reached this stage of the argument.

Taking everything into account, All things considered, All in all. These indicate that you are making a balanced judgement of all the points raised, whether they form a consistent list or not.

In brief, in short, in a word (the last two more conversational). These indicate that you are going to summarise the points made briefly, and should only be used if that is the case:

In brief, we have no alternative to this course of action.

3 Developing an Argument (Example)

For example, for instance, A case in point is . . . The last normally introduces an extended example ('a case') to illustrate the point made.

4 Developing an Argument (Contrast)

When people can see points both for and against an argument, they tend to modify their first statement by placing another in contrast. This can be done in a simple sentence, using **but** or in a sentence using **although** or **in spite of** for greater effect, emphasising that the second consideration is more important than the first.

His argument is interesting **but** it does not convince me.

Although his argument is interesting, it does not convince me.

In spite of the strength of his argument, it does not convince me.

Reservations about an initial statement are most frequently expressed in written argument with the following connectors:

However, Nevertheless, All the same, At the same time:

The argument put forward in this article is an interesting one.

However, it is not altogether convincing, because . . . .

Yet can be used in the same way as a stronger form of **but** without the comma that must always follow the other expressions.

After all means 'in spite of all other considerations'. It tends to suggest a conclusive negative to arguments previously presented.

These arguments are interesting but not convincing. **After all**, similar measures have been attempted in the past without success.

5 Developing an Argument (Balance)

While the phrases used for argument by contrast tend to throw the emphasis on the second point, the following maintain a balance.

On the one hand . . . **on the other hand.** In this case, the writer is neutral.

On the other hand is frequently used alone, simply to put forward an alternative point of view, without favouring it:

Businessmen will no doubt welcome the Government's decision to restore some nationalised industries to private enterprise; the unions, **on the other hand**, fear that it will lead to greater unemployment.

A balanced argument can be presented in a single sentence by the use of **while** – see the first sentence of this section.

6 Developing an Argument (Cause and Effect)

The following phrases indicate the reasons why an action has taken place or is proposed:

Because of . . ., **Owing to** . . .:

Because of the world situation at present, we do not think it advisable for the company to proceed with this project.

Due to should, strictly speaking, be used as a complement:

Our decision not to proceed is **due to** the world situation.

Having explained the reason(s) for an action, we can continue the presentation of an argument with **For this reason, For these reasons.** Note that **For one reason or another** suggests that we do not know the reasons:

For one reason or another, the Government has decided to raise the tax on red wine, but not on white.

Therefore and **thus** indicate the logical continuation or conclusion of an argument.

In concluding a logical argument based on cause and effect we can employ the following:

As a result, Consequently, In consequence.

7 Expressing Personal Opinion

The most common general phrases to indicate a personal, as distinct from a general, opinion are: **In my opinion, In my view, As I see it, To my mind.** The last two are more often found in conversation.

Personally emphasises the individual opinion, often in contrast to that of the majority:

A lot of people believe such statements. **Personally,** I think they are nonsense.

As far as I am concerned means 'in so far as the matter affects me' and is less likely to appear in written argument than in such contexts as:

They can do what they like, **as far as I am concerned.** I don't care (It's not my business).

For my part is similar in meaning, though it tends to stress contrast, like **personally**:

I do not know what their decision will be. **For my part,** I would be happy to forget the whole business.

8 Modifying what is said or written

There are many ways in which we modify statements, limiting their meaning or in some cases pointing to specific circumstances in which they are correct.
a) Expressing truth in general terms though not in all circumstances:
   In general, As a rule, As a general rule, On the whole, In the main, For the most part.
b) Indicating that the statement is only partly correct:
   To some extent, To a certain extent, Up to a point, In a way, In a sense. The last indicates a limitation in interpretation:

   I agree with you **in a sense** (if the words mean one of the possible interpretations that could be placed on them).

c) Indicating a limitation in the speaker's responsibility for the statement:
   As far as I know, To the best of my knowledge.

   For all I know suggests ignorance:

   I have no idea where they are. **For all I know,** they may be in the south of France.

d) Indicating that the responsibility for the statement lies with someone else:
   According to . . ., By all accounts (indicating that the opinion is generally held).
e) Limiting the validity of a statement:

In these circumstances (but not necessarily in others).
At least (commonly used for avoiding responsibility):

The Government has no intention of raising taxes. **At least**, that is what they say. (I am only repeating what I have heard.)

At any rate is used in the same way.
As it is, Things being as they are (= 'as the situation is at present', but not in ideal circumstances).

9 Intensifying the statement

a) By making it in such a way that the reader is expected to believe it is common knowledge:
   Clearly, Obviously, Of course, Needless to say, As everyone knows.
b) By drawing attention to a particular aspect or group of circumstances:
   In particular.
   Here, **especially** is commonly used within the sentence; also **above all** can be used:

   The new law has caused a great deal of hardship, **especially** among the poor.

c) By referring to a more noticeable example of the same thing:
   let alone.

   They are incapable of organising themselves properly, **let alone** running the country.

   We use **not to mention** in a similar way, usually by referring to specific things or people:

   Society as a whole has suffered from the effects of the assassination, **not to mention** the family of the victim.

10 Rephrasing a statement

In other words, That is to say.

11 Referring to someone or something

As regards . . . With regard to . . ., In this connection.
As far as . . . is concerned
For that matter suggests an additional reference to the same point:

Our customers abroad have not shown much interest in the new model, and **for that matter,** neither have people here.

As for . . . tends to imply lack of interest or contempt for the person or argument in question:

As for Jones, I do not think we need to take his opinions into account.

12 Suggesting that further discussion will serve no purpose

In any case (= 'whatever happens', 'whatever the facts are')
At all events (= 'whether that is true or not')
Anyway is used as an equivalent, usually in conversation.

Grammatical reference

Definite article

Adjectives: comparison

Adjectives: word order

It's + adjective + for/that

Adverbs: word order

Adverbs of Manner, Place and Time

Prepositions

Modals: Formulae for different situations

Verbs not usually used in Continuous forms

Verb + gerund/infinitive

Active and Passive

Double object verbs

Direct and reported speech

Relative clauses

Reflexive verbs

Clauses

Definite article

1   Omission of **the**

We do not use **the** with the following:

a) Games and sports

I **play football** every week. My sister **plays tennis** and **likes swimming**, too.

b) Subjects of study

I **studied literature** at university and now I **teach English**.

c) Languages

Many Welsh people **speak Welsh**, but most Scots **speak English**.

Note that we say **the English** (noun) or **English people**, but nationality as an adjective has no definite article.

I'm English.

d) Meals and clock time

What time do you **have breakfast**?
— **About eight o'clock**.

e) Gerunds

Horse-racing is more popular in Britain than **fox-hunting**.

f) Collocations (proposition + noun)

Notice that there is no **the** after these sentences:

Is he still **in bed**?
— No, he's **at church**.
I was **at school** for thirteen years and then I went **to university**.

A number of common phrases in English made up of a preposition and a noun do not take **the**.

Here is a list of the most common ones:

bed (**in, to**)	market (**at, to**)
church (**at, in = inside, to**)	paper (**on**)
court (**in, to**)	prison (**in, to**)
dock (**in**)	school (**at, to**)
harbour (**in, to**)	sea (**at, to**) university (**at,**
home (**at**)	**to**)
hospital (**in, to**)	work (**at, to**)

The definite article is only used when we clearly refer to a particular school, hospital, etc.

My mother's **in hospital**.
I'm going **to the hospital** this afternoon to take her some flowers.

Modes of travel and transport take **by** + noun, without **the**.

By air/sea/road
By car/bus/plane/train, etc.

Note that we say **on foot**.

2   Use of the

We use **the** with the following:

a) Weights and measures

Petrol is sold **by the litre**.

b) Groups or classes of people

The young often get impatient with their parents.

We can say either **the young** or **young people**. The verb that follows expressions of this kind is plural.

c) Rivers, seas, mountain ranges

The Amazon is longer than **the River Thames**.
The Mediterranean flows into **the Atlantic Ocean**.
Mount Everest is the highest mountain in **the Himalayas**.

Note that we use **the** in all cases, except for the name of a single mountain:

Mount Everest, Kilimanjaro.

d) Unique objects, points of the compass, some time expressions

The sun rises in **the east**.
The past is often more real to old people than **the present**.

We use **the** when there is only one of something:

the sun, the moon, the earth, the world.

We use **the** with points of the compass:

the north, the south, the east, the west.

But compare these sentences:

We were travelling **north**.
We were travelling **towards the north**.

We usually use **the** when we speak of **the past, the present** and **the future**. The exceptions are **at present**, which means 'now, at this time' and **in future**, which means 'from now on'.

I'll drive more carefully **in future** (from now on, from this moment).
In the future (but not from now on) men may live on the moon.

3   Use and omission of **the**

We use **the** when we are talking about something *specific*.
We don't use **the** when we are speaking in a more *general* sense.

a) Plural count nouns and mass nouns

She likes **flowers**. (General)
She likes **the flowers** that I gave her. (Specific)
Coffee is expensive nowadays. (General)
The coffee that you bought is very bitter. (Specific)

b) Abstract nouns

I always admire **honesty**. (General)
I was surprised at **the honesty** with which he answered the questions. (Specific)

c) Species of animals

Elephants are said to have long memories.

When we talk about animals in general, we usually use the plural without **the**.
When we refer to a particular species we can use either **the** and a singular noun,

The Indian elephant is smaller than **the African elephant**

or a plural noun without **the**,

Indian elephants are smaller than **African elephants**.

d) Noun + modifying phrase/clause

Life is always valuable.
Modern life is often tiring.
Albert Schweitzer's life was devoted to the sick.
The life he is leading bores him.
The life of our grandparents was very different from the life we lead today.

The is used when the noun is modified by a relative clause, or by a phrase including **of**.

Adjectives: comparison

1   One-syllable and three-syllable adjectives

He's **taller** than his sister; in fact he's **the tallest** in the family.
But she's **more intelligent** than he is. She's **the most intelligent** person I've ever met.

One-syllable adjectives form the comparative with **-er** and the superlative with **-est**;
adjectives with three syllables or more form the comparative with **more** and the superlative with **most**.
Note the irregular forms: **good, better, best; bad, worse, worst**.

2 Two-syllable adjectives

That house is **prettier** than the last one we looked at; in fact, I think it's **the prettiest** we've seen so far.
Cathy is **more cheerful** than her sister; actually she's **the most cheerful** person I know.

Two-syllable adjectives usually form the comparative with **more** and the superlative with **most**. But an important group, those ending in **-y** (e.g. **happy, easy, lucky**), form the comparative with **-er** and the superlative with **-est**. Note the **-y** changes to **i** (e.g. **happier, happiest**).

Other groups taking **-er** and **-est** are those ending in **-le** (e.g. **noble, gentle**), **-ow** (e.g. **narrow, yellow**) and **-er** (e.g. **clever, tender**).

All others (e.g. those ending in **-ful, -less**, such as **cheerful, useless**), usually take **more** and **most**.

In a few cases (e.g. **common, stupid, unfair, unkind, pleasant**), both the **-er/-est** and **more/most** forms are found.

Adjectives: word order

It is difficult to give clear rules to follow about the position of adjectives before the noun. The table below, however, should be of value as a useful check in given cases. The following general points should also be remembered:

1 When there are more than two adjectives, they are usually linked by commas.

2 We seldom use **and** except when the adjectives are a complement, following **be**:

His work is untidy **and** unsatisfactory.

3 We usually put the more or most precise adjective nearest the noun, but it is not always easy to decide which is more precise. When in doubt, consult the examples and order given below:

All the first three competitors broke the record. (1,2,3,4)
The beautiful, intelligent girl fell in love with **the tall young** man. (2,5,6 and 2,7,8)
There was a **round, green** spot on **the carved, wooden Japanese** screen. (9,10 and 2,11,12,13)
He had a **beautiful, old, ivory chess** piece. (5,8,12,14)

1) **both, all** or **half**
2) **the**
3) Ordinal number (**first, last**)
4) Cardinal number (**one, three**)
5) General judgement (**good, bad, nice**)
6) Measurement (**big, tall**)
7) Physical characteristics (**beautiful, handsome**)
8) Mental characteristics (**intelligent, stupid**)
9) Age or temperature (**old, young, hot**)
10) Shape (**round, square**)
11) Colour (**red, green**)
12) Verb participle form (**carved, boiling**)
13) Material (**wooden**)
14) Origin, nationality (**French, Mediterranean**)
15) Noun in apposition (**steel, cigarette**)

Some of these categories are reversed at times, particularly the following:

6 and 7 for emphasis on 6. In this case, the comma must always be used.

A **little, intelligent** man. (7,6)

10 and 13 in a phrase like:

Yugoslavian white wine. (13,10)

Here **white** is used to describe a type, in contrast to **red**, rather than as an indication of colour.

It's + adjective + for/that

It's easy (for you) to say that.
It's obvious that you don't know what you're talking about.

In some cases, the adjective may be followed by either construction but usually we prefer one or the other. Among the adjectives followed by **for** are: **boring, dangerous, difficult, easy, expensive, healthy, necessary**.

Among those followed by **that** are: **certain, clear, curious, likely, lucky, probable, surprising, true**. Note the use of **interesting** with the two constructions:

It would be interesting for you to study abroad. (You would find it interesting.)
It's interesting that he made you that offer. (I find it interesting.)

Adverbs: word order

1   Adverbs of frequency (**often, always, usually**, etc.)

   a) **Be** (including negatives and passives)

   The opposite **is usually** the case.
   He **isn't often** late.
   Headlines **are often designed** to puzzle the reader.

   b) **Be** with auxiliary (including negatives and passives)

   He **has always been** very kind to me.
   They **may not always be** the best newspapers for foreign students.
   I **have never been asked** a question like that before.

   c) Other verbs (including negatives and one auxiliary)

   It **often confuses** foreigners.
   I **don't usually look at** my mail till after breakfast.
   He **has always taken** a great personal interest in my career.

   d) Other verbs with two auxiliaries

   I **could never have done** it without your help.

Adverbs of Manner, Place and Time

a) Time expressions (WHEN) can come at the beginning or end of the sentence. We usually put them at the beginning if the time expression or the sentence is very long, or for emphasis.

b) We sometimes put one-word adverbs of manner (HOW) in front of the main verb for emphasis – in the example in the table, we could say:
   The film fans **frantically** besieged the airport.

Prepositions

Prepositions of place

at, in

At is used for particular points, **in** for larger areas.

I was waiting **at** the bus stop.
He is staying **at** the Ritz Hotel.
She lives **in** London.
There are a lot of mountains **in** Switzerland.

Confusion is only possible when the point of view of the speaker is different.

Someone who lives in a city may say:

My friend, Mary, lives **at** Farley. (a small village)

but a farmer who lives outside the village may say:

Mary lives **in** Farley.

In the same way, a housewife answering the phone may say:

My husband's **at** his office. (= at his place of work)

but his secretary, sitting outside the office, may say to a visitor:

Mr Jones is **in** his office. I'll tell him you're here.

c) We usually put the adverb of place (WHERE) before the adverb of manner (HOW) after verbs of movement:
   She went to London (WHERE) by train (HOW) yesterday (WHEN).

	SUBJECT	VERB	OBJECT	ADVERBIAL
HOW	I	miss	him	**very much.**
WHERE	They	haven't got	a man	**around the house.**
WHEN	They	had fallen off	a wall	**while they were playing.**

(WHEN)		HOW	WHERE	WHEN
	She acted	**terribly**	**in the film.**	
(Yesterday)	The film fans besieged the airport	**frantically**		**yesterday.**
(An hour later)	I interviewed him		**in his flat**	**an hour later.**

in, out, on, off, into, out of, on to

Notice the prepositions in these sentences:

Look, there's a boat **on** the lake. (floating on the surface)
He's **in** the water. (swimming)
He took his hat **off**. (It was on his head.)
The dentist took my tooth **out**. (It was in my head.)

He got **into** the car. He got **on to** his bicycle.
He fell **out of** his pram. He fell **off** the roof.

In almost always suggests 'inside' in English;
on means 'on the surface of'.

Out is the opposite of **in**, and **off** is the opposite of **on**.
With verbs of movement, when there is an object, we use **into** and **out of, on to** and **off**.

We say **get on** and **get off** for a bus and **get in** and **get out of** for a train,

You must **get out** at the next station. (train)
You must **get off** at the next stop. (bus)

This is because buses did not have closing doors until recently in Britain.
We would normally use **get out of** for a coach, because coaches have always had doors.

On or **at the corner** is used for corners outside (of a street, for example).
In is used for corners inside (of a room, for example).

opposite, in front of

Opposite is often confused with **in front of**.
Compare:

I asked the woman sitting **in front of** me at the cinema to take her hat off. (We were both facing in the same direction.)
I sat **opposite** my wife at the table. (facing her)

2   Prepositions of time

at

Exact points of time – **at 5 o'clock, at dinner time, at this moment.**
Festivals – **at Christmas, at Easter, at New Year.**
At night, (but: **during the day**), **at weekends, at the weekend.**

on

Days and dates – **on Monday, on June 10th, on Christmas Day, on a summer evening, on a Sunday morning, on Wednesday night.**

in

Longer periods of time – **in August, in spring, in 1968, in the twentieth century, in the Middle Ages, in the past, in the future.**
Periods of time within which or at the end of which something may happen – **in five minutes, in three years' time.**
In the morning, in the afternoon, in the evening.

by

By = 'at some time not later than'.

I'll pay you **at** the end of the month. (on the 30th or 31st)
I'll pay you **by** the end of the month. (perhaps during the month at any time, but certainly not later than the 31st)

3   Some useful time expressions

At first, in the beginning (not used for points in argument – *see Appendix: Connectors and Modifiers, page 164*).
In the end, finally (The first is not used for points in argument.)
Eventually = after a long period of time.
At last comes at the end of a long series of events.
For the time being = until things change.
In the meantime = meanwhile.
In due course = in the future, at the proper time.
Now and then = from time to time (at irregular intervals).
These days = at the present time.
In those days refers to the past.
Nowadays refers to the present in contrast to the past.
At the moment = now; **at this moment** may mean 'now' but may mean the time being referred to.
At present/at the present time = now, but **presently** (in British English) = soon.

Modals: Formulae for different situations

All phrases we use here are polite but we have indicated differences, where necessary, between what you normally say to a friend (informal, marked **I** in the left/hand margin); what you say formally to someone you know (formal, marked **F**); and what you say to someone you do not know (very formal, marked **VF**).

1 You want someone (not) to do something.

   I   **Help me** with these cases, will you?
       Will/Can you help me with these cases, please?
       Would/Could you help me with these cases, (please)?

       (The last is the most polite.)

       Please don't make a noise. The baby's asleep. (Negative)

   F   **I want you to** help me.
       I'd like you to help me.

       (The second is more polite.)

       I don't want you to make the same mistake again. (Negative)

  VF **Would you mind** helping me with these cases?
       Would you mind not smoking in the waiting room? (Negative)

2 You are asking permission to do something.

   I   **Can/May I** borrow the car, please?
       Could I borrow the car, please?

       (The second is more polite, or you are less sure that the person will say 'Yes'.)

   F   **Do you mind if I** open the window?
       Would you mind if I opened the window?

       (Again, the second is more polite, or you are less sure that the person will say 'Yes'.)

3 You are offering something to someone.

   I   **Do you want** some tea?
       Do you want to watch TV?
  I/F **Would you like** some tea?
       Would you like to watch TV?

Remember that the relationships between people in a society affect the formality of the language they use. In general shop assistants are more polite and formal towards customers than customers towards shop assistants. This is not always true, but it is a good rule to remember.

4 You are offering to do something.

   I   **Do you want me to** help you with the washing-up?
  I/F **Shall I** help you with the washing-up?
       Would you like me to help you with the washing-up?
  VF **Can I** help you?

       (This is used as a formula in shops, etc.)

5 You are suggesting something you want to do with the other person.

   I   **Shall we** go to London this weekend?
       How about going to London this weekend?
       Why don't we go to London this weekend?
       Let's go to London this weekend.

       (Each is more positive than the one before. The last is not a question.)

(In making suggestions to solve problems (F), the second and third are the most common.)

6 You are suggesting something to the other person or trying to advise him/her.

       Why don't you go to the doctor?
       Why not go to the doctor?

       (These phrases show less concern than those below.)

       Don't you think you should/ought to go to the doctor?
       I think you should/ought to/had better go to the doctor.
       You should go to the doctor.
       You'd better go to the doctor.

       (Each is stronger and more urgent than the other one before.)

Note: 'You **ought to** go to the doctor' usually suggests 'but I don't suppose you will'.

7 You are giving orders or explaining obligations.

a) Positive forms:

Write your name in ink.
You **must** write your name in ink.

(The second is an explanation, not an order.)

You **have to** write your name in ink.

(The speaker is not responsible for the rule.)

You **should** write your name in ink.

(The speaker is only giving advice; see 6 above.)

b) Negative forms (prohibition):

Don't drive so fast! You're breaking the speed limit.
You **mustn't** drive so fast. You're breaking the speed limit. (It is against the law.)
You **shouldn't** drive so fast. You'll have an accident one day. (It is not necessarily against the law.) (The speaker is giving advice, not an order.)

c) You are telling someone that there is no obligation:

You **needn't** write in ink (if you don't want to).
You **don't have to** write in ink.

Note: See 9 below for past forms.

8 You are explaining your own obligations or prohibitions to someone else.

a) Obligations:

I **must** give up smoking. It's bad for my health.
I **have to** give up smoking. I don't want to, but the doctor says it will kill me.
I **should** give up smoking, I know it's bad for me, but I find it difficult to stop.

Note: It is polite to say 'I **have to** go now' when you say goodbye to someone, because it suggests that you don't want to go. The obligation comes from outside.

b) Probitions:

I **mustn't** smoke. I've got a bad cold.

c) You have no obligation:

I **needn't** go to work tomorrow. They've given us a holiday.
I **haven't got to** go to work tomorrow. They've given us a holiday.

Note: I **don't have to** (see 7 above) is usually used in general terms.

I **don't have to** go to work on Saturdays.

9 Past forms expressing obligation and prohibition.

a) Obligation:

We **had to** walk home because our car broke down.

b) Prohibition (see 7b and 8b above):

We **weren't allowed to** stay up late when I was young.
We **couldn't** stay up late when I was young.

c) There was no obligation (see 7c and 8c above):

We **didn't need to** book the tickets in advance. It wasn't a very popular film.

Note: 'We **needn't have** booked the tickets in advance.' This means that we booked the tickets, but it wasn't necessary.

10 You are complaining about someone or blaming him/her.

Why didn't you shut the gate?
You should have shut the gate.
Why did you park your car there?
You shouldn't have parked your car there.

11 You are wondering about something and thinking about possible explanations. (Present)

Situation: You are in the street outside a church. A wedding is going to take place and you are waiting to see the bride arrive. A man about sixty years old arrives and someone asks, 'Who's that?'

a) Possibilities:

He **may be** one of the guests.
He **could be** the best man.
He **might be** the bridegroom.

(The first is a reasonable possibility. The second is possible but not likely – the man is old. The third is possible but very unlikely for the same reason.)

b) Negative forms:

He **may not be** one of the guests. He may be a stranger, like us.
He **might not be** one of the guests, but he's talking to the other people there.

c) Logical conclusions:

He **must know** the bridegroom. Look! He's shaking hands with him.
He **can't be** one of the guests. He's going away. (Negative)
He **couldn't be** one of the guests. He's wearing an old suit. (Negative)

(In the last example, the conclusion is not clear. You are saying, 'I can't believe it'.)

Note: If you are wondering about people's actions, use the same forms with Continuous tenses.

He **may/could/might be working** late this evening. That's why he hasn't arrived.

12 You are wondering about something and thinking of possible events. (Future)

Question: Is it going to rain tonight?

a) Possibilities:

It **may** rain. It often does at this time of year.
It **might** rain, but I don't think it will.

b) Negative forms:

Don't look so sad. It **may not** rain this evening.
It **might not** rain tonight but the sky looks very dark.

13 You are wondering about something that (has) happened and thinking of possible explanations. (Past)

Problem: What (has) happened to your umbrella?

a) Possibilities:

I **may have** left it at the office.
Someone **might have** borrowed it.

(The second is possible, but you don't think this is the explanation.)

Note: We normally use **could have** when someone has not taken advantage of a possibility. See 10 above, but you are not complaining or blaming the other person.

Why did you come by train? You **could have** come by air.

b) Negative forms:

I **may not have** left it at the office. I may have left it on the train. Of course I **might not have** taken it to the office this morning, but I'm sure I did.

c) Logical conclusions:

Now I remember. I had it when I got off the train but I bought some cigarettes on the way home. I **must have** left it in the tobacconist's shop.
I **can't have** left it anywhere else. (Negative)

Note: The difference between **can't have** and

couldn't have in the negative is not very clear, but the first suggests 'I'm sure he hasn't' and the second 'I'm sure he didn't'.

He **can't have** seen the letter. It's still on his desk and he hasn't opened it.
He **couldn't have** seen the letter. He was on holiday when it arrived.

14 You are telling someone that you know how to do something, or you have the physical ability to do something.

a) Present forms:

I **can** play the piano but I **can't** play the violin.
I **can** run 100 metres in 11 seconds but I **can't** run as fast as John.

b) Past forms:

I **could** speak French when I was ten but I **couldn't** speak English.
He **could** throw a ball a long way but he **couldn't** catch very well.

c) Future forms:

I'**ll be able to** speak English quite well when I go to England.
We **won't be able to** climb the mountain tomorrow. The weather isn't good enough.

15 You are telling someone that an action will (not) be possible or was (not) possible.

a) Future forms:

I **can (can't)** come to the meeting tomorrow.
I'**ll (I won't) be able to** come to the meeting tomorrow.

(The second is perhaps more polite and is better as an excuse, but there is not much difference.)

b) Past forms (Negative):

I **couldn't** go to the meeting yesterday. I was very busy.
I **wasn't able to** go to the meeting yesterday. I was very busy.

Note: In the affirmative, you say, 'I went to the meeting'. If you went but it was difficult because you were busy, see 16 below.

c) Present Perfect forms:

I'**ve been able to** work better since we moved to the country.
I'm sorry the job isn't finished. I've been ill, so I **haven't been able to** do anything.

16 You are telling someone that an action was difficult for you but you (finally) did it.

My car crashed and I hurt my leg, but I **was able to** get out and shout for help.
My car crashed and I hurt my leg, but I **managed to** get out and shout for help.

Note: If the action was too difficult (therefore impossible), use **couldn't** or **wasn't able to** (see 15b above).

Verbs not usually used in Continuous forms

Certain verbs are almost never found in continuous forms. They are mainly verbs connected with senses, mental processes, wishes, appearance and possession. Here is a list of the most common ones:

hear, notice, recognise, see, smell*, taste;
believe, feel (that), think (that)*;
know, mean, suppose, understand;
forget, remember*;
care, dislike, hate, love, want, wish;
appear (= seem), **seem;**
belong to, consist of, contain, have (= own, possess);
matter;
refuse.

* Note the following:

That **smells** good. (Intransitive)
She **is smelling** the rose. (Transitive)
What **do** you **think?** (What is your opinion?)
What **are** you **thinking?** (What thoughts are going through your mind?)
Do you **remember** our schooldays? (Have you any memory of them?)
Are you **remembering** our schooldays? (Are memories going through your mind?)

Verb + gerund/infinitive

1 Gerund (only)
Some common verbs followed by a gerund are:
avoid, dislike, enjoy, finish, not mind, practise, can't help, can't stand.

Note: I **enjoy working** here.
I **can't understand him (his) working** so hard.

A gerund follows a verb + preposition.

He **kept on working.**

Note in particular the following, using the preposition **to:**
amount to, be (get) accustomed to, be given to,

be opposed to, be (get) used to, come near to, limit oneself to, look forward to, object to, resign oneself to.

2 Infinitive without **to**
Let and **make** take the infinitive without **to.**

Let him **go.**

Note: **Help** can be used with or without **to.**

Help him (**to**) **do** it.

Most auxiliary verbs: **can, must, had better,** etc.

Exceptions are **have to, ought to** and **used to.** (Compare **be used to, get used to** in 1 above.)

3 Verbs taking gerund and infinitive, including changes in meaning

allow	The doctor doesn't **allow me to smoke.** We don't **allow smoking** in the classroom.
	Allow takes an infinitive with a personal object, a gerund where there is none.
begin	I'm **beginning to feel** tired.
	Begin (and **start**) are not normally used with a gerund in continuous tenses (e.g. **I'm beginning**).
continue forget hate	(see **remember**) The gerund is the usual form, but the infinitive occurs:
	I **hate to interrupt** you while you're working. (I'm sorry to interrupt you.)
	I'**d hate to live** there.
	(Conditional form, see **like**).
intend like love	The gerund is used in general terms, meaning 'enjoy, find agreeable'. The infinitive is used when **like** means 'prefer'.
	I **like** people **to be** polite. I **like to have** a good breakfast before I go to work.
	In the negative, when **don't like** means 'dislike' (see 1 above), **like** takes the gerund. If it means 'I'm sorry to' (see **hate** above), it takes the infinitive. The Conditional form of **like** and **love** is followed by the infinitive (see **hate**). I'**d like to go** home now.

prefer   I **prefer driving** to **walking**.

This is a much easier construction than:

I **prefer to drive**, rather than **to walk**.

Infinitive in Conditional form, but for particular preference on a certain occasion we usually use **would rather** (auxiliary, infinitive without **to**, see 2 above).

I'**d rather drive** than **walk** this afternoon.

remember   I **remember smoking** my first cigarette. (have the memory of)
I **remembered to post** the letter. (didn't forget)

Remember with gerund after the event.
Remember with infinitive before the event.

stop   He **stopped talking**. (He was silent.)
He **stopped to talk** to his friend.
This is really a use of **to** for purpose because the meaning is 'He stopped (walking because he wanted) to talk to his friend'.

try   I **tried to understand** it. (made an effort, attempted)
I **tried smoking** a cigarette for the first time. (experimented with it to see if I would like it)

Active and Passive

1   Formation

The Passive is formed by the verb **be** in the appropriate tense and the past participle of the main verb (**used, made, built,** etc.)

	ACTIVE	PASSIVE
Present Simple	They **grow** wheat here.	Wheat **is grown** here.
Future Simple	They'**ll open** it next week.	It **will be opened** next week.
Past Simple	They **began** the castle in 1108.	The castle **was begun** in 1108.
Present Perfect	They **have restored** the tower.	The tower **has been restored.**
Modals	They **may finish** it soon.	It **may be finished** soon.
	They **must do** it again.	It **must be done** again.
Continuous forms	They'**re laying** the foundations.	The foundations **are being laid**.

The Passive sometimes occurs with an agent (**by . . .**) when our main interest is in a thing – a building, a book, a picture, etc:

The Mona Lisa **was painted by** Leonardo da Vinci.

But in general it is wiser to avoid it and use the Active form.

The Passive is necessary, however, in sentences where the agent is not mentioned:

The Mona Lisa **was painted** at the end of the fifteenth century.

Double object verbs: Passive forms

Some verbs can have two objects and most of them have alternative constructions.

John **gave me** some money.
John **gave** some money **to me**.

We prefer the Passive when we are not interested in the person who did the action.

Someone gave John some money. (Active)
John was given **some money**.

(We are interested in John and perhaps in the effect of the gift on him.)

Someone gave some money to John. (Active)
Some money was given to John.

(We are interested primarily in the money.)

Double object verbs

Most of these verbs are found in two constructions:

He lent me some money.
He lent some money **to me.**

In the Passive two possibilities also exist:

I was lent some money.
Some money was lent to me.

In each case the first form is more common.

a) The commonest verbs of this type are:
give, guarantee, leave (money), **lend, make** (an offer, a present), **offer, owe, promise** (a reward), **read** (a story), **refuse** (a loan),

sell, send, show, teach (a language, etc.), **tell** (a story), **write** (a letter).

b) **Buy** is used in the same way but the preposition used is **for**, not **to**.

He **bought** a present **for his wife**. (He bought her a present.)

c) **Ask** is only found in the first construction with a few phrases:

I **asked him** a question (his name/the way).

Ask for is also only found in the first construction:

I **asked them for** help. (Active)
They were asked for help. (Passive)

d) **Pay** is like type a) if it refers to money, but like **ask for** if it refers to goods or services.

I **paid him** the money.
I **paid him for** the goods.
The goods were paid for. (Passive)

e) **Rent** belongs to type a), except that only the second form exists in the Passive. When the person who pays the money becomes the subject, an Active form is used.

He **rented me** the car.
He **rented** the car **to me.**
BUT: I **rented** the car **from him.**

The car was rented to me/from him. (Passive)

In British English we prefer **let** for houses and only the second construction is possible.

He **let** the house **to me.** (Active)
The house was let to me. (Passive)

f) Note that **borrow** cannot be used with these constructions.

I **borrowed** the money **from him.**

g) Certain verbs are only found in the second construction. The most common are:
announce, describe, entrust, explain, introduce, propose, suggest.

He **explained** it **to me.**
It was explained to me. (Passive)

But NOT: 'He explained me the subject.'

Direct and reported speech

He said, 'I don't like onions'. (Direct)
He said **he didn't like onions.** (Reported)
She said, 'I visited my aunt yesterday'. (Direct)
She said **that she had visited her aunt the day before.** (Reported)

Notice that when we change direct speech to reported speech, expressions of time and place (e.g. **yesterday**) often change. The tense will change also if the verb introducing the reported speech is in the past tense (e.g. **said**). Use these lists of rules for reference.

1   Tense changes

DIRECT	REPORTED
'I'm working very hard.'	He said he was working . . .
'I earn £100 a week.'	He said he earned . . .
'I'm going to change my job.'	He said he was going to . . .
'I'll finish it soon.'	He said he would finish it . . .
'I've never seen her before.'	He said he had never seen her . . .
'I didn't break it.'	He said he hadn't broken it.
'I can run faster than Mary.'	He said he could run faster . . .
'It may be too late.'	He said it might be . . .

2   Time and place changes

DIRECT	REPORTED
here	there
this	that
now	then
yesterday	the day before
tomorrow	the day after
last week	the week before
next week	the week after
ago	before

Relative clauses

1 Defining relative clauses

	SUBJECT PRONOUN	OBJECT PRONOUN
Person Thing Possessive Prepositional	**who (that)** **that (which)** **whose**	____ **(whom) (that)** ____ **(that) (which)** **whose** ____ **+ preposition** (or: prep. + **whom/which**)

2 Non-defining relative clauses

	SUBECT PRONOUN	OBJECT PRONOUN
Person Thing Possessive Prepositional	**who** **which** **whose**	**whom** **which** **whose** prep. + **whom/which**

a) Defining relative clauses identify the person or thing we are talking about. Without them, the sentence would be meaningless.

The man who repaired the TV was called Fred.

b) **That** is preferred to **who** or **which** following **all, every, everything, some, something, any, anything, no, nothing, none, little, few, much, only** and superlative forms.

The only thing that matters to him is winning.
She is **the best secretary that** ever worked here.

c) When these clauses refer to the object of the sentence, the relative pronoun is usually omitted (contact clause).

The man she married had a red beard.

d) It is normal to avoid pronouns in prepositional clauses either by putting the preposition at the end in a contact clause:

That's **the man I was talking to.**

or by using **where** or **when** as relative adverbs in references to place and time:

That's **the house where I was born.** (NOT 'in which')
Do you know **the time when your plane takes off?** (NOT 'at which')

a) Non-defining clauses do not identify the people or things we are talking about, but give us additional information about them.

Jack Briggs, **who used to live next door to me**, has just got married.

In spoken English this information would usually be conveyed in two sentences.

You remember Jack Briggs – **he used to live next door to me.** Well, he's just got married.

b) Clauses like this are usually placed between commas but if the person or thing referred to is the object of the main clause, the relative clause can appear at the end.

I've just met Jack Briggs, **who got married last month**.

c) **Where** can be used in these clauses as a relative adverb.

Farley, **where I was born**, is a small town north of London.

d) The use of a proper name always indicates that the clause following is non-defining, not defining, because the name itself is a definition (see b) and c) above), except in cases where one of those talking may know two people or places, etc. of the same name.

3 Co-ordinating relative clauses

These refer to the whole of the main clause, and the only pronoun ever used is **which**.

I've just spent the weekend with Uncle Harold, **which ought to qualify me for some kind of a medal.**

Clearly, **which** does not refer to Uncle Harold but to the experience of spending the weekend with him.

Compare the following:

Someone stole her car, **which was parked outside her house.** (Non-defining, where **which** refers to the car.)
Someone stole her car, **which naturally annoyed her.** (Co-ordinating, **which** refers to the fact that the car was stolen.)

Reflexive verbs

A number of common verbs in English are often found in reflexive constructions.

Don't do that! You'll **hurt yourself**.

These are listed below in Section 1 with notes on usage. In many cases, however, verbs whose equivalents in other languages are reflexive are more often used in English in a form employing **get** or **be** (Section 2 below), or are used without a reflexive form (Section 3 below).

1 Verbs commonly found in reflexive forms.

a) Action, pain, danger:
burn, cut, defend, hurt, kill (drown, shoot).
(But we say 'commit suicide'.)

b) Behaviour, emotion:
amuse, behave, blame, control, deceive, enjoy, express, be ashamed of, be sorry for.
(**Behave** is the only intransitive verb in this list.)

c) Thought, speech:
consider, count, say to, talk to, tell, think.
Count and **think** are included here with the meaning of 'consider':

Consider/count/think yourself lucky.

d) Action not normally reflexive:
congratulate, educate, introduce, invite, teach.

e) Others:
can't help, prevent, stop, weigh.

f) Idiomatic uses:
help, let, please.

Help yourself = serve yourself (with food, a drink, etc.)

Let yourself go = relax, lose inhibitions.
Please yourself = do as you like (usually suggesting 'if you don't agree with my suggestion').

2 Forms employing **get**, etc, instead of a reflexive form.
get accustomed to, get confused, get dressed, get engaged, get excited, get lost, get married, get tired, get upset, get wet, be self-employed, fall asleep.

3 Forms where a reflexive is not necessary or is usually incorrect.
apologise (for), decide, find out, forget, get up, hide, hurry, improve, join, move, prepare (for), remember, resign (from a job), **retire** (from work), **shave, sit down, stand up, wake up, wash, wonder, worry.**
Note, too, that we do not use a reflexive in sentences like:
I cut my hand.
I hurt my arm.
Compare this with:
I cut myself.
I hurt myself.

Clauses

1 Future time clauses

Look at these sentences:

As soon as I get home, **I'll ring** him.
I'm going to have a party **when** the examinations **are** over.
Raise the flag **when I give** you the signal.
He **may not do** anything **until** he **hears** from you.
I won't be able to confirm the dates **until I can talk** to the manager.

The Present tense is always used in the part of a future time clause containing the time expression (**when, until, as soon as,** etc.). The main clause may be in the Future (**will, going to**) but can also be formed with the imperative or **may**, for example.

Note: Other patterns are:
When I've spoken to Joan, **I'll know** what to do. (referring to a completed action in the time clause)
While you**'re ringing** Joan, **I'll be waiting** here. (two simultaneous actions taking place in the future)

2 Clauses of concession

a) **although, in spite of**, etc.; **however**, etc. Compare these sentences:

Although Though Even though	he played brilliantly,	he still lost the match.
In spite of Despite	(his) playing brilliantly,	

He lost the match.	He played brilliantly,	**though. however. nevertheless. all the same.**
	However, Nevertheless, All the same,	he played brilliantly.

Even though is a stronger form of **although**.
In spite of and **despite** are followed by a noun or a gerund.
The clauses in the first five examples can be in reverse order, so that in all cases the sentences can begin: **He still lost the match . . .**
Though can appear at the end of a sentence, but not **although** or **even though**.

b) **on the other hand, while**
Compare these sentences:

The Government would like to stop people smoking; **on the other hand,** they need the money they obtain from taxes on tobacco.
While the Government would like to stop people smoking, they need the money they obtain from taxes on tobacco.

All the same and **nevertheless** may be used in the same way as **on the other hand** in the first example.

c) **whatever, whoever, however, wherever**
Compare these sentences:

**I don't care
It doesn't matter** } **what** she says. I don't believe her.
I don't believe her, **whatever** she says.

**I don't care
It doesn't matter** } **who** he is or **what** his business is. He's not coming in.

He's not coming in, **whoever** he is and **whatever** his business is.

**I don't care
It doesn't matter** } **how urgent** it is. I'm not going to stay here all night to finish it.
I'm not going to stay here all night to finish it, **however urgent** it is.

**I don't care
It doesn't matter** } **where** they are. We'll find them.
We'll find them, **wherever** they are.

3 if, whether . . . (or not)

a) **if, whether**
Notice the use of **if** and **whether** in these sentences:

1   I don't know { **if
whether** } she'll be able to come **(or not)**.
2a Tell me **if** you want me to come. (But if you don't want me to come, don't tell me anything.)
2b Tell me **whether** you want me to come **(or not)**. (You must tell me what you've decided.)
3   I don't know **whether** to invite him **(or not)**.

In Sentence *1* either **if** or **whether** may be used. There is no difference in meaning.
In Sentence *2a* the meaning is 'only tell me if you want me to come'.
In Sentence *2b* the meaning is 'tell me either to come or not to come'.
In Sentence *3* we can only use **whether** with the infinitive.

b) **whether, it doesn't matter/it makes no difference**
Compare the following sentence structures:

Whether she feels like composing music **or not**, she has to practise.

**It doesn't matter
It makes no difference** } **whether** she feels like composing music **or not**. She has to practise.

c) Concessive clauses with **if** and **whether**

Compare these sentences:

If you **don't** pay me, I won't do it. (*or:* **Unless** you pay me, I won't do it.)

I've decided to do it, **even if** I am not paid for it.

I've decided to do it, $\left\{ \begin{array}{l} \textbf{although} \\ \textbf{even though} \end{array} \right\}$ I am not paid for it.

I've decided to do it, **whether** they pay me **or not.**

In the first example, I will only do it *if* I am paid. In the others, I will do it in any case. The difference is that **although** and **even though** imply that I will not be paid, while **even if** and **whether . . . or not** imply that I may be paid, but payment is not the decisive factor.

d) **whether** and **either . . . or**

Compare these sentences:

Either he's at home **or** at work. He can't be anywhere else.
Whether he's at home **or** at work, we must get in touch with him.

The first sentence puts forward two alternatives. The second is not so much concerned with the alternatives as with the action to be taken.

Compare: **We must get in touch with him, wherever he is.**
Note that all sentences of this kind can be written with the **whether** clause first or second.

4 provided (that)

Provided (that), as long as and **so long as**
are all strong forms of **if**, meaning 'if and only if'. Look at the alternative expressions in this sentence:

You can stay up late tonight $\left\{ \begin{array}{l} \textbf{provided (that)} \\ \textbf{so long as} \\ \textbf{as long as} \end{array} \right\}$ you do your homework first.

The negative of these expressions (with the meaning **if not**) is formed by using **provided (that)**, etc. followed by the negative form of the verb, or by using **unless** and the affirmative.

5 **as if/as though**

Notice that the forms are interchangeable:

It looks **as if/as though** it's **going** to rain.
It looks **as if/as though** it **was going** to rain.

You talk **as if/as though** it **rained** all the time in England. (It doesn't.)
He behaves **as if/as though** he **were/was** the king. (He isn't.)
He speaks **as if/as though** he **had won** the Nobel Prize. (He hasn't.)

The first two sentences refer to real possibilities in the present and past. The forms can also be used to express unreal or untrue comparisons, as in the last three examples. Here the tenses are the same as those used in conditionals for hypothetical conditions in the present and past.

6 **In case**

Look at these sentences:

I'll leave some food in the fridge for her. **She may arrive late.**
I'll leave some food in the fridge for her, **in case she arrives late.**
He left some food in the fridge for her **because he thought she might arrive late.**
He left some food in the fridge for her **in case she arrived late.**

In case means 'because . . . may' in reference to present or future time and 'because . . . might' in reference to past time. It is followed by a verb in the Present tense when it refers to present or future, and by a verb in the Past tense when it refers to the past.

You can stay up late	provided (that) so long as as long as	you **don't feel**	too tired.
	unless	you **feel**	

7 so, such and result clauses

Compare the forms used in these examples:

She's **so pretty.**
She's **such a pretty girl.** (singular, countable)
She's **so pretty that** everyone looks at her.
She's **such a pretty girl that** everyone looks at her.
The weather was **so awful.**
It was **such awful weather.** (uncountable)
The weather was **so awful that** we couldn't go out.
It was **such awful weather that** we couldn't go out.
His manners are **so bad.**
He has **such bad manners.** (plural)
His manners are **so bad that** no one ever invites him to a party.
He has **such bad manners that** no one ever invites him to a party.

8 Purpose clauses

a) Purpose: **for, to, because**; cause: **because**
Compare these sentences:

A **What**'s that brush **for?**
B It's **for cleaning** typewriters (with).

A **What** do you want that brush **for?**
B **To clean** my typewriter (with).

A **Why** do you want that brush?
B **Because I want to clean** my typewriter (with it).

A **Why** are you cleaning your typewriter?
B **Because** it's dirty.

We use **for** with the gerund to talk about the function of a thing; we use the infinitive to talk about the purpose of an action.
Why? questions can refer to purpose, as in the third example (answered by the infinitive or a clause with **because**), or cause, as in the fourth example (answered by a clause with **because**).

b) **to, in order (not) to, so as (not) to**
Compare these sentences:

We took the children to the cinema
{
to keep them happy.
in order to keep them happy.
so as to keep them happy.
in order not to disappoint them.
so as not to disappoint them.
}

Note that the order of the clauses could be reversed in all cases, but this is most common with **in order to** and **so as to**, which usually appear in more formal contexts,

e.g. **In order to** avoid disturbance of the peace, the Government has decreed that no public meetings will be held in the square until further notice.
The infinitive without **in order** or **so as** cannot be used in the negative.

c) **so that** with change of subject
Compare these sentences:

He spoke slowly **to help** them understand him.
He spoke slowly **so that they would** understand him.

When the subject is understood from the main clause, we use the infinitive; if the subject changes, we use **so that** or **in order that**. Exceptions are verbs taking two objects (**give, send**, etc.),
e.g. I gave her a ring **to wear** on her finger. (She wore it.)
I sent him to the baker's **to buy** some bread. (He bought it.)
However, this is only true if there is no doubt about who did the action.

9 avoid, prevent, make (im)possible (for) and purpose clauses

a) **avoid, so as not to, in order not to**
Compare these sentences:

The thief wore gloves
{
to avoid leaving
so as not to leave
in order not to leave
}
} fingerprints.

b) **so that, make it possible for**
Compare these sentences:

He has set up the school **so that poor children can have** a good education.
He set up the school **so that poor children could have** a good education.
He set up/has set up the school **to make it possible for poor children to have** a good education.

c) **so that . . . not, prevent, make it impossible for**
Compare these sentences:

They have built a high wall **so that the prisoners cannot escape.**
They built a high wall **so that the prisoners could not escape.**
They built/have built a high wall **to prevent the prisoners from escaping.**
They built/have built a high wall **to make it impossible for the prisoners to escape.**

Answers

Unit 3   How much do you know about Britain   (page 13)

1   46,222,000 live in England, which is over 80%. 5,117,000 live in Scotland, 2,790,000 in Wales and 1,547,000 in N. Ireland.

2   Birmingham   (1,006,900)
Glasgow   (762,200)
Leeds   (705,000)
Sheffield   (536,800)
Liverpool   (510,300)

3   November is the wettest month. The highest average rainfall is in the west of Scotland, Cumberland and Wales. The driest months are March and April.

4   b) 11·9 million out of a total of 21·5 million households (55%). 6·8 million rent from local authorities, and 2·8 million from private landlords.

5   The correct order, significantly, is the reverse!
the *Sun*   (4,077,000 copies daily)
the *Daily Mirror*   (3,355,000)
the *Daily Express*   (2,034,000)
the *Daily Telegraph*   (1,305,000)
the *Guardian*   (420,000)
The Times   (300,000)

6   We do not import eggs and milk. We import 53% of sugar used. Other imports are fish (30%), meat (16%), wheat (12%), potatoes (8%).

7   West Germany   (11·1%)
USA   (10·4%)
France   (7·7%)
Holland   (7·5%)
Eire   (4·6%)
Japan   (2·6%)

8   Shops   (3,159,000)
Factories – Engineering, manufacturing   (3,150,000)
Civil Service   (1,596,000)
Transport   (1,582,000)
Agriculture   (less than a million)

9   Food, housing   (16%)
Drink   (8%)
Running the car   (7%)
Fuel and light   (5%)
Tobacco   (4%)

10   Sheep   (32 million)
Cows   (13 million)
Cats   (9 million)
Pigs   (8 million)
Dogs   (4 million)

Unit 7   Quiz   (page 37)

A   1 c) 587   Tenerife, Canary Islands, 1977
2 c) about 5,000   Peru, 1941
3 c) 830,000   China, 1556
4 c) 1,670   China, 1845
5 c) 3,700,000   China, 1931
6 a) 689   United States, 1925
7 a) 543   France, 1917
8 b) 127   Egypt, 1973
9 c) 7,700   off Poland, 1945
10 c) 436   India, 1907

B   5 A collision on the runway – Aircraft accident
10 Snow melting – Avalanche
9 Seismic movement – Earthquake
1 A lighted match – Fire
2 A river bursting its banks – Flood
4 Atmospheric pressure – Hurricane/tornado
6 Brakes which failed – Railway accident
7 The driver ignoring a signal – Road accident
3 A torpedo – Shipwreck
8 Hunger – Tiger

C   1 Killed by the impact
2 Buried
3 Buried in most cases
4 More likely to have choked or been trodden on than burnt
5 Drowned
6 Killed by the impact resulting, or buried
7 Killed by the impact
8 In fact, they were drowned
9 Drowned
10 Eaten, but first killed by blow from paw or claws

D   1 b) Because the greatest risk is that the house will fall on you.
2 b) Because the ceilings will collapse before the room itself catches fire, if the fire is elsewhere.

3 a) According to most sailors, there is more chance of your being seen by another ship if you remain with your boat.

Unit 7   Rail and road accidents (page 40)

1 The other driver was to blame, because he was not looking.
Legally, my wife was to blame, because he was coming from the right and the local council has forgotten to put up a 'STOP' sign on that intersection!
2 The woman was to blame, in fact and legally.
3 Both were to blame, but the driver coming from the left was legally responsible.
4 The woman was to blame, but each of the cars that crashed into the back of the one in front was legally responsible, because they had not kept their distance.

Unit 9   Cities   (page 48)

1D, 2B, 3A, 4E, 5C, 6F, (Nero was the politician/musician who was said to have watched while Rome burned)

Unit 15   Grading Students (page 85)

Task 1   54% opposed: 37% favoured: 9% neutral
Task 2   2 to 1 in favour: B/C evenly divided:
D/F unanimously opposed.

Unit 27   Arousing interest (page 151)

1 The novel is political, connected with the first relatively democratic elections of 1832 in Britain. The heir to the estate returns home and stands for Parliament. We read to find out who was expected and are made aware of 'the memorable year'.
2 About a young American girl in Europe in the 1870s. We realise we are likely to read about travellers in Europe.
3 A parody of romantic novels in 1800. We learn that Catherine is the heroine, but not typical. We read to find out what is different about her.

4 Theme is the corruption of different levels of Victorian society. Opening provides the moral and physical atmosphere.
5 Science-fiction story. We are curious. What was wrong?